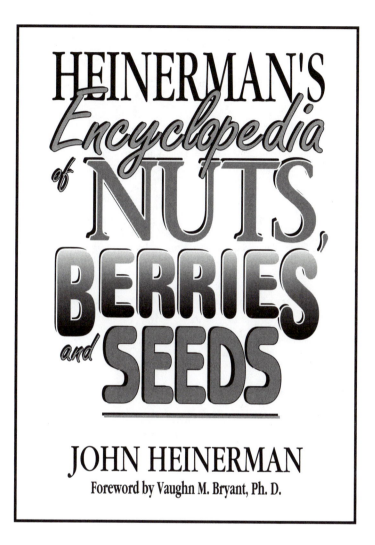

HEINERMAN'S
Encyclopedia of
NUTS,
BERRIES
and SEEDS

JOHN HEINERMAN
Foreword by Vaughn M. Bryant, Ph. D.

PARKER PUBLISHING COMPANY
West Nyack, New York 10995

10   9   8   7   6   5   4   3   2   1

This book is a reference work based on research by the author. The
opinions expressed herein are not necessarily those of or endorsed by
the publisher. The directions stated in this book are in no way to be
considered as a substitute for consultation with a duly licensed doctor.

Library of Congress Cataloging-in-Publication Data
Heinerman, John.
    [Encyclopedia of nuts, berries, and seeds]
    Heinerman's encyclopedia of nuts, berries, and seeds / John
Heinerman ;   foreword by Vaughn M. Bryant.
        p.   cm.
    Includes index.
    ISBN 0–13–310301–3 (c). — ISBN 0–13–310285–8 (p). — ISBN
0–13–228305–0 (pc)
    1. Nuts—Therapeutic use—Encyclopedias.   2. Berries—Therapeutic
use—Encyclopedias.   3. Seeds—Therapeutic use—Encyclopedias.
I. Title.
RM216.H35   1995
615'.321—dc20   95–11512
                                                                      CIP

ISBN 0-13-310301-3 (C)
ISBN 0-13-228305-0 (PC)
ISBN 0-13-310285-8 (P)

PARKER PUBLISHING COMPANY
Career and Personal Development
West Nyack, NY 10995
A Simon & Schuster Company

PRINTED IN THE UNITED STATES OF AMERICA

To

Hyrum Smith,
patriarch of the latter days, martyr for his religion, and devoted
brother to the Prophet Joseph Smith, founder of Mormonism

PREFACE

This is the third in the best-selling series of *Heinerman's Encyclopedias*. First came the one of *Fruits, Vegetables and Herbs*. Then six years later *Healing Juices* made its appearance. In 1995 there appeared this work—the most comprehensive reference book you'll ever find on the *remedial* side to nuts, berries, and seeds.

I've always been a strong advocate of "food therapy" to "cure what ails you." I once had a TV talk-show host test my ability of instant recall for different health problems that she came up with. The segment was unrehearsed and very spontaneous on both ends. Here's a sampling of how some of the dialogue went.

> *TV Host:* "Dr. Heinerman, what would you tell someone to do for a bad case of diarrhea?"
>
> *Myself:* "I'd have that individual drink a glass of blackberry juice, which will stop even the worse case of loose bowels within 30 minutes or less!"
>
> *TV Host:* "How about an excruciating toothache?"
>
> *Myself:* "I would, of course, suggest visiting a dentist as soon as possible. But in the meantime, I'd have that person peel and crush one clove of garlic. Then he or she would apply a little Jiffy peanut butter to a 2 × 2-inch-square corner of white bread. The crushed garlic would be laid on top of this, the specified size cut out, the piece inserted into the mouth and firmly affixed on the site of the pain. Within minutes the aching sensation is gone and the peanut butter bread combination helps hold the garlic in place for several hours."
>
> *TV Host:* "Amazing, truly amazing! How about ringing in the ears?"

Myself: "First of all I'd inquire about the person's particular occupation. Who knows but that the individual might be a bell ringer in the local cathedral. If so, then I'd have him change jobs immediately! (Laughter on the set.) Otherwise, I'd have that person drink one cup of very warm fenugreek seed tea every three hours on an empty stomach until the problem subsided. That really works you know!"

TV Host: "Hmmm...let's see what else I can throw at you. How about horrible heartburn where your insides feel like they're about to explode?"

Myself: "Oh, that's a very simple problem to deal with. I'd recommend slowly eating and thoroughly chewing some fresh alfalfa or bean sprouts. Also, taking several capsules of ginger root with a glass of water, chewing some parsley, or else drinking a cup of warm catnip or peppermint tea or a small glass of papaya juice helps, too."

And so the interview moved merrily along in this fashion. But from that one network television show came the inspiration for this book. In these pages you will learn many fascinating things you never knew before about nuts, berries, and seeds.

But above all, you will learn their *medicinal* values for many different types of health complaints. *Specific* remedies for *particular* problems is what this book is all about! Enjoy and use its accumulated wisdom for years to come!

Your friend, John Heinerman, Ph.D., 1995
POB 11471, Salt Lake City, UT 84147

CONTENTS

PART I

Health Problems/Natural Solutions

vii

PART II

Natural Solutions/Health Problems

PART III

Appendices

FOREWORD

Humans are remarkable. We have explored all the regions of our world, we have landed on the moon, and our space craft are now traveling beyond our solar system. Yet, not long ago there were no cities, no fields of cultivated crops, nor any of the technological advancements that are now so commonplace and so much a part of our daily lives.

The first humans emerged in Africa as a new species of primates more than five million years ago, yet the time of this precise event is still in question. From that first instant, and for the next 99 percent of all human existence on earth, our ancestors lived as hunters and gatherers who relied on their skills and knowledge to survive. They beat the odds against extinction to become the paragon of animals.

Most of human development happened at a time before farming, which began about 10,000 years ago; before city markets and the grocery stores we rely on today; before modern medical advancements and hospitals, which have only become commonplace during the last few hundred years; and before today's pampered lifestyle we have come to expect and enjoy. Before the advent of farming and cities our ancestors lived what many call "a perfect lifestyle." They ate a mixed diet of natural foods, relied on herbal medicine to cure their ills, and led active lives full of exercise. Archaeologists tell us that these peoples were slim and trim, and enjoyed diets that were low in fat, high in fiber, and lacked the large quantities of salt and refined sugar most of us consume daily. Many of our ancestors didn't live as long as we do today, but those who did enjoyed strength and stamina even into the last days of their lives. But, their shorter average lifespans were not caused by poor diets, or a lack of an active lifestyle. Instead, many died from infection, accidents, and from the rigors of living a demanding and physical lifestyle.

Today we have the added benefit of increased longevity, and that should be of great concern to each of us. For most of us, healthiness remains fairly constant from childhood through our twenties. But with each increasing decade the gap begins to widen between those who remain in excellent health and those who begin to suffer from an ever increasing list of illnesses. Until recently, the medical profession believed that the degenerative process, seen in so many of our elderly, was inevitable and was part of the natural aging process. However, growing evidence now suggests that the degenerative process is caused more by our own lifestyle of careless neglect than by some genetic flaw in the human species.

The choice is there for each of us to make. We need not give up the many advantages we have learned through technology, nor those advances developed as part of our modern civilization. Instead, we need to learn to live in harmony with our body's physiology. By getting daily exercise and choosing natural foods unblemished by modern chemical additives and the addition of unneeded sodium, by reducing our intake of refined sugar and saturated fats, by eating more foods containing natural fiber and complex carbohydrates, and by avoiding tobacco and other harmful substances, we can approach the "perfect" lifestyle and excellent physical health enjoyed by our ancestors.

John Heinerman's *Encyclopedia of Nuts, Berries and Seeds* is an important step guiding us in the right direction. For thousands, and even millions of years our ancestors learned by trial and error which natural foods were good for our bodies and which ones could be used to cure various types of aches and illnesses. Eventually, much of that plant knowledge became the foundation for many of the medical remedies we now take in pill or powder form.

Today, some members of the medical profession dismiss various types of "cures" derived from natural plant sources. Instead, these doctors prefer to dispense their own variety of pharmaceutical drugs, many of which have unpronounceable names. This is not to say that we should dismiss many of the important advancements made by modern medicine, but nor should we dismiss the vast knowledge of botanicals that has been handed down to us over thousands of years of successful use.

The choice is ours to make. We have an ability to direct our own destiny. If we are willing to heed the advice given to us by our bodies, and make the needed changes in our diets and lifestyle, then we can better our chances for enjoying lives that will be healthy, even into the last decades of our own existences.

Vaughn M. Bryant, Jr.
Professor and Chairman
Department of Anthropology
Texas A & M University
College Station, TX

ACORN
(Quercus Alba)

BRIEF DESCRIPTION

The term "acorn" refers in a general sense to the nut of any oak tree. All true oaks belong to the genus *Quercus* (Latin for "oak tree") and are placed in the beech family along with the chestnut and beechnut. The oak genus is native to the temperate regions of the northern hemisphere and to high altitudes in the tropics. Worldwide, more than 450 species of oak are known, some 60 of which occur in North America. Edible, sweet acorns are found in Europe, Asia, and North America. The white oak *(Quercus alba)* is a noble, deciduous tree of the northern United States and produces the most popular acorns. Requiring no special planting or cultivation, the annual nut crop from oaks is larger than that of all other tree nut crops combined, despite the fact that oaks are not even grown as a tree crop in America. Acorns are scarcely utilized commercially at the present time in this country, although they are traditionally sought after by wildlife and livestock.

The oak is mentioned frequently throughout the Bible. The oak in Genesis (35:4-8) is thought to have been the holm oak *(Quercus ilex)*; other species of oak are prevalent in the mountainous regions of Syria, Lebanon, and Palestine. Some biblical scholars

1

think that it was the branches of a wide-spreading oak tree in which Absalom, the third son of King David, was caught in its branches by his thick, flowing hair when his mule rode out from under him (2 Samuel 18:9–14). The oak has played a prominent role in religion and mythology as a symbol of strength and sturdiness. Merlin, the renowned medieval magician of the fabled King Arthur's Court, carried out his enchantments beneath an oak. And the Druids, those ancient priests of Celtic Britain, Ireland, and Gaul of 300 B.C. and later, performed mystic ceremonies beneath oaks; their diet consisted mainly of acorns and berries. In fact, they believed that the consumption of both items together enhanced their psychic perceptions for supernatural experiences.

Species of the white oaks are the most widely distributed and best known, ranging all around the northern hemisphere. These majestic trees reach heights of 80 to 120 feet, with sturdy trunks 3 to 5 feet in diameter, stout, wide-spreading branches, and stately, rounded crowns. Their bark is light gray, rough and often deeply furrowed, while the black-oak bark is usually blackish. The light brown oblong-ovoid acorns of the white oak, with their familiar, bowl-like cup, are about three fourths of an inch long; they mature in one year, fall to the ground, and germinate soon thereafter. The white oak grows slowly and may attain an age of 500 years or more. Yields of acorns vary with region and site; annual production may vary from a few pounds to several hundred pounds per tree.

The state tree of Maryland, the white oak, is generally considered to be the most valuable hardwood species in the United States; the wood is strong, durable, light brown in color, and an excellent timber for furniture, flooring, and cooperage. White-oak barrels are universally employed for aging whiskey and rum. In the early history of America, oak wood played an important role—it was utilized to construct block houses, forts, cabins, bridges, tools, and countless necessities of daily living.

Acorns Make Suitable Food and Beverage

Acorns were the staff of life for many Native American tribes in the United States and Canada. They gathered them for food to prepare their daily mush and bread. They used both sweet and bitter types.

The latter were not consumed directly, but were ground and then leached or stored in water before being eaten. The astringent characteristics of bitter acorns are caused by tannin, a substance readily soluble in water, which in most cases can be leached out to leave a sweeter, nut-flavored product. Sweet acorns, such as those from the white oak, were eaten raw or roasted, or were ground into a meal and formed into dark brown cakes for baking in crude ovens.

Sometimes acorn meal was mixed with corn meal to make tasty biscuits, or to thicken venison stew. I've watched several Native American friends of mine in the eastern United States grind sweet acorns into a fine meal and thicken the gravy of beef stew with it. Fresh acorns were also boiled to obtain nut oil for cooking, or for use as a liniment; the boiling process yielded an oil that was skimmed off. In the autumn, Native Americans gathered large quantities of acorns and spread them in the sun to dry before storing them for winter food.

In December of 1620, the Pilgrims in Massachusetts came upon baskets of roasted acorns, hidden in the ground by Native Americans in that region. The New England settlers prepared a rather palatable dish of boiled sweet acorns, whose flavor was supposed to compare favorably with that of the European chestnut. During the Civil War, when coffee was hard to come by, a tolerable substitute beverage was obtained through roasting and cracking white oak acorns. Yankee and Rebel soldiers made the most of their crude but adequate "wakeup beverage," but without the caffeine.

A Cure for Stinky Feet

Many younger people suffer from sweaty feet, the smell of which is strong enough to knock the nostrils and brain for a loop! But early Native Americans had a sure cure for this and for smelly armpits and groins. They boiled handsful of crushed, green acorns in plenty of water until half of the original liquid remained. This they managed to strain off and preserve in crude containers. Smelly feet were routinely soaked in some of this green-acorn water each day until the problem cleared up. Other body parts were regularly washed with this same acorn water with good results.

Stops Diarrhea Quickly

An old Indian cure for diarrhea calls for 4 crushed acorns to be boiled in 1 quart of water on low heat for about 40 minutes, then strained. When cool, 1 cup of the tea is consumed. Within a matter of minutes even the worst case of diarrhea is known to stop, on account of the powerful astringency of the tannic acid present in the tea.

ALFALFA SEED
(Medicago Sativa)

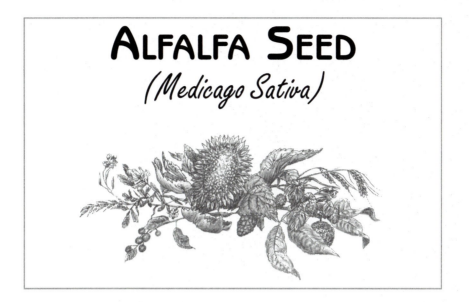

BRIEF DESCRIPTION

For all practical purposes, alfalfa may be considered a tall clover because of its three-part leaves. The herb is a many-stemmed and branched perennial, usually two to three feet tall when mature. The flowers are typical clovers, with purple, lavender, or blue tufts of blossoms interspersed at the ends of the stems. It is rather hard to distinguish between alfalfa and yellow and white clover until they are in full bloom, even though yellow sweet clover grows earlier and white sweet clover is larger.

Alfalfa is pretty common throughout the United States and Canada, especially where a lot of livestock are raised. It is a very popular pasture hay used for fodder and crop rotation. On our large family ranch in the wilderness of southern Utah, we've seeded poor ground with alfalfa, let it go an entire summer without cutting, and then plowed it under come fall; the result is richer soil the following year on account of the high nitrogen and mineral content of this herb. Most people have never seen alfalfa in bloom; a field of it is as one old Texas cowhand from Fort Worth said awhile back, "purtier than the purtiest hussy you find downtown."

5

Alfalfa seed is exceedingly small and was once used by the Paiute or Digger Indians of Utah and Nevada as a source of food. The seeds are a great favorite for sprouting by many health enthusiasts. They are rich in potassium, phosphorus, calcium, and magnesium.

Alfalfa herb has estrogen-like properties. In natural medicine it is used as a tincture or in capsule form for balancing estrogen levels within the system.

The Art of Sprouting

Almost an seed, grain, or legume can be sprouted, although some are tastier than others. While I will be specifically referring to alfalfa sprouts here, the reader is encouraged to try all of them in sprouted form. Alfalfa seeds can be found in most natural-foods stores. Be sure that they haven't been chemically treated, though. If they have been, the germination rate will drop. Figure on getting about one cup of alfalfa sprouts from just an ounce of tiny alfalfa seeds.

There are two different ways you can go with the equipment needed for sprouting. The first and easiest way is to simply buy one of several different up-to-date sprouters. One that I recommend is called the Sproutmaster. It doesn't sour sprouts as would be the case if you failed to change the water in a glass jar. Several sprouting trays can be stacked with the tray lid in place without losing necessary air circulation (you can't achieve this extra growing space with the old fruit-jar method). The rectangular shape also permits easier cabinet and refrigerator storage. A removable divider in the center allows you to grow a half crop or a full crop of alfalfa and some other kind of seed crop (mung bean) at the same time. With a lid placed under the bottom as a drip tray and a lid placed over the top, your sprouts remain crisper a lot longer in the fridge without souring or losing vital nutrients. Finally, this unit disassembles quickly for easy cleaning. To inquire about ordering one, write or call: Life Sprouts, P.O. Box 150, Paradise, UT 84328 (801) 245-3891.

But for those still interested in the old-fashioned way of doing things, here is what you'll need to get started:

➤ A wide-mouth jar, such as a Mason fruit jar
➤ Cheesecloth or wire mesh to cover the mouth
➤ A rubber band or string with which to secure the mesh

➤ The alfalfa seeds you intend to sprout

Be sure that the jar has enough room for your seeds to expand at least eight times their present size. For instance, three tablespoons of tiny alfalfa seeds will fill an entire quart jar!

Next comes the soaking. Put the alfalfa seeds into the jar and cover with mesh or cheesecloth and secure with rubber band or string. Wash the seeds several times by rinsing them under cold water. Then fill up the jar about halfway with lukewarm water, preferably, spring water. Now, each type of seed will vary in its own soaking time, but a good rule of thumb is to leave them overnight. In the morning pour off the soaking water into another container and save it; it makes a very nutritious addition for soup stocks, juice blends, or as a growth stimulant for your house plants. (One lady in Pasadena told me that she followed by advice and poured her alfalfa soaking water into her potted begonias and noticed incredible growth within less than a week.)

Now rinse the sprouts under the tap with water and pour off. Let them rest by tilting the jar upside down, at a 45 degree angle, making sure that the mesh opening allows air in and isn't completely covered up by sprouts. A dish rack is quite useful for this.

Rinse and drain the alfalfa seeds morning and evening. Use lukewarm water each time you do this. Be sure to inspect them carefully; any seeds not sprouting properly should be discarded. Do this for about 4 days. Always be on the lookout for possible development of mold; if this becomes apparent, *do not use the seeds but promptly discard them*! However, if they are thoroughly rinsed at least twice daily (or even three times, with one rinse at noon), there should be no danger of harmful mold forming. The main reason for rinsing is merely to keep the sprouts moist.

During the sprouting process, the outer case or husk of the seed will gradually loosen. Generally speaking, you'll want to float the husks away during the rinsing process. But do it gently; many seeds, like alfalfa, tend to split into their two halves if the husk is wrenched away and the seed will then not continue to sprout properly.

Most seeds such as alfalfa will sprout at temperatures ranging from 60–80 degrees; in other words, at normal room temperatures. Exceptions to this would be soybeans and chickpeas, which do well at somewhat lower temperatures.

Technically, the sprouting process should take place in a darkened situation. However, cereal and grain seeds—alfalfa, barley, clover, millet, rye, and wheat—can be permitted a few hours each day in artificial light or in *indirect* sunlight after their initial sprouting to let them develop chlorophyll. This is called "greening" and adds a mild, sweet taste, not to mention a nice touch of color, to what otherwise might be anemic-looking sprouts. An average length for a good alfalfa sprout is 1 $^1/_2$–2 inches. There you have it—perfect sprouts!

Seizures Stopped with Alfalfa Sprouts

One of the most incredible health success stories I've heard in years came to me from a friend I've known for a number of years. Her name is Loretta Harmony Kohn. During the 1970s she underwent medical treatment for a number of problems. The most serious of them were two brain seizures that were eventually diagnosed as epilepsy. And as if this weren't bad enough, she suffered from acute hypoglycemia as well.

She struggled with brief bouts of depression because of her deplorable physical conditions. The proverbial "straw that (nearly) broke the camel's back," however, came when her driver's license was revoked following her second epileptic seizure in January 1979. This left her virtually stranded in a rural part of central Pennsylvania. "Nobody else seemed to be helping me at the time," she recalled. "I had just about given up all hope and figured my life was finished for good at age 47!"

Then she read a book entitled *Be Your Own Doctor: Let Living Food Be Your Medicine* by the late Ann Wigmore, who founded The Hippocrates Health Institute in Boston, Massachusetts, some years ago. "Doctor Wigmore," as she was fondly called by hundreds of her patients, incorporated sprouts of all kinds as the main feature of her unique dietary program.

Alfalfa seed and wheat berry sprouts reigned supreme over the many different seeds she used. Loretta decided to visit her institute in Boston and stay a month in hopes of getting well again. "There were no other options left," she wistfully recalled. "Either I died or I lived—it was just that simple. And I chose to live!"

In one of her little booklets, *Spiritual-Physical Survival Thru Sprouting* (p. 20), written some years ago, Ann wrote this: "No disease can exist when the bloodstream is clean. The nourishment we grow in the kitchen will keep our blood clean. The cells are well nourished, enabling the circulation system to carry away wastes and toxins. We have a wonderful cleaning system: the lungs, liver, kidneys, skin and colon."

She told my friend Loretta that her seizures were due to "a big backup of toxic wastes" that had accumulated in her system over a period of many years. Medical doctors, of course, would have laughed themselves silly at such a simplistic explanation by someone without proper scientific accreditation. Yet, for all of her backward ways and limited academic education, Ann Wigmore had a lot of common sense and ingenious thinking about her. She implemented this rather elementary philosophy about health many years before Loretta ever visited her Boston institute. She worked with hundreds of sick patients, using her "live foods" in the form of sprouted salads, sprouted juices, and other sprouted foods to purge basic disease-causing sludge from their ravaged and decrepit bodies. And she did so with amazing results! People who came in barely able to walk or speak soon had enough energy to play tennis or volleyball, go swimming or jogging, or engage in other physically challenging activities of equal effort.

"Ann put me on a total raw foods diet," Loretta informed me. "I had a juice blend in the morning made from equal parts of alfalfa and wheat sprouts. Then a salad or sandwich for lunch teeming with alfalfa and wheat sprouts. Then another drink of the same sprouts in the evening with dinner, which usually included both types of sprouts in a baked vegetarian loaf or else in fried vegeburgers. I felt better after just a few days of being on this diet. I mean, my energy levels started coming up and I began losing weight, because obesity had plagued me for much of my adult life. In about four months I want to a physician at Brigham and Women's Hospital in Boston and submitted myself to an electroencephalogram (EEG) because I was curious as to what Ann's very restricted diet was doing for me internally. Imagine my great joy and delight when my doctor showed me normal results, telling me that as far as he was concerned, *I was free of epileptic seizures*! It wasn't to long after this that I got my driver's license reinstated!"

Loretta smiled a calm smile and said, as she looked away nowhere in particular, "Ann, wherever you are now, thank you for giving me my life and health back again!"

Gangrene Cured with Alfalfa Sprout Juice

On Sunday, November 6, 1983, Ann Wigmore and I were featured speakers at the Health Horizons Expo in the old Soldiers and Sailors Memorial Hall, situated on the corners of Fifth Avenue and Bigelow Street in downtown Pittsburgh. Ann told the audience of 2,000 people about a middle-aged man who came to her institute suffering from gangrene in his right leg, due to poor circulation brought on by acute diabetes.

I heard her describe in detail how she cured him of this disease. She gave him four glasses of alfalfa and wheat sprout juice to drink a day, made by putting equal parts with a little water in a blender for three minutes and also bathing the afflicted limb each day with the same sprout juice combination. Within two weeks the gangrene had *completely disappeared* to return no more. He was discharged and went home a healthier and much happier fellow after that.

Almond
(Prunus Dulcis)

Brief Description

The almond formerly went by the Latin binomial of *Prunus amygdalus*. It is a graceful tree of medium height (12–14 feet) of the rose family and closely allied to and resembling in some ways the peach, plum, and apricot.

There are numerous biblical references to the almond. The one I like best occurs in Numbers 17:8 and describes its fast-sprouting properties. After the famous exodus from Egypt, the rods of the princess of Israel were placed in the Tabernacle. Of the dozen staffs, only one sprouted and it was the almond: "…and, behold, the rod of Aaron for the house of Levi was budded, and brought forth buds, and bloomed blossoms, and yielded *almonds*." Almond branches are still known for the quickness with which they prematurely bloom when placed in water in a warm place. In biblical times the Hebrews looked upon the almond tree as a symbol of haste because of its sudden blossoming.

The peachlike almond fruit consists of the edible seed or kernel, the shell, and the outer hull. At maturity the hull splits open . When dry it may be readily separated from the shell. The sweet, luscious outer flesh of the peach is eaten and the pit containing the seed thrown away, while the almond pit is kept and the thin, fibrous outer flesh is discarded. The almond pit, containing a kernel or edible seed, is the nut of commerce we're speaking of here.

Almonds may be grouped into two distinct types: the sweet kind and bitter ones. There are also some intermediate almonds. The sweet almond is grown for its edible nuts. Bitter almonds provide the main source of oil of bitter almond, which is used both as flavoring and as an ingredient in cosmetic skin preparations.

The earliest almond trees in America were those grown from seed introduced from Mexico and Spain when the missions were established in California. Apparently, these trees died after the missions were abandoned. No further attempts at almond growing in the United States were made until 1840, when some trees imported from Europe were planted in the New England States. The climate was too severe there and the attempt wasn't successful. In time, however, plantings were made up and down the Atlantic seaboard and over into the Gulf States.

Eventually, some of these almonds found their way to California with the huge migrations westward during the 1840s and 1850s. California is now the only important almond-producing state in the Union. Almond orchards in California provide a living for some 7,500 growers and their families. For the most part, the trees are grown in the central valleys and watered by the Sacramento and San Joaquin Rivers and their tributaries.

Almonds for Indigestion

Almonds were very popular in England, where they had been introduced by the Romans at an early date. Among the recipes in the *Form of Cury*, a fourteenth-century cookbook written by the master chefs of King Richard III, mention is made of "Creme of Almand, Grewel of Almand, Cawdel of Almand Mylke," and others. The consumption of almonds in French medieval cookery was substantial. A inventory of the household goods of the queen of France in 1372 listed only 20 pounds of sugar—but included over 500 pounds of almonds.

Now, in medieval times, cookery was known more as *cury*, wherein chefs became recognized not only for the fabulous dishes they could whip up for their royalty bosses, but also for the different remedies they could provide to bring relief to such dietary-related health problems as obesity, gout, flatulence, heartburn, acid indigestion, hypertension, enlarged heart or liver, and constipation.

Through repeated trial-and-error testing such "kitchen doctors" discovered that when crushed almonds were slowly simmered in thin barley gruel or cow's milk over a hot fire for 30 minutes or more and then given to their gluttonous kings to eat or drink, the agonies of different gastrointestinal discomforts ceased within minutes. The same kind of almond gruel can be made today using oatmeal, barley, or wheat. The cereal should be quite watery, almost soupy, in fact, when a tablespoonful of crushed almond is added to 2 $1/2$ cups of this liquid mixture. Or one level teaspoonful of crushed almond can be added to 1 $1/2$ cups of regular milk. Allow either to gently steep on low heat, uncovered, for at least half an hour. Then strain and eat or sip when lukewarm.

Aging Without the Wrinkles

In the seventeenth century, Ninon de Lenclos, a French woman of fashion, recommended an almond-based cold cream that was said to have preserved her beauty and kept her face free of wrinkles until she was well into her seventies. The *Nonon de Le enclos Ointment* contained four ounces oil of almonds, three ounces of hog's lard, and one ounce of spermaceti (a yellowish, waxy solid obtained from sperm whale oil). After onion juice had been added, the ingredients were melted, stirred until cool, and scented with rose water. Almond oil is still used today as a base for cosmetics employed in theatrical makeup.

Here is a modern version of the same thing to make at home. Melt 2 tablespoons of Crisco shortening, $1/2$ tablespoons grated candlewax, and 3 tablespoons almond oil in a stainless-steel saucepan, over low heat. Put $1/8$ section of onion into a garlic press and squeeze until $1/2$ teaspoon onion juice has been obtained; then add this to the mixture. Be sure to stir often. Remove from heat and add 1 teaspoon of rose water. Then pour into some clean, empty baby-food jars, letting it cool and set up before capping with screw-on lids. Apply this almond antiwrinkle cream on the forehead, face, and neck every night before retiring. Cover these areas with some strips of plastic wrap to prevent staining pillow slips and bed sheets. Wipe off the next morning with cotton balls soaked with rubbing alcohol.

Then use the following mixture to thoroughly cleanse the face. All of the ingredients listed below are available at supermarkets or, better, at health-food stores. To make the *Daily Facial Scrub*, combine 4 tablespoons each of oatmeal, yellow cornmeal, and whole almonds, along with 2 tablespoons granulated kelp in a Vita-Mix Nutrition Center or equivalent food machine for 15 seconds on low speed and 10 seconds on high speed. This amount of scrub, stored in a glass jar, will last for 1 week and is safe to use every day. It's great for all skin types. For daily use on oily skin, place 2 tablespoons of the scrub in a bowl and add 4-6 tbsps. water. For daily use on dry skin, add 4–6 tablespoons water and 1 tablespoon olive oil. Rinse with cold water.

Follow this up with a *Wonderful Fruity Toner*. In your Vita-Mix Nutrition Center or equivalent food machine, combine $1/4$ cup each of strawberries, unpeeled applies, peeled banana, and orange juice for 15 seconds on high speed; strain, store in a glass bottle, and refrigerate. Splash it on your face or put some into an empty spray bottle and mist onto your skin.

Finally, add this *Delightful Moisturizer*. In your Vita-Mix Nutrition Center or equivalent food machine, blend together $3/4$ cup each of aloe vera gel, almond or olive oil, and vegetable glycerin, along with an essential oil fragrance of your choice. Blend on medium speed for 10 seconds; store in a dark glass container. This moisturizer can, as can the scrub and toner, be used over the entire body if desired. It is a fantastic beauty regimen to help you age "gracefully" and virtually wrinkle-free.

Proven Cancer Remedy

The bitterness in the bitter almond is due to the presence of the glycoside *amygdalin*, which readily hydrolyzes or breaks down to produce a cyanide. During extraction of the oil of bitter almond, the cyanide, also known as prussic acid, is eliminated so that the oil may safely be used for flavoring. But what may be dangerous to some, can, in fact, be quite life-saving to others.

The Merck Index (9th Ed.) (Rahway, NJ: Merck & Co., Inc., 1976; p. 81) legitimized the efficacy of amygdalin in its encyclopedia of chemicals and drugs by pointing out that this extract from bitter almonds, peaches, and apricots, has "been used in cancer chemotherapy since 1845…". Its other name, which most people are more familiar with, is *laetrile.*

In my controversial best-seller, *The Treatment of Cancer with Herbs* (Orem, UT: BiWorld Publishers, 1980, pp. 171–182), I wrote at considerable length on laetrile. I presented hard evidence to show that the initial research done by Dr. Kanematsu Sugiura at the Sloan-Kettering Institute in New York City proved laetrile "had a definite inhibitory effect on lung cancer" in test animals. But his work "was summarily suppressed by his superiors," who informed the press that "all the tests with laetrile had turned out to be negative…".

By the early 1980s nearly two dozen states had bypassed legislation legalizing laetrile's use by doctors; well over 75,000 cancer patients nationwide were then being treated with laetrile.

One scientist, who gave up a promising career to champion the use of laetrile, was the late Dr. Harold W. Manner, formerly chairman of the Department of Biology at Loyola University in Chicago. When I interviewed him for my book back in 1979, he told me that his own research had shown that the cyanide in laetrile "is not a poison when it is part of a *complete chemical complex,*" that is, used *intact* with other things. Dr. Manner believed that cancer patients could safely take small amounts of bitter almonds (up to ten) each day without suffering serious consequences. His main point was that "almonds could do no more harm than chemotherapy or radiation does, and probably at lot *less.*" He quit his lucrative job and went to Tijuana, Mexico, to open the Manner Clinic, which has helped hundreds of people recover from a number of different cancers in the past decade.

In recent years, laetrile has fallen into disfavor with many of the alternative cancer clinics in Tijuana. But there are still a few doctors in Mexico and here in the United States who continue prescribing it to their cancer patients. And there are still those I meet every so often at alternative health conventions who tell me they regularly chew small mouthfuls of almonds to prevent getting cancer or to treat existing tumors they may have.

Almonds Are Good for the Heart

Imagine this—eating almonds might just curb dangerously high blood cholesterol. At least that's the scientific opinion of Dr. Gene

A. Spiller, a noted researcher and director of the Health Research and Studies Center in California.

In tests, Dr. Spiller asked a group of men and women with relatively elevated cholesterol, averaging approximately 240, to consume 3 $\frac{1}{2}$ ounces of almonds each day for a little over two months. Other groups ate equal amounts of fat from cheese or olive oil. They all ate comparable amounts of whole grains, vegetables, and fruits.

But what Dr. Spiller found intriguing was that the almond-consumers' cholesterol dropped from 10–15 percent compared to that of the cheese-eaters. The almonds also reduced cholesterol slightly better than olive oil did. He things the findings make sense in light of the fact that most of the fat in almonds and olive oil is the same type—monounsaturated. If olive oil is good for the heart as has been repeatedly demonstrated in a lot of research, then so is almond oil. There is just one small drawback, though. All fats are high in calories; 3 $\frac{1}{2}$ ounces of almonds has 636 calories. But the good doctor thinks they're still okay to substitute for meat and dairy fats if you're to bring down your cholesterol.

Hemorrhoid Treatment with Almond Oil

Over three decades ago, the *British Medical Journal* carried a report in its January 27, 1962, issue on "Injection Treatment of Hemorrhoids [with Almond Oil]." Doctors at St. Thomas's Hospital in London injected a solution of 3 milliliters of 5 percent phenol with almond oil into the submucousal tissue just above each hemorrhoid. Additional injections later on are given, if necessary.

It was noticed that almond oil helped to stop bleeding, itching, and swelling almost immediately. The article recommended *that doctors* give serious consideration to the use of pure almond oil with phenol for treatment of hemorrhoids. (Note: phenol can be toxic without proper medical supervision.)

Amazon Nut (see Brazil Nut)

AMERICAN HOLLYBERRY
(Ilex Opaca)

BRIEF DESCRIPTION

The hollies include almost 500 different species of evergreen shrubs and trees that occur in temperate and tropical regions of the eastern and western hemispheres. Roughly 20 species are native to eastern North America. Most are highly prized for ornamental plantings, and all serve as useful food sources for wildlife.

The wood of American holly in particular is used in cabinetry and for the construction of novelties and specialized wood products. Black alder berry or winterberry (*I. verticillata*) is a close cousin to American holly. (For a discussion of it, see Black Alder Berry.)

Small greenish-white flowers first appear in the spring on trees averaging about 103 feet in height. The holly fruit is rounded, berry-like, and contains 2–9 bony, one-seeded, flattened nutlets called pyrenes. They usually mature sometime in September or October, turning from green to various shades of red, yellow, or black.

The ripe berries may be picked by hand or else flailed from the branches with some kind of long instrument onto ground sheets below. Seeds removal can be accomplished in several different ways. One is to run the berries through a macerator and then separate the seeds by flotation in water. Another way is to hand-rub the ripe berries across a screen in order to remove the pulp from the small amounts of seed.

The American holly is quite similar in appearance to the English holly (*I. aquifolium*), which is commonly associated with Christmas tradition. Two other types of holly berries are used along with their shrub or tree leaves in South America as popular tealike beverages. These would be the yerba maté (*I. paraguariensis*) of Brazil and Paraguay and the guayusa (*I. guayusa*) of Ecuador.

Fever Buster

Several folk healers from the rural parts of North Carolina have utilized a tea made from the dried berries to "bust fevers," so I was informed some years ago. Generally 1 cup of boiling water was sufficient to brew 5–7 small berries on low heat, covered, for 3 minutes. After it had cooled a spell, the liquid was then slowly sipped.

It is bitter as gall, but quite effective, I discovered, as a reliable "fever buster" in cases of influenza and other diseases where a rise in body temperature may be common. The tea, when cool, has also been injected into the rectum via a syringe and hot-water bottle.

The berries can be toxic but not fatal if taken in large amounts. Small $1/4$-cup doses every few hours will not produce vomiting as a rule, but slight purgative action may be evident nevertheless.

Chinese Treatment for Coronary Heart Disease

In the summer of 1980, I accompanied a group of third- and fourth-year medical students who were part of the American Medical Students association, and their faculty, to mainland China. Our purpose in going was to observe firsthand the medical procedures and techniques of China's "barefoot doctors" and better trained physicians.

We discovered in our tours through many different clinics and hospitals that a tea made from the berries and roots of a related holly (*I. pubescens*) was then being used in the treatment of coronary heart disease. Upon inquiring about the specific reason for this, we were informed through interpreters that the berries have a wonderful vasodilation action: they expanded blood vessels, which allowed for more blood to circulate through them.

Skin Wash

Certain types of skin disorders will ofttimes yield runny matter from open sores. A strong tea (10–14 berries to 1 cup of boiling water simmered on low heat, covered, for 5 minutes), when refrigerated and later strained, makes an ideal skin wash for such conditions.

Some nineteenth-century physicians employed this remedy when treating cases of smallpox. It not only relieved the itching, but also kept the scarring to a minimum. Its use externally for infectious skin diseases of children, such as measles, mumps, and chickenpox, is highly encouraged.

BARBERRY
(Berberis Vulgaris)

BRIEF DESCRIPTION

There are roughly 280 different species of barberry found in Asia, Europe, North America, and throughout the western hemisphere. Most of these deciduous and spiny shrubs are in the genus *Berberis*, but about 90 species, which are usually evergreen and unarmed plants, are placed by some botanists in the separate genus of *Mahonia*.

Those naturalized in eastern North America, often for ornamental purposes, carry the name of barberry. However, out West the shrub is equally well known by another common name, wild Oregon grape. (The term "grape" is used on account of the flowers that appear in little grapelike bright-yellow bunches in late spring and early summer. At higher elevations the ripening berries turn a dull purple, again giving them the appearance of grapes.)

The maturing berries can also be bright red and in juicy clusters similar to currants. Or else they can be dry and hollow and of a yellowish-tan hue.

All barberries have a yellow alkaloid in their root and bark systems called berberine. It is antibacterial, anticonvulsant, antihypertensive, amebicidal, and sedative in its operations. Berberine can also stimulate (due to its unpleasant taste) salivary and parotid secretions and, by reflex, hydrochloric acid and pedsinogen secretions from the gut lining.

Leaf appearances vary with different types of barberries. While most of them yield five or seven leaflets, *Manonia trifoliata* has just three leaflets. The only one that doesn't have the small prickly-leafed, large blue-green desert shrub appearance is *Mahonia wilcoxii*. It is a dark-green, large-leafed and open-foliaged moist barberry, more similar to a giant wild Oregon grape than any of the others.

The acidic flavor of the berries, while somewhat mouth puckering in nature, have made tasty preserves that are a nice accompaniment to wild game and help to better digest especially fatty or greasy meats such as duck or mutton.

In medical applications, barberry should not be used by women during their periods of pregnancy.

Gall Bladder Attack Cured

Ellen Martin (her real name) is a secondary-school teacher of 27 years in a small, middle-America town. One day while writing on the blackboard in her classroom, she suddenly experienced a sharp stabbing pain that started high in her abdomen and shot upward toward her right shoulder blade. "It felt as if I had been stabbed in the back with a knife," she recalled of her terrible ordeal.

A few days later, while correcting some test papers at home, "I suddenly grabbed my gut as an agonizing pain swept through it," she said. "I began sweating profusely and felt nauseous. I barely made it to the bathroom in time before I vomited up the remains of my previous meal."

Obviously very concerned and "somewhat frightened," she went to a naturopathic physician the next day to find out the exact nature of her problem and just how serious it was. Her doctor informed her that all these miseries had been produced by a stone passing down the narrow pipe from the gall bladder.

He prescribed for her three barberry capsules with a full glass of water on an empty stomach every other day for two weeks. Following this course of treatment, Ellen claimed that she had no further problems. "Barberry cured me of my all bladder attacks!" she emphasized.

Marvelous Eye Wash

The late Rudolf F. Weiss, M.D., routinely prescribed barberry tea for various eye disorders in his *Lehrbuch der Phytotherapie* (Stuttgart: Hippokrates Verlag, 1985). He wrote that barberry tea was an effective treatment for hypersensitive eyes, inflamed lids, and chronic and allergic conjunctivitis.

To make the tea, bring one pint of *distilled* water to a boil. Add one level teaspoonful of dried barberry, stir, cover with lid, and reduce heat. Simmer for three minutes. Remove from the heat and steep for an additional half hour. Strain through a fine-mesh sieve or double-layered cheese cloth. With an eye dropper put several drops into each eye, one at a time, with the head tilted back. A compress can also be applied to acute inflammatory eye conditions by soaking a clean handkerchief or similar cotton cloth material in the tea, gently wringing out excess liquid, folding it lengthwise and placing it over both eyes with the body in a reclined position. Repeat as often as necessary. Tolerance is good and the results are fairly rapid.

Guaranteed Hangover Treatment

Different remedies have been used for treating alcoholic hangovers. Some of them have ranged from hot black coffee and spicy tomato or tomato-vegetable juice.

One that isn't so common but quite effective, nevertheless, is barberry tea or fluid extract. One cup of the warm tea or 25 drops of the fluid extract in half a cup of *lukewarm* water will stimulate the liver into action and help eradicate the tension headache that often accompanies a hangover.

Alcohol causes dilation of the blood vessels, especially those within the skull as well as those that produce a flushed face. Barberry causes an expansion of these blood vessels and sends more blood circulating through the liver at a slightly increased rate. These actions enable the sufferer to start his or her day more clear-eyed and clear-headed than would otherwise be the case.

BAYBERRY
(Myrica Cerifera)

BRIEF DESCRIPTION

Bay is a perennial shrub that can reach treelike heights of up to 30 feet in the more hot and humid regions of the South. Essentially, it is a waterside shrub, preferring the moist and sandy soils of the Pacific and Atlantic coasts. One species, *M. californica*, may be found all along the lower western ridges of the California coastal ranges, from the Santa Monica mountains north to British Columbia, sometimes descending nearly to the surf. It is sometimes confused with an actual tree called the California bay.

You'll be able to find bayberry from Florida (*M. cerifera*) all the way northward to the New England coastline (*M. pensylvanica*). It is quite resistant to harsh winds, salt spray, and salt fog. I've discovered it growing wild rooted on bluffs overlooking the Atlantic in Maine. But some of it also grows in clumps as far inland as the Great Lakes area.

What makes bayberry so special is its unique odor and the waxy berries that mature from August to October. Break off a cluster of bayberry in the wild and you will detect that universally appreciated aroma; it seems to embody the untamed beauty of its surroundings. Even the narrow, tapering, evergreen leaves yield a pleasant fragrance.

The charming fruit is heavily coated with a whitish-green dry wax, creating a ghostly looking mantle of surreal-silvery beauty to the landscape. Actually a nutlet, the fruit is, in reality, a delicately coated stone, directly covered with memorable grains resembling gunpowder, inside of which is a twin-seeded kernel.

The early American colonists often referred to it as waxberry to indicate the service for which it was usually rendered. Animal fats were not too plentiful in those times. But the Puritans and Pilgrims soon discovered a cheaper and more abundant substitute in bayberry. Candles were made from bayberry wax and were more brittle and less greasy than those made from tallow. Candles are still made by some craftspeople in parts of New England and sold to tourists who pass through these regions. These candles, when lit, are a curious, almost transparent green, and when the flame is put out the resulting odor is as sweet and pungent as burnt incense.

The color of the ripe fruit varies with the species to which it belongs. Mature bayberries range in hue from brownish purple and light green to lustrous and grayish white.

Scottish Remedy for Skin Sores

When I wrote my first book in this series back in 1988—*Heinerman's Encyclopedia of Fruits, Vegetables and Herbs* (West Nyack, NY: Parker Publishing Co., Inc., 1988)—I had no idea it would be selling so well all over the world. I've received letters from France, Germany, England, Canada, Malaysia, New Zealand, and Australia from admiring fans who loved the book very much.

One letter came from a reader in Scotland telling me of some new uses for bayberry that, he said, "you overlooked." His name is Malcolm Campbell, "one of the Highlander clans," he bragged. "We wear the sweet gale [the Scot edition of the bayberry] right proud as our family badge," he noted.

For those unfamiliar with Scottish clans, let me digress a moment for a simple explanation. The word itself comes from the ancient Gaelic tongue. Most clans stress mutual obligations and duties. Clan descent is traced in one line only, male or female. A Scottish clan may include several family groups. A clan is distinguished from a lineage in that a clan merely claims common ancestry, whereas a lineage can be traced to a common progenitor. (For further information see Sir Iaian Moncreiffie's *The Highland Clans* (1967).]

In his wonderful letter, Malcolm explained how clan members had used the bayberry fruit for generations to treat open wounds, runny sores, bedsores, itchy and scaly skin, and similar external afflictions. He said that the remedy he included, "never failed in its desired actions."

The Highlanders bring a small amount of water to a boil in a pot (a pint or a quart, depending on the size of the area to be treated). "One generous handful [about 2 $1/_2$ level tablespoons] is thrown in [to 1 quart of water]; put your lid on and let it cook awhile [approximately 25 minutes] on a low fire [steep on low heat]," he wrote.

"After this, the brew can be strained and used to wash the skin with. It is very soothing and healing. Sometimes we make compresses using clean cloth to apply directly to a wound or sore. We also dry the sweet gale [Scottish bayberry] berries, crush them into powder, wet an open wound or sore with some water, then dust the area with some of this pulverized berry matter. We find that nothing equals this or works as well for any skin disturbance clan members may be afflicted with. I heartily recommend it to you for your next book," he concluded.

Great Shaving Agent

Peter Kalm was a Swedish botanist who traveled by canoe and on foot from the last U.S. fort north of Albany, New York, Fort Nicholson, through "no-man's land" to the first French fort, Fort St. Frederic, to reach Quebec where he spent many months as a guest of the French government. Jean François Gualtier was his guide, interpreter, and companion on this thrilling expedition. Kalm captured the adventure of his travels in a two-volume work entitled *Travels in North America* (1770).

Before starting his heroic trip northward, Kalm spent some time in Philadelphia. On October 13, 1748, he wrote (pp. 101–103): "Bayberries. There is a plant here from whose berries the settlers make a kind of wax...From that wax...they likewise make a soap here, which has an agreeable scent, and is the best for shaving. This wax is also used by doctors and surgeons who reckon it exceedingly good for plaster upon wounds."

During one of my periodic trips to the New England states, I briefly experimented with this as a shaving agent for myself. I took

about 15 of the nutlets, with their waxy coats intact, and dried them
in a friend's oven on a metal cookie sheet, after which they were
crushed by hand between two layers of wax paper with a heavy
stone rolling pin.

Then I shaved a few slivers of soap from a bar of Ivory into an
empty coffee mug, added only a tiny amount of water to moisten,
and then vigorously stirred the mixture up with a shaving brush
until I got enough lather. I then added the dried bayberry powder
and mixed it into the later with my brush, after which proceeded to
dab this mixture on my face.

While using my razor to get off the previous night's whiskers,
I was amazed at how smooth and easy a shave I was able to get
from this. In fact, when I was done and after rinsing and drying my
face, I ran my hand over both cheeks, across my chin, and under
my throat to get a better idea of how my skin felt after this unique
experience. It felt, well, kind of waxy, to be quite honest with you,
almost as if I had shaved with particles of candle. My skin didn't feel
rough at all and was nice and slick. I've sometimes thought about
that moment since then and wished I had access to some more bayberries.

For those with ready access to bayberries who would like to
collect the wax for shaving purposes, the process is quite simple.
Boil them in water until the wax collects to the surface and is either
skimmed off, strained, or else permitted to coagulate as the liquid
cools, after which it can then be removed in a solid state. To work
back into soap, simply melt some of it and a little grated Ivory bar
soap together in an old pan; then allow the mixture to set up again
before using in a shaving mug, just as I did.

Terrific for Oral Problems

Dr. Samuel Thomson, an early nineteenth-century practitioner of
eclectic medicine, had this to say about bayberry in his *Botanic
Family Physician* (Albany, NY: J. Munsell, 1841, p. 597):

"This valuable article…is the best remedy for canker [sores]
that I have ever found. It…causes the saliva to flow freely. It is an
admirable article to cleanse the teeth and mouth, and to remove the
scurvy from the gums. If taken, about a teaspoonful of the fine powder in water once a day, for a few days in succession, it removes
the most offensive breath…."

BEARBERRY/MANZANITA
(Arctostaphylos Uva-Ursi)

BRIEF DESCRIPTION

Bearberry has often been mistaken for cranberry by the uninformed. Not only does it grow in the same environments as the cranberry, but its brilliant red berry also resembles cranberry's. The berry derived its curious common name from early New England colonists, who noticed that black bears were very partial to it.

Bearberry is found worldwide. The medicinal properties of this hard red berry were known to Kublai Khan, founder of the Mongol dynasty in ancient China, and to Italian traveler Marco Polo.

The leaves of bearberry or manzanita are leathery and plastic to the touch. The early Algonquian Indians enjoyed mixing the leaves with tobacco and having a good smoke. They called this interesting mixture "kinnikinnick." In Scandinavia the leaves have been used for tanning leather.

The flowers are either white, pink, or flesh colored, each with five segments and formed like tiny narrow-mouthed urns, which eventually mature into small fruits with five seeds apiece.

The plant is a trailing vine and grows in thick carpets, depending on where it is. New growth in the spring can reach up to ten inches in height. The long trailing stems run just below ground level, usually in loose mulch.

Bearberry is intended more for medicinal purposes than for culinary use on account of the disagreeable taste; it has a cottony, mealy flavor. Also, the high tannin content can irritate the stomach lining and the liver, which suggests short-term use only.

Kidney Complaints Cured

Uva-ursi or manzanita is terrific for treating kidney problems. Nephritis (inflammation of the kidneys) and renal calculi (kidney stones) are overcome with a tea made from the berries and leaves of this plant. Cystitis (inflammation of the urinary bladder) and urethritis in women (inflammation of the urethra) have been successfully treated using the same tea. It is the astringency of the tannin acid in the berries and leaves that makes them work so well in such medical conditions.

It may be of interest to the reader to know that bearberry has been an official drug in the pharmacopoeias of Dublin, Ireland, Edinburgh, Scotland, and London, England, as well as in the United States pharmacopoeia from 1820 to 1936, and the National Formulary from 1936 to 1950. Besides being recommended for the aforementioned kidney problems in some of these texts, it has also found favor in allaying the usual irritations that follow catheterization.

To make an all-purpose tea, bring a quart of water to a boil. Then add 3 tablespoons of dried, chopped berries and leaves. Reduce heat, cover, and simmer about 5 minutes. Turn off the stove and let the brew steep for a half hour. Strain one cup at a time and take when lukewarm on an empty stomach.

Bearberry Baths Useful for Female Problems

One of the most helpful recommendations I've given to many pregnant women over the years is for them to utilize a sitz bath made from bearberry tea immediately following childbirth. The tannins, including another compound called arbutin, act as mild vasconstrictors to the endometrium of the uterus and reduce inflammation, infection, and further bleeding. This is only possible, though, if it is taken as a tea internally. However, a bearberry wash will eliminate inflammation on the perineum (the strip of tissue between the vagina and anus). This is particularly useful if a woman has torn her perineum or had an episiotomy (surgical widening of the vagina).

Normally, a sitz bath is made by putting enough warm or hot herbal bath water in the tub so that it reaches your navel when you sit in it. The feet are propped up on a hassock set beside the tub. The body is wrapped from the neck down with large beach towels or blankets. About 4 inches of water are put into the bathtub, the knees are kept up, and the water is splashed continually with the hand onto the abdomen. The person should remain in the tub for 30 minutes, then rinse with a short cold bath or shower.

However, a large oval-shaped enamel pan large enough for the average person to sit in will suffice in lieu of the tub. This space requires less liquid. The legs can hang over either side of the rim with the knees arched high. About three quarts of warm *uva-ursi* tea should suffice. An old cotton blanket or beach towel can be loosely draped over the person's midsection, while the individual washes the urogenital area with a cupped hand, while supporting the body upright with the other hand if necessary. Sitting with the back against a wall will help keep the upper torso erect while in this position.

Make the tea according to the instructions previously given. I should point out that this simple sitz bath arrangement will also go far in getting rid of hemorrhoids in the rectum. The buttock cheeks need to be firmly grasped by each hand and pulled apart in order for the tea to work this way. Hemorrhoids are quite common during pregnancy.

Cardiac Edema Helped

Cardiac edema means edema (fluid accumulation or swelling) of the limbs and other parts of the body due to congestive heart failure (CHF), not an accumulation of fluid around the heart per se. Pulmonary edema can occur, that is excess water in the lungs, when CHF is bad. Decreased kidney function (actually a compensatory function due to the CHF) causes the edema but it does not cause CHF. CHF results from a variety of health problems. For example, hypertension, mitral stenosis, and coronary artery disease. Dropsy is an old term formerly used to denote cardiac edema.

René Suscheaux lives in one of the parishes south of New Orleans. His diet has been fairly typical of most native Louisianians: a lot of fatty meat, greasy foods, white bread, mashed potatoes and gravy, and pastries. And when he has sat down to such meals, they have always been consumed with gusto.

By the time he checked in with his physician to get a complete diagnosis of what was wrong, René was experiencing shortness of breath accompanied by an added sound every time he breathed. He had noticeable fluid accumulation in his hands and feet, engorged neck veins, and an enlarged liver that was very tender to surface skin touch.

Not happy with the drugs the doctor prescribed for his problems, René turned to a local Cajun folk healer who used herbs in her treatment program. She put him on a program of two cups of *uva-ursi* tea for the first two weeks and then two capsules of the powdered berries every day for the next six weeks. By that time his condition had improved enough to allow him to discontinue this natural medication.

Unfortunately, René didn't change his lifestyle habits and went back to his old ways of eatings. He died several years later of congestive heart failure. But during the short time he took bearberry, he did feel a lot better.

Manzanita Cider for Allergies

Manzanita is the Spanish name given to bearberry. It means "little apple" and is quite apropos since the red berries do, indeed, look like miniature apples.

Here is an old recipe I got from an Hispanic curandera in Albuquerque some years ago. She washed approximately 4 cups of bearberries to remove accumulated debris. The berries were placed in a saucepan, covered with water, and gently simmered for about 20 minutes or until they were soft. She then drained them, reserving the liquid. The berries were mashed up a bit using a flat metal potato masher, but were not reduced to a pulp.

My friend then measured out the fruit and put it into a large mixing bowl. An equal amount of reserved liquid was added to the fruit. A cloth was put over the bowl and the mixture allowed to set for a day and a half until everything had properly settled. She then strained off the liquid and refrigerated it.

She mixed equal parts of this manzanita cider with orange or grapefruit juice, added one tablespoon of apple cider vinegar, and gave it to those who came to her with allergy problems.

BEECHNUT
(Fagus Grandifolia)

BRIEF DESCRIPTION

Another edible nut and cousin to the acorn is the beech. For bibliophiles such as myself, it comes as a pleasant surprise to learn that the beechnut has been more intimately associated with books and writing since early times than any other nut. Before books were written, messages were indelibly scratched on the smooth, light-gray surface of the bark of the European beech (*F. sylvatica*) or on beechen boards. The word "beech" comes from *bōece,* the Anglo-Saxon name for the tree which eventually became *Buch* in German, and *book* in English. As a tree to commemorate remembrances, the beech has absolutely no rivals: For many centuries its bark has served as a convenient place to register challenges to the enemy, epitaphs. and most frequently the carved initials of loved ones.

American beech trees are native to the eastern part of the United States, the same range as the white oak. But in contrast to the many species of oak, North America has just a single species of beech. The American beech is a medium-sized tree, reaching a height of 60 to 80 feet, with a diameter of 2 to 3 feet. Slow-growing, it may live 400 years or more. This deciduous tree has a rounded crown and oval, pointed leaves, 3 to 6 inches long, which resemble the chestnut's.

The beech bears fruit in the form of woody burs that enclose two to three small, triangular nuts about three-eighths to one-half inch across. The burs open and the nuts ripen and fall to the ground in October; a few seeds, not consumed by squirrels, birds, wildlife, or humans, germinate and possess enough vitality to establish themselves even in the deep shade of the forest.

In southern Germany the beech is still considered useful for forecasting the season in the same way as the oak. The peasants there expect a hard winter with plenty of snow if there are acorns on the oak. But the beech is carefully watched by the grain merchants: If there are plenty of beechnuts in the fall, the next corn harvest will be especially good. And if the beech starts shooting at the bottom of the tree, the price of grain will rise. If it starts at the top of the tree, however, the price will tumble, as that means there will be a good crop that year.

Good Food for the Underweight

During both world wars fought in this century, many peasants of battle-ravaged Europe took to the gathering and grinding of beech nuts in order to provide themselves with adequate fat and protein when no milk, eggs, or meat were readily available for them. During more normal times, the farmers in the southern parts of France and Germany made beechnut cakes from the ground meal to feed to their pigs, goats, rabbits, and poultry. These cakes are always mixed with the animals' other food and are never given alone. Farmers throughout Europe have reported substantial improvement in their bacon, the fur of goats and rabbits, and the laying capacity as well as the feathers of barnyard poultry. People, domestic livestock, and poultry all seem to put on weight and do well when beechnut is made a regular part of their diets.

Although similar to the chestnut in flavor, the beechnut is much richer in fat content (50 percent) as opposed to about 4 percent for the chestnut. The protein content of beech nut is almost 20 percent, carbohydrates 20.3 percent, and its energy value 2,576 calories per pound. In Germany, the oil of the European beechnut is routinely utilized by nutritionists and doctors as a salad oil and butter substitute in patients who are underweight. When placed on special hospital or clinic diets that include plenty of beechnut oil and "butter," skinny patients soon become plump and full in flesh. During times of famine in Scandinavia, beechwood sawdust was boiled in water and mixed with flour and baked to make bread. In France, roasted and ground beechnuts have occasionally served as a coffee substitute for those recuperating from lengthy illnesses.

Nut Tea Reduces Fevers

The rinds of immature nuts and young twigs and branches, collected in the spring, have been used in Germany either fresh or dried as a sure remedy in the case of intermittent fevers. The following remedies for this were obtained from two old German books and apply both to beechnuts as well as to acorns and oak bark: Bruno Schoenfelder's *Welche Heilpflanze ist das?* (Stuttgart: Frankh'sche Verlagshandlung, 1941, pp. 48, 50, 68) and E. M. Zimmerer's *Kraeutersegen* (Donauwoerth: Ludwig Auer, 1910, pp. 102–3; 146–50).

Put 1–2 teaspoons of nut rinds (fresh or dried) into one cup of cold water. Either bring it slowly to a rolling boil and then simmer for 10 minutes, or it can be left cold, allowing it to stand in a cup of cold water for 12–14 hours and straining it before drinking. About 2 cups a day are recommended.

Another method is to add 1 tablespoon of young rinds (fresh or dried) to 1 pint of cold water, bring slowly to a rolling boil, and then simmer for 15 minutes on low heat. After that, 1 teaspoonful of honey is stirred in while the liquid is still hot. Once it has cooled and been strained, a cup may be taken twice daily with good results on an empty stomach for fevers.

Effective Gargle for Sore Throat and Bleeding Gums

The aforementioned home remedies can be used for treating sore throat by gargling with some of the warm contents or by soaking some cotton balls in the same tea and swabbing gums with it to stop bleeding.

Compresses for Swollen Glands and Hemorrhoids

Make a strong decoction by adding 3 tablespoons of beechnuts or acorns to 2 pints of water and slowly boiling for up to 15 minutes. Allow to cool for a few minutes, but not too long; the tea should still be warm enough to work with. Soak a clean washcloth in some of the tea, gently squeeze out any excess liquid, and apply to the neck, throat, or under the armpit to any swollen glands. Cover with a dry hand towel and keep in place until the compress becomes dry and requires changing. For hemorrhoids, fold a length of gauze strip several times, soak in the tea, squeeze out any excess fluid, and insert into the rectum. Leave there for at least 20 minutes.

Intestinal Parasites

Because beechnuts and acorns contain certain amounts of tannic acid, they make excellent teas to take internally to expel worms and other parasites from the intestines.

BETEL NUT
(Areca Catechu)

BRIEF DESCRIPTION

The betel or areca nut is the seed of a plant of the same name, belonging to the palm family. The betel is a single-stemmed, slender, graceful tree that grows up to 100 feet in height, with a crown of featherlike pinnate leaves 4 to 6 feet in length. Annually, the tree bears 2 to 6 bunches of conical fruits, each one about the size of a hen's egg, which ripen to an orange-yellow color. Although the original habitat of this palm is uncertain, since it has never been found in the wild, it is sometimes considered to be indigenous to Malaysia.

    The hard seed or kernel of the betel, miscalled a "nut," is a masticatory; it is never swallowed but is chewed in much the same way as is plug tobacco. The chewer of the betel nut derives a mild narcotic effect from it. Betel ranks as one of the world's major stimulants. It is estimated that at least 10 percent of the human race indulges in the habit of betel-nut chewing—some 400 million people from India and southeast Asia to the central Pacific islands, East Africa, the Philippines, and southeastern China. On a global basis, it is more popular than chewing gum.

Preparation of betel for chewing commences with the harvest of partially ripened fruits which are boiled and then dried in the sun. Although betel may be chewed alone, more commonly a few thin slices of the kernel are made into a quid, smeared with a dab of fine, slaked lime, and wrapped in a fresh leaf of the perennial, climbing betel pepper vine (*Piper betle*), to add piquancy. This quid is chewed slowly, usually after meals as a breath sweetener and is spit out when the flavor is gone. On ceremonial occasions, the quid may be flavored with spices such as cloves or cardamom, or sometimes tobacco. Betel chewing stimulates a copious flow of red saliva, which is constantly expectorated. When I've walked the streets of Calcutta, India, I've noticed the scarlet-splashed sidewalks as evidence of the notorious popularity of betel chewing.

Chewing betel occasionally is helpful in certain medical conditions, but should not become a ritual. The habit causes the lips, tongue, and teeth to become brown, and eventually black. If used with increased frequency, it can become very addictive.

A Sure Cure for Dysentery

The betel nut contains various alkaloids, the most important one of which is arecoline (about 0.1 percent) This is what gives the nut its narcotic properties. Cured nuts contain up to 15 percent tannic acid. Both compounds are very helpful in the treatment of dysentery. I've had doctors in East Africa tell me that they've turned to betel nut as a last resort, when all other Western drugs at their disposal failed to completely eradicate dysentery. They would make quids of the nut and give it to their sick patients to chew. The red saliva would be swallowed in small amounts, while the rest of it was spit out. This would be done several times throughout the day. Invariably the amoeba (*Entamoeba histolytica*) causing this ulcerative inflammation of the colon and diarrhea would be knocked out and soon eliminated from the bowels.

Fantastic for Tapeworm, Roundworm, and Hookworm

Ayurvedic physicians whom I have interviewed in Bombay and Calcutta in past years have routinely used betel nut in the treatment

of certain intestinal parasites. In fact, it was considered so efficacious against tapeworms and roundworms in Rudyard Kipling's day
that it was introduced into the British pharmacopoeia, where it
remained as a useful drug agent for many years.

I observed how Dr. Vany Singh administered betel nut to some
of his patients in his Bombay clinic. He stirred $1\frac{1}{2}$ tablespoons of
the powdered betel nut in $\frac{1}{2}$ cup of lime juice and had each patient
who was afflicted with worms drink this nasty-tasting concoction. It
never failed to discharge the parasites from their intestinal tracts.

Stops Tropical Diarrhea

I've spent a lot of time over the years doing research throughout
most of the countries in Southeast Asia. While on such ethnobotanical expeditions, I always try to be careful about the water I drink
and the food I eat. In most cases I've been pretty successful in not
contracting diarrhea in these tropical environs.

On a couple of occasions, however, I haven't been so fortunate. In Malaysia, an old native folk healer living on the edge of a
deep jungle made me a quid of betel nut and insisted that I slowly
chew it, being sure to swallow my red-colored saliva. I did this for
about an hour until he finally told me to spit it out. After that I
passed only solid stools, the tannic acid in the betel nut having
tightened up the watery feces within my bowels.

BILBERRY
(Vaccinium Myrtilloides)

BRIEF DESCRIPTION

Confusion often ensues when trying to distinguish between blueberry and its closest European relative, the bilberry or whortleberry. It is a favorite of berry pickers in northern European climes and is quite similar to the blueberry in appearance and taste. The key to differentiating between the two of them is by the flowers of each. The blueberry has u-shaped flowers, while those of the bilberry are star shaped. In addition to this, the fruit of the bilberry is, generally speaking, darker in hue than that of blueberries and grows singly on axils, as opposed to the familiar clusters with blueberries.

The Finns give the bilberry an evocative name, *mustikka,* which is often translated as blueberry or huckleberry; that only adds to the confusion surrounding them already. Bilberry grows carefree in forests, interspersed with lingonberries, forming colorful patterns on woodland floors. In the "Land Down Under" Australians often call the bilberry fruit by the name of blueberry, much to the consternation of some botanists who know the difference.

Bilberry shrubs growing along north slopes of the California coastal ranges, sporadic from San Diego to Santa Barbara, and a smaller but very different version of bilberry forming large colonies in spruce forests in Arizona, New Mexico, and points northward, both go by the misnomers of blueberry or huckleberry.

The evidence, therefore, indicates that there is a great deal of confusion surrounding the correct identification of true bilberry. But when properly identified, bilberries are found to be very sweet and delicious. Samuel de Champlain, a French explorer of Eastern Canada and the founder of Quebec City, mentioned their food use by early Native American tribes of the time that he and his exploration party often encountered. In the translated edition of the *Journal of Champlain for the Years 1615–1618* (Paris: 1619, p. 34), he had this to say of a large growth of bilberries discovered by his nearly famished party: "Without them we might have starved to death." A little later on, page 36 of this extremely rare and priceless work—a copy of which, by the way, I found in the library at Laval University in Quebec City some years ago—he mentioned "a tribe we called the cheveaux relevés or long hairs," who had been drying great quantities of bilberries, "so they would have something to eat that winter when their other supplies had been used up."

Further along in his journal (p. 78), he furnished his readers with an Indian bread recipe, which called for "boiling the dough, as if they were making corn soup." "This makes it easier to whip," he explains. "After it is thoroughly boiled," he continues, dried bilberries or dried raspberries along with "occasional piece of suet" are added. "After moistening the batter with warm water they make it up into loaves or biscuits which they bake under hot coals."

A Treatment for Diabetes

While I was doing research at Laval University in Quebec City, Quebec, Canada, back in the late part of the 1970s, I came across an interesting item in the Archives of Folklore there. It was in the form of a research paper entitled, "Traditional use of herbs in Quebec Province" by Catherine Jolicoeur.

She recorded the statements of different Quebecois folk healers and herbalists whom she had apparently interviewed. There was a collective assessment among all of them that an alcoholic fluid extract of fresh bilberries was one of the best remedies for diabetes mellitus. It also helps to prevent leg ulcers and possible gangrene from occurring, she noted—two conditions frequently accompanying diabetes in its more advanced stages.

"With the fresh berries," she wrote, "you make a tincture which...[according to her informants] 'is the first and most indispensable of all the tinctures in our household pharmacy.' The instructions she obtained from them for making this useful fluid extract are as follows:

> In a liter jar put 100 to 150 grams of fresh berries and fill with alcohol or brandy. It is ready in 15 days but stronger and better if left longer. It is taken [for diabetes]..., 10–30 drops [under the tongue]. A second dose after 3 to 10 hours [may be necessary]....

A similar remedy for the same disease is verified by Czechoslovakian authors Frantisek Stary and Vaclac Jirasek in their *Herb* book (London: Hamlyn, 1973, p. 210).

Oral Inflammation Disappears

Inflammation of the mouth, throat, and gums can be a real problem for some children and adults because such conditions won't always respond to antibiotics and are, therefore, quite difficult to get rid of. The usual culprit is some type of infection that can induce colds and influenza, or else to a yeast such as *Candida albicans.*

Almost two decades ago, a German pharmacist and doctor by the name of Mannfried Pahlow compiled a little work entitled *Heilpflanzen heute* (Munich: Gräfe und Unzer GmbH, 1976, p. 43) in which he gave a nifty remedy for such oral problems. He stated in his book that much of his herbal data was "Volks Heilmittel von Oma und Opa" or folk remedies handed down through successive generations of grandparents.

I have taken the liberty of translating his instructions for making this. Dried bilberries can be taken as they are, but it is better to prepare a concentrated solution of the fruit juice and drink a small wineglassful as required. To prepare bilberry tea: Pour a pint ($^1/_2$ liter) of cold water over three dessertspoonsful of dried berries and boil for ten minutes. Strain and cool and the tea will be ready to drink. For the best effects drink a glass of tea several times a day, being sure to swirl each sip around in the mouth and retaining it there for a couple of minutes before finally swallowing it.

I've given this remedy to several alternative-minded dentists I know, and they've passed it on to some of their patients with very good results, they've told me.

Effective Ulcer Healing

Italian scientists working out of the Inverni Della Beffa Research Laboratories in Milan, Italy, discovered not too long ago that bilberries contain "a significant preventive and curative antiulcer activity," which they attributed to the a group of compounds in the berries themselves called anthocyanosides. (This flavonoid is also common to all red and blue berries such as blackberries, cherries, blueberries, and hawthorn).

As reported in the Italian pharmacological journal *Il Farmaco* (42[2]:29–43, February 1987), a variety of ulcers were induced different ways in male rats of the Wistar or Sprague-Dawley strains. Some stomach ulcers were prompted by administering several kinds of irritating chemicals via gastric lavage.

Following the inducement of different types of ulcers, all the test animals were given fluid extracts of bilberries by gastric tube twice daily, usually at 8 A.M. and again in the late afternoon, at 4 P.M. The animals were later sacrificed after a treatment period of 6 at 12 days, and the areas of the ulcers measured and carefully evaluated.

Quoting directly from the report prepared by A. Cristoni and M. J. Magistretti: "The results of this study show that VMA [*Vaccinium myrtillus anthocyanosides*] are endowed with a strong preventive and curative antiulcer activity." The bilberry extract was very effective in every type of ulcer induced. They reasoned that bilberry acts on the biosynthesis of protein-carbohydrate complexes found in the blood called mucopolysaccharides, which seems to "improve the efficiency of the mucus barrier at [the] gastric level and may increase the connective tissue ground substance at cutaneous and capillary levels."

Circulatory Disorders Helped

The fluid extract or powder of dried bilberries has been amply documented to benefit problems of circulatory insufficiency in the extremities including feet and legs, hands and arms, as well as the head area. For older or obese people suffering from "cold hands and feet" syndrome or a "pins-and-needles" effect, this berry would be the right thing for them to use on a continuous basis.

In fact, the extract is well documented to reduce and even reverse damage caused by actual blood-vessel deterioration or inflammation. It strengthens the entire vascular system and prevents leakage of fluids or cells from capillaries. It also strengthens coronary arteries and helps prevent obstruction of heart arteries by accumulations of digested fat. Bilberry also inhibits the degradation of blood platelets.

Extract of bilberry is quite useful for the prevention and treatment of hemorrhaging and the formation of blood clots. It prevents venous insufficiency causing swelling of the ankles and feet—especially during pregnancy or as people age.

The Italians have been doing a great deal of work in this area with bilberry and a common weed from Southeast Asia called gotu kola. Both are available in health food stores and should be used together for the aforementioned problems.

Vision Dramatically Improved

The eyes have a rich supply of blood vessels. But impaired circulation to the eyes may decrease the normal delivery of adequate nutrients and may also induce oxidation, which can lead to cataracts, glaucoma, macular degeneration, and even blindness in certain cases.

Again, Italian scientists have been in the forefront of the medical research into the wonderful benefits of bilberry for the eyes. Their investigations have demonstrated that bilberry extract can increase circulation to the eyes by as much as 80 percent, which soon leads to an 80 percent improvement in vision for the person taking bilberry consistently.

The Italian studies say that bilberry increases enzymatic activity and energy production in the eye. Thus, it enables the eyes to receive and transmit signals better and more rapidly. A German ophthalmologist whom I spoke with by phone from my home in Salt Lake City to his clinic in Frankfurt enthusiastically related how a combination of bilberry extract and dandelion flowers helped many of his patients suffering from night blindness to better adapt to bright or dim light.

Further research by another Italian scientist, Dr. Bravetti (as reported in the medical journal *Ann. Ottalmol. Clin. Ocul.* 115:109, 1989) showed that when vitamin E (600 I.U.) and bilberry extract (3 capsules) were both taken orally, once a day, they stopped the progression of cataract formation in 97 percent of subjects tested. Another study showed that bilberry alone produced significant improvement in 75 percent of people tested with nearsightedness and myopia.

Bilberry is terrific for vision problems, but I suggest it be used in conjunction with dandelion, gotu kola, and ginkgo biloba for maximum efficiency.

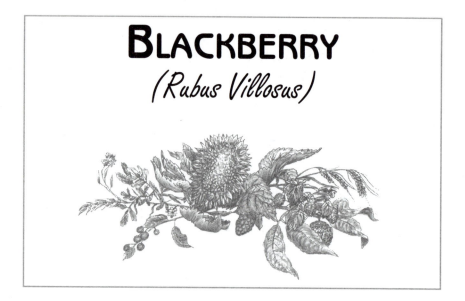

BLACKBERRY
(Rubus Villosus)

BRIEF DESCRIPTION

Blackberries have been divided into hundreds of species, with two major kinds occurring both in Europe and in America and Canada. These are the upright growing forms and the prostrate, or trailing forms, often called dewberries in the South. How on earth this name ever originated beats me, unless it was because the berries were frequently covered with dew when they were gathered in the early morning hours.

The upright blackberries not only have stiff, erect canes but are generally very thorny as well. They propagate by suckers from the roots. In contrast, the trailing blackberries found in North America have slender canes, are much less heavily thorned than their European counterparts, and don't sucker. The tips of the canes, if in contact with the soil, strike root and establish new plants. In general. the upright forms have a strong flavor, with a somewhat bitter aftertaste. The trailing forms are usually milder flavored as a rule.

In North America blackberries thrive in all except the coldest or driest parts of the country. They are especially abundant along the eastern seaboard, west to the Plains, and throughout the South. Texas is particularly rich in this fruit. Two very high quality species of dewberries also grow along the Pacific Coast.

Most species produce black or reddish-black berries, but I've seen and tasted a few that are yellow or orange. The berry pulls away with its soft, fleshy and edible corelike torus attached. The stones are oval, pointed, and wrinkled. The juice is deep purple, the fragrance agreeable, and the taste rather sweet.

I've discovered in years past that the blackberry is also quite profuse in the English country roadside hedgerows, where it takes on a less formidable appearance. The British garden author William Robinson was very much a champion of the natural hedgerow. He opined that it is "very interesting...to observe the differences between some of the sub-species and varieties of blackberries, and the beauty, both in fruit and flower, of the family." His words undoubtedly inspired many a gardener to let the bramble into the home landscape—one potential explanation for the existence of so many blackberry thickets throughout Great Britain.

Blackberry became immortalized in the writings of an American journalist by the name of Joel Chandler Harris, who worked for the Savannah *Morning News* (1870–1875) and the Atlanta *Constitution* (1876–1900). His claim to glory rests on his creation of the Uncle Remus tales. In his *Uncle Remus and Brer Rabbit* (published in 1906), Brer Rabbit begs his assailants to *not* throw him into a nearby briar patch, which, in this case, happened to have been a patch of dewberries. Not realizing that this is the very thing he hoped they would do, they threw him in anyway, and he settled down to a nice meal of dewberries unmolested by his enemies, who couldn't reach him again on account of the many thorns they encountered.

Versatile Blackberry

Ethnobotanist and naturalist Judith L. Bolyard spent some time among the residents of rural southeastern Kentucky and Rabun Gap, Georgia, interviewing them regarding their medical lore. She found that the inhabitants of both regions are primarily descendants of people from the British Isles. She chose these areas to conduct her research because both cultures have remained relatively isolated from the homogenizing influences of mainstream American values and attitudes. Both cultures have developed a tradition which has been transmitted orally from generation to generation, using folk medicine. Historically, neither culture has had much contact with trained medical care. Similarities between them are based either on a common shared ancestry, contacts with Native American medical practices in the past, or a common knowledge gained from herbalists who have utilized common sources such as published herbals.

In her book *Medicinal Plants and Home Remedies of Appalachia* (Springfield, IL: Charles C. Thomas, 1981, pp. 128–130), she described the diverse uses for blackberries. Hemorrhaging and hemophilia have been successfully treated with blackberry tea. Fresh blackberries are picked with gloves, washed under water in a colander to remove debris, and then laid out in the sun on an old but clean bed sheet to dry. Afterwards, they are stored in a closed fruit jar in a cool, dry place until needed. A handful of dried berries is added to a pint of boiling water and simmered for 15 minutes, then allowed to steep for an additional 30 minutes. The brew is strained, and a cup is drunk twice daily for both problems.

Dried dew berries (dried in the manner just described) made into a simple tea and taken warm with a meal will prevent intestinal discomforts such as heartburn and flatulence. The tea should be made as needed and then only enough for the purposes intended. In a cup of boiling water, add one level tablespoonful of dried dewberries. Cover and simmer for 20 minutes, strain, and drink when it has cooled a bit.

Stings from bees, wasps, or hornets, and bites from chiggers, red ants, and mosquitoes may be alleviated by soaking a cotton ball with some blackberry juice and then immediately applying it over the afflicted area and holding it in place with a bandage or a strip of tape.

Diarrhea, dysentery, and cholera have been successfully treated with blackberry cordial. In the Appalachias, the cordial is made with fresh berries, some spices, sugar, and a little moonshine whiskey, but brandy can be substituted if the former is unavailable. Pick and wash a quart of blackberries. Mash them thoroughly in a large pan with a flat metal potato masher. Add 1 teaspoonful each of powdered cinnamon, cloves, and allspice. Add $1\frac{1}{2}$ pints water and cover; simmer slowly for two hours before straining. Add 3–4 tablespoons of brown sugar, cover and simmer some more until only a pint or slightly less remains. Finally, add $\frac{1}{4}$ as much brandy to the mixture and you have your blackberry cordial. Two tablespoons every few hours is recommended. In the hillbilly culture of the Appalachias, moonshine or homemade corn liquor is consumed by adults and children alike for medicinal and social reasons. However, it is a good idea to *not* give very young children herbal extracts which are alcohol-based.

The mountain folks of the Appalachias have long relied on blackberry juice or tea for treating a goiter. How this exactly works in the system still isn't known. Ordinarily an iodine-rich supplement of some kind, such as kelp or other seaweeds, have been routinely prescribed for goiter. But folks afflicted with goiter in those two regions of Kentucky and Georgia visited by Ms. Bolyard some years ago took nothing but blackberry for getting rid goiter.

An efficient salve for burns suffered from kerosene lanterns or coal and wood stoves is made from blackberries and lard. Wash one cup of blackberries in a colander under some running water to remove debris. Mash thoroughly in a pan and strain into another container. Heat a large iron skillet and over a low heat slowly melt some Crisco or other shortening (substituted for beef tallow or hog lard), about 5 tablespoonfuls to start with. Pour in the blackberry juice, a little at a time. Don't allow the shortening to get hot enough to smoke! If there is more juice than shortening, a little more shortening might be necessary in order to reduce the liquidity of the mixture. Pour the contents into clean, empty baby-food jars and allow to harden while still warm. When cooled and set up, screw on the lids and store in a cool place until needed. The salve is quite effective in reducing blistering that always occurs when the skin is injured with heat.

Hemorrhoids may be shrunk by soaking two cotton balls with blackberry juice, squeezing out the excess fluid, and inserting into the rectum. Uterine hemorrhages may be stopped by douching with blackberry juice as well as by drinking some of it, too.

BLACKHAW BERRY
(Viburnum Prunifolium)

BRIEF DESCRIPTION

Blackhaw is part of the honeysuckle family. There are about 120 species of Viburnum that occur in the northern hemisphere. Many species are important for environmental plantings and for ornamentals. In England they are especially abundant in hedgerows and borders surrounding forests.

Blackhaw species are either large shrubs or small trees. They are densely branched, opposite-leaved, and many of the branches bear thorny branchlets. The flowers are very abundant, in terminal corymbs, white in color, and quite showy and fragrant in late spring. They are succeeded by small flattish-oval drupes, which, after the first frost, become purple black, glaucous, sweet, and rather edible once they are cooked to neutralize their toxic components.

Miscarriages Avoided

In the nineteenth century blackhaw berry was a popular ingredient in many proprietary preparations intended for gynecological conditions. It was generally administered in an alcoholic fluid extract (20 drops beneath the tongue twice daily) or a simple tea (2 cups daily in the very early stages of pregnancy).

To make a fluid extract of the same, combine three table-spoonsful of the dried, crushed, powdered berries in one pint of brandy or rum. Shake daily, allowing the powdered berries to be extracted for about 15 days. Let them settle to the bottom of the container they're in before pouring the contents out, straining out the powdered material through a fine cloth or paper filter. Mountain folk in the Ozarks swear that the best time to put up the fluid extract is on the new moon and to strain it off on the full moon so that the drawing power of the waxing moon will help extract the properties from the berries themselves.

A very simple tea is made by bringing a pint of water to a boil and adding two heaping teaspoonfuls of blackhaw berries, either fresh or dried. Cover and simmer at a reduced setting for ten minutes. Steep another ten minutes before straining and sipping one cup while it is still somewhat warm.

Painful Menstruation Eased

For a long time in the nineteenth and early part of the twentieth centuries, blackhaw berry was considered almost a specific remedy for cases of difficult and painful menstruation. Both the dried berries and bark were used, with a peculiar valerianlike odor coming from the combination. They were made into a fluid extract according to the instructions already given. A full teaspoonful, about 20–30 drops, was given to women several times a day on an empty stomach to ease their pain. A tea made the same way for miscarriages and taken as often also proved useful.

Now it seems to have fallen in disfavor in lieu of other herbs such as squawvine, chamomile, and yarrow. But where blackhaw berries can be obtained, they are still helpful gynecological aids for women who need them.

BLUEBERRY
(Vaccinium Corymbosum)

BRIEF DESCRIPTION

The blueberry group is probably the most widely distributed fruit in the world. Species of this group are distributed over much of Asia, Europe, and North and South America. They extend from the tropics to the northern limits of human habitation. Blueberries have been extensively exploited for their food and medicinal values by tribal shamans residing in the rain forests of northwest and north Amazonia. Richard E. Schultes and Robert F. Raffauf, authors of *The Healing Forest: Medicinal and Toxic Plants of the Northwest Amazonia* (Portland, OR: Dioscorides Press, 1990) explain how edible berries such as these and others are employed by witch doctors as an internal drink to help calm patients whose bodies are wracked with fever. Dr. Mark J. Plotkin in *Tales of a Shaman's Apprentice* (New York: Penguin Books, USA, 1993), gives the juice of blueberry to those suffering from malaria.

At the opposite end of the hemisphere (quite literally), in the Koyukon region of north-central Alaska, one can still find many Athapaskan Indians gathering and preserving blueberries the way their ancestors probably did centuries ago. Having an old-fashioned

Native American dinner in the middle of a subfreezing winter at any of the nearly snow-covered homes in villages lining the banks of the frozen Yukon can be a meal experience all to itself. Patricia Semakan served up one such repast complete with roast moose, pine needle-acorn dressing, gravy, and wild greens salad. For dessert, she dished up a bowl of blueberries that had been carefully preserved all winter long in seal oil and stored inside a sealskin bag! While the taste took some getting used to and was certainly very different from the typical blueberries I had been previously accustomed to eating, it wasn't all that bad. The closest comparison I can find is mushy blueberries soaked in sardine oil for several months! But that dessert alone was packed with a walloping amount of vitamins A and C; little wonder then that there are hardly any nutritional deficiencies among these people in spite of their lack of abundant produce.

There is still some confusion between blueberry and huckleberry. In some parts of the country the names are occasionally used interchangeably. But a concerted effort by U.S. Dept. of Agriculture botanists and horticulturists now confine the name of blueberry to those berries having a large number of very small, inconspicuous seeds—so small, in fact, that they're not noticed when eating the fruit. Huckleberry, on the other hand, is applied to those berries having ten rather large bony seeds that are definitely noticeable and somewhat objectionable when the fruit is being consumed.

Blueberries indigenous to North America are either high bush or low bush. The high bush types, especially *V. corymbosum*, have large, sweet, deep-blue berries; these are the blueberries that grow in cultivation. They can reach heights of twenty feet, creating their own close societies in deciduous forest, hillsides, or acid bogs.

The low bush sorts, such as *V. angustifolium*, dote on sandy or rocky acid soils, are quite hardy, and have a wide range. These petite plants grow from only 8 inches to $1\frac{1}{2}$ feet high. The small, tart fruits, which vary from cadet blue to purplish black, inspire pickers to trek deep into the woods to procure them. Low bush plants have an independent spirit all their own that can't be broken, even by the most skilled horticulturist. These very fussy berries strongly resist cultivation in the home garden but thrive like crazy in the wild.

Yanomamo Cure for Fevers

The Yanomamo Indians reside in a dense jungle area bordering Brazil and Venezuela in the northeast part of the huge Amazon basin. They have a reputation for fierceness that in part, is fully justified but in another respect has been greatly exaggerated by imaginative foreigners who've visited them from time to time.

Upon entering a typical Yanomamo roundhouse in one village some years ago, my guide and I were instantly greeted by what, at first, seemed like pandemonium. Natives were running around with machetes or axes in their hands, making either chopping motions toward the ground or else in the air and howling and wailing at the top of their lungs. The air inside resembled Los Angeles smog, only worse, due to the thick smoke of cooking fires and the smell of perspiring bodies. My first uttered exclamation was, "What in the hell is going on here?"

But I was informed by my guide, a Methodist missionary-doctor well acquainted with these parts, that we had just entered while a "curing ceremony" was going on. Now this roundhouse was about half the size of a high school football field and completely circular. A middle-aged, pot-bellied man with black serpentine lines running the full length of his body was squatting on his haunches and chanting at the top of his lungs, while holding a wooden bowl between his hands. Every few minutes he would cease his hullabaloo long enough to give his patient, a young boy lying on the ground stark naked, a sip of the liquid contents from it; then he would resume his caterwaul with the same fiendish enthusiasm.

After the ceremony was finished, we inquired of the witch doctor concerning the type of beverage he had just given his young patient. We were taken outside to a nearby hut, where a handful of luscious blueberries were produced. With grinding motions of his hands and jabbering away in Yanomamo dialect, he gave us to understand that the berries were crushed and the juicy pulp taken internally to quell fevers of all types. He claimed the blueberry juice was like "wind from the gods" to put out the "fire demons" that raged in the body.

In the course of time since then I have had ample opportunity to prescribe this jungle remedy to different people across the United States and Canada in my many speaking engagements on health-related topics. I used to credit the old witch doctor as my source for this wonderful fever remedy, but stopped doing this after one born-again Christian lady accused me of spreading "malicious evil" simply because my informant "had not accepted Jesus Christ as his Lord and Savior." After that, I said only, "This came from an aboriginal doctor trained in the ways of natural healing."

Jungle Cure for Diarrhea and Dysentery

In treks like these through the tropics, where a combination of bad water, extreme heat and humidity, and blood-sucking insects of every description can render even the strongest man as weak and helpless as a baby within hours, diarrhea ceases to be a joke within conversation and becomes a serious matter where one's life can literally hang in the balance. My missionary-doctor friend discovered when he first entered the vast Amazon Basin that all of his regular conventional drugs brought along to treat conditions such as these were no match for something as simple and readily available as blueberries.

"I've eaten them right off the bushes," he asserted, as well as to "pound a bunch of them up into a thick juice to drink. And I tell you, quite frankly, John, that *nothing* in my years of medical experience has proven as effective in settling even the worst case of diarrhea or dysentery as these berries have been."

BOYSENBERRY
(Rubus Loganobaccus)

BRIEF DESCRIPTION

Anyone who has ever enjoyed a piece of boysenberry pie will surely know just how delicious this tart-flavored, purplish berry is. Boysenberry is believed to have originated either from a variety of the Pacific dewberry (*R. ursinus*) or else as a hybrid between this and the red raspberry.

The original plant appeared in the California orchard of Judge J. H. Logan in 1881 (after whom the loganberry derived its name). Boysenberry, like other brambles, is a shrub with prickly stems (called "canes"). The underground part is perennial and the canes are biennial; only second-year canes bear flowers and fruit, however.

The edible fruit, botanically speaking, isn't really a berry at all, but is rather aggregates of drupelets. Boysenberries are grown commercially in the United States for sale as fresh, canned, and frozen fruit and for use in pies, ice cream, and some preserves.

"Stomach" Flu Disappears

Lorraine Walton of Appleton, Wisconsin, told me once how she cured herself of "stomach" flu (not an actual flue but an upset stomach of unknown origin). "I wasn't able to keep any food down," she began. "My stool was watery, I felt weak, lacked an appetite, and was beside myself as to what I was going to do. But then my grandmother, bless her soul, recommended that I eat some boysenberries. I followed her health hint and within 18 hours was totally over my symptoms! I suggest anyone bothered with the same problem eat them whole and drink some boysenberry juice, too."

"Sure Cure" for Atopic Dermatitis, Impetigo, Itching, and Rash

Ms. Watson also informed me that her 27-year-old brother developed atopic dermatitis on the back of his neck, on his eyelids and wrists, and behind his ears. Doctors attributed this condition to certain pollen and food allergies. He was given several prescription medications and put on a restricted diet that excluded the offending foods. These measures helped his runny nose and itchy eyes, hay fever and asthma, but did nothing for his skin problem.

His sister decided to experiment with boysenberry to see if it might help her brother. "I didn't know for sure if it would even work or not," she confessed, "but I figured we had nothing to lose by giving it our best shot." She showed him and his wife how to gently bathe the afflicted areas of his skin with four to six cotton balls soaked in boysenberry juice and to squeeze out the excess liquid lightly. "This was done several times each day," she added. "Within days we began seeing results. And by the end of two weeks most of the contact dermatitis disappeared."

She didn't know what there was in boysenberries to attribute this to, but was happy, nevertheless, that the remedy worked so well. "Since the healing episode with my brother," she explained, "I've recommended it to my neighbor, who used it on her young children afflicted with impetigo and diaper rash; in both instances, they cleared up. And my uncle in Camden, Ohio, made contact with some poison ivy and broke out in a severe rash. He soaked gauze pads in some boysenberry juice and placed them directly on the skin; the itching ceased, the inflammation disappeared, and he was over it in one and a half weeks."

Brazil Nut
(Bertholletia Excelsa)

Brief Description

The tree on which this nut grows is a handsome giant evergreen with a long straight trunk branched only in the uppermost part. The tree is capable of reaching heights exceeding 145 feet with a trunk diameter of almost 8 feet. The crown spreads out to a breadth of 100 feet or more as it towers over other tropical vegetation in the Amazon forests of South America.

Its large, glossy, dark-green leaves are 12 to 15 inches long, about 6 inches wide, and deeply ribbed. Pale-yellow flowers with 6 large petals are borne in clusters at the ends of the branches. The spherical dark-brown fruits, which take about 14 months to mature, are 4 to 6 inches in diameter and weigh 2 to 4 pounds each. They resemble large coconuts with a hard, woody casing.

The nuts have to be gathered deep from within the jungle forest. It is a hazardous occupation, to say the least. Nut gatherers must contend with terrific heat and humidity, clouds of thirsty mosquitoes and gnats, malaria, giant boa constrictors big enough to swallow an adult German shepherd in several good gulps, deadly poisonous vipers, and even the falling nut fruit itself!

As one nut gatherer, Carlos Ramañchos, told me some years ago: "The *cocos* [the hard spherical shells] fall from the height of 12-

56

to-15-story buildings and present a life-threatening hazard to those of us who work below. They fall to the ground during the rain season, which lasts from November to February. We must work very quickly, throwing the *cocos* into a pile away from the *almendro* to minimize the danger of getting our skulls split open by one of these hard, four-pound fruits crashing down like a fired cannon ball!"

Carlos paused a moment to wipe the beads of sweat from his glistening dark forehead with the back of one hand before continuing with his narrative.

"Cutting open the *coca* requires great skill. Several full-length blows with a razor-sharp machete in just the right place are needed to release the nuts without damaging them. Here, let me show you how it's done." With that he took one of these coconutlike spheres and laid it on the ground. He drew a big, wicked-looking machete from an old leather scabbard slung across his back. Lifting his right arm all the way back, he swung with all his might, bringing the instrument down onto the tough, woody shell, which measured about one-quarter of an inch in thickness. He repeated this stroke with several more carefully calculated swings.

The shell fell neatly apart revealing a dozen to two dozen Brazil nuts, closely packed together, with their thin edges facing inward, like the sections of an orange. It was amazing to see how nicely arranged and expertly packaged they came from nature! Because they were still green when they came out of their open shell, Carlos threw them into a large pile of other Brazil nuts. "We have to keep turning them over every day with a shovel," he said, "to let those at the bottom dry out" (they have a high water content—roughly 35 percent).

Fattening Food for Cancer, AIDS, and Other Flesh-Wasting Diseases

Some years ago when I met this *castanheiro* named Carlos, it was at the municipality of Marabá, near the Tocantins river and bordering the then relatively new Transamazonian Highway in the Brazilian state of Pará. I accompanied him to a rather rustic dwelling in one of the slum sections of the town, where I was introduced to a *curandero* who went by the odd name of Diké (pronounced dee-kay).

This small, middle-aged folk healer with dark, wrinkled skin and a toothsome grin picked up one of the medium-sized *tocs,* as

Brazil nuts are called down there, and commenced a dialogue with me in a clipped mixed Portuguese-Indian accent. Fortunately for me, Carlos was there to interpret as I hastily jotted down highlights of what was being said in my little spiral flip-open notebook that I always carried in my shirt pocket for just such information emergencies.

Diké explained to us that *tocs* were one of the best foods to give sick people who had diseases that made them "look like skeletons." He attributed this, in part, to "the goodness of the gods," which he claimed they had put into every single Brazil nut. If a patient didn't have the strength to chew whole nuts for himself, then he would grind some of the shelled *tocs* into a fine meal and mix it with a little water to form a crude paste. This he would feed to the invalid patient with a wooden spoon. He swore that it put flesh back on emaciated frames, no matter how wasted they were.

As a medical anthropologist, I've learned to keep an open mind to everything I hear, rejecting none of it until I've had a chance to digest the information for myself and eventually test it out in some type of clinical setting, if at all possible. My work a few years ago with Lawrence Badgley, M.D. in west Los Angeles with a number of his AIDS patients who were in the advanced stages of illness, allowed me such an opportunity.

At first, I made several of them rather angry with me because they got sick of chewing the whole, shelled nuts. So remembering what Diké had told me about crushing them into a powder, I secured a small stone wheat grinder and each day ground up enough of the shelled Brazil nuts to provide several half-cup servings to three other AIDS patients who volunteered to be my guinea pigs. But this was done without Lawrence's knowledge or approval.

I showed some healthy friends of each of these three patients how to make the meal from the shelled nuts. These three sick men would then consume the nut powder mixed in with some thick banana, papaya, mango or carrot juice, yogurt, or cottage cheese. I then returned home to Utah, but kept in touch with them or their care-giving friends by phone and also by mail. One of the three patients unfortunately died several weeks later, so I was never able to learn whether or not he ever gained any weight before his demise. With the remaining two, however, there was a noticeable weight gain (in about 1 $\frac{1}{2}$ months) of 10 pounds in one fellow and

13 pounds in the other guy. Complications due to pneumonia contracted by the latter person terminated his existence four months
later. But his lover wrote to thank me for the food remedy I had
given him, saying in the letters "...at least Eric didn't die with just
skin and bones." I never heard anything further from the final
patient, so cannot say what the final outcome with him was. But, at
least, what Diké said proved to be true.

Based on this casual experiment, I recommend Brazil nuts for
any flesh-wasting diseases. The nuts should be shelled before using.
The best machine to use for making them into a nice flour is the Vita-
Mix Nutrition Center or an equivalent food machine. Be sure to use
the plastic container with the heavier blade intended for grinding
wheat and making nut butters. (See the Appendix section of this book
for more information on where to get the excellent Vita-Mix unit.)

A Hint on Shelling Brazil Nuts

Cover unshelled nuts with boiling, salted water, allowing one tablespoon salt to a quart water. Boil gently for 3 minutes. Strain and
cool. Crack and quickly remove shells. Unshelled nuts may be roasted, too, in a hot oven (400°F) for about 20 minutes. Cool, crack, and
shell. The nuts come out whole with considerable ease.

Brazil Nuts Pack Anticancer Wallop

Researchers at Roswell Park Cancer Institute recently announced in
the early winter of 1995 that animals fed Brazil nuts showed an
increased cancer resistance. The tropical nut contains exceptionally
high levels of selenium, a trace element with potent anticancer
properties. Animals fed a diet enriched with Brazil nuts were better
able to resist tumors than were those fed a walnut-enriched diet
(walnuts are low in selenium). The researchers then compared the
Brazil nut's anticancer potential to selenium supplements and discovered the nut to be "just as powerful as sodium selenite, if not
more so, at similar levels of dietary selenium intake." The Roswell
Park research group advises eating a *few* Brazil nuts a day to bol-
ster selenium reserves.

BUFFALO BERRY
(Shepherdia Argentea)

BRIEF DESCRIPTION

Silver buffalo berry and russet buffalo berry (*S. canadensis*) are deciduous shrubs that can reach almost ten feet in height. Silver buffalo berry is a thorny species, but russet buffalo berry is smaller and thornless. Both species are nitrogen fixers and have been used in shelterbelt plantings in some parts of the Midwest and the West.

Both shrubs have silvery foliage and bear small, yellowish male and female flowers on different plants, either solitary or else in clusters on the branchlets. Drupelike, ovoid berries, about 0.3 to 0.6 centimeters long, develop during the summer months. The fruit resembles currants and turns either golden yellow or a fine scarlet color after fully ripening.

When I assisted Joy Yellowtail Toinetta, a Crow Indian residing in eastern Montana, in collecting some of these berries, it was in the late fall after the first frost. They are usually collected earlier by white folks, but she insisted that they taste better and are much easier to harvest after the first good cold snap. We spread a large tanned buckskin tarp under the shrubs, then with gloved hands and sticks gently flailed the branches causing the silver buffalo berries to drop.

Afterwards, we gathered them up into several handmade wicker baskets and drove back to her house where we poured them into a couple of large pans. Joy let them fill and run over with tap water, which brought a lot of debris such as leaves, twigs, and thorns to the top. She drained off the water and washed them this way a second time.

Then the berries were put through a manual-operated food grinder fastened to the edge of her kitchen table with a screwlike vise from beneath. Half of the ground berries were then spread out on a clean bedsheet on top of the table and left in the sun to dry, while being stirred often with a wooden ladle. The rest of the mashed berries were then dusted with a little white flour and formed into patties, which were placed around the edges of the sheet and turned over daily to assure thorough drying.

In a couple of days the drying process was completed, and I assisted her in storing both patties and berries in airtight Mason jars. Sometimes she would place the whole berries in zippered plastic bags and freeze them for later uses.

Buffalo berries may be found throughout the central and western United States and Canada. They are still enjoyed to some extent by a few Native American tribes such as the Sioux, Crow, and Blackfoot.

Crow Indian Cough Syrup

Joy's grandmother taught her how to make a tribal cough syrup from buffalo berries over 50 years ago. She still makes it for her own children and grandchildren today. Wash and clean several cups of buffalo berries as previously described. Then place in a large pot and add just enough water to cover them. Boil the berries until they are thoroughly cooked. *Do not drain* the liquid, but mash the berries with a metal potato masher or round-bottomed wooden object. Place the wet pulp into a jelly bag or small, clean flour sack, tie the top with some twine, and suspend over a large enamel pan for the night. This will allow all the juice to drip out.

Next morning pour the collected juice into a smaller pot and add an equal amount of blackstrap molasses. Stir thoroughly with a wooden ladle and then bring to a boil until it *starts* thickening. Remove from the stove and pour into sterilized fruit or baby food jars. Permit to cool, uncovered. Add a few drops of glycerin to each jar as a natural preservative, then seal and store.

When someone has a bad cough, give that person two table-spoonsful of this syrup every hour until the condition clears up.

Medicine Woman's Stomachache Cure

Some years ago while traveling on Vancouver Island in British Columbia, Canada, I met an old Indian medicine woman belonging to the Nanaimo tribe. She informed me how her people used buf-falo berries to get rid of abdominal distress and constipation.

Bird Woman, as she was called, picked the berries in mid-August, peeled them, and then rolled them in a little shortening or bear grease and stored them in an airtight can in a cool place.

Then, when necessity required it, she would take some of these greasy berries (about $1/2$ cup) and boil them in 2 cups of water for approximately 20 minutes. The broth would be strained and drunk warm on an empty stomach. Usually in less than half an hour the worst stomach-ache would disappear or else in an hour the most stubborn constipation would be remedied.

I tasted some of her "special brew" myself and pronounced it as being "godawful." When asked how it was possible for a person to keep this stuff down, she smiled and said, "By thinking good thoughts."

I noticed a distinct difference in the degree of tartness between those that Joy Toinetta and that Bird Woman had collected. It seems that the first cold snap reduces some of the bitterness and brings an improvement in the flavor.

Recuperation Stew

During the time I spent with Joy in the early 1970s, I watched her make a stew out of buffalo berries that she fed to a neighbor of hers who was recuperating from a lengthy illness. Joy claimed that the berry stew was good for giving a weakened physical system much needed strength and vitality.

Joy took some old elk bones that she had kept in her freezer and boiled them up in water for an hour to get a rich stock (beef marrow bones can be substituted). She then soaked some of her dried berry patties in just enough bone marrow broth to cover and added at least $2\,^1\!/_2$ cups more liquid to replace what had been soaked up.

After this she made a simple paste from white flour and water before adding it to the berry patty soup. She stirred vigorously with a wooden ladle to prevent lumping, then added a tablespoon of white sugar and a lump of marrow fat for taste. This she took to her bedridden neighbor, who ate it accompanied with some fried bread. (Note: Honey and butter may be substituted for the sugar and fat.)

Indian Ice Cream

"Soopalalie" have been used by the Chinook Indians of Vancouver Island in the past for making a favorite dessert treat. Anthropologists like myself who've tasted this have dubbed it "Indian ice cream."

Buffalo berries were picked at the end of July or early August, crushed in water, and then beaten with bundles of grass or maple leaves into a salmon-colored froth. In olden times, other fresh berries or *camas* (an edible lily bulb common to the western United States and Canada) were added to sweeten it; but more recently, white sugar has been used.

This dessert was usually consumed with a special type of flat wooden spoon.

Other western and northwestern Native American tribes whom I've visited in the past never prepared such a treat as this, though they used buffalo berries in different ways. I would assume that it is original to the Coast Salish Indians inhabiting all of Vancouver Island.

BUTTERNUT
(Juglans Cinerea)

BRIEF DESCRIPTION

The butternut is the most northern and cold-resistant member of the walnut family. Indigenous to eastern North America and growing mainly in the northeastern quarter of the United States, its native range extends northward well into Canada.

As a devout Latter-Day Saint, I have stood in the peaceful splendor of the Sacred Grove directly across the road from the Joseph Smith family home just outside Palmyra New York. Here in this stand of closely grown trees, according to Mormon tradition and the Prophet Joseph Smith's own testimony, is where God appeared to him sometime in his fourteenth year.

During one such visit, I leaned against a stately butternut tree approximately 50 feet in height and 3 feet in circumference. It was sometime in the fall and I was alone with my thoughts. At the base of this tree lay some ripe butternuts. I stooped down and picked a couple of them up. I quickly discovered that the thick and bony shells made it virtually impossible for me to crack them between my back molars, unless I wanted some broken teeth and a sore jaw for my troubles. So I pocketed them for opening later on with a nut-cracker. I found the flavor of each thin kernel to have a very distinctive, delicious flavor.

I marveled to myself at how long this particular butternut and many other very old trees in my immediate vicinity had been silent witnesses to Joseph Smith's religious experience, sturdy sentinels watching over the unfolding of this momentous event.

Effective Folk Medicine for Diarrhea

On Thursday, April 13, 1843, at 10:00 A.M. in Nauvoo, Illinois, the Mormon Prophet addressed a large congregation of emigrant converts, newly arrived from England. In speaking to them about the strange climate and country into which they had just come, he warned against drinking the spring water and instead advised that wells be dug in order to obtain good water.

But in the event they suffered any intestinal discomforts, he had some simple home remedies for them to try. "If you feel any inconvenience" he said, "take some mild physic two or three times, and follow that up with some good bitters. If you cannot get anything else, take a little salts and cayenne pepper. If you cannot get salts, take ipecacuanha [an emetic herb still used by the medical profession in case of poisoning]" Then, in a typical moment of natural humor, he dryly observed with a straight face: "Or [go] gnaw down a butternut tree, or use boneset or horehound!" (Joseph Smith, *History of The Church of Jesus Christ of Latter-Day Saints* (Salt Lake City: Deseret News, 1909, 5:357).

What he meant, of course, was for them to use the crushed shells and thin kernels in the form of a tea. Mormon pioneers would often take one quarter pound of butternut hulls and kernels and cook them uncovered in 1 pint of boiling water over a low fire for approximately 20 minutes, after which the liquid would be strained off, permitted to cool, and a full cup of the nut tea would be drunk on an empty stomach to reduce fevers and stop loose bowels.

Fever Cure from the Revolutionary War

Francis Marion was born sometime in 1732 in South Carolina. He became a famous American general during our nation's War of Independence (1775–1783), earning for himself the nickname "The Swamp Fox" by the British for his elusive tactics. He and his band of guerrillas often defeated larger bodies of British troops by the surprise and rapidity of their movement over swampy terrain. For a daring rescue of Americans surrounded by the British at Parkers Ferry, South Carolina, in August, 1781, General Marion received the thanks of Congress.

According to a Civil War physician, Francis Peyre Porcher, M.D., some butternut trees growing in South Carolina were frequently utilized by The Swamp Fox to make a warm tea to give his sick men who had contracted fever, to drink. The tea, made from the tree bark and nut hulls and kernels helped them to quickly recover from their debilitating ordeals so they could resume fighting the enemy. (Francis P. Porcher, "Report on the Indigenous Medical Plants of South Carolina,"; in *Transactions of the American Medical Association* (Philadelphia: T. K. and P. G. Collins, 1849, 2:760).

CARAWAY SEED
(Carum Carvi)

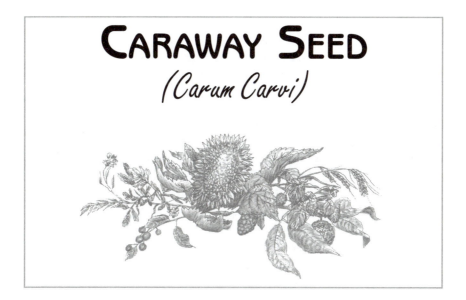

BRIEF DESCRIPTION

Caraway is a biennial that grows over two feet tall with umbelliferous cream-white flowers and feathery leaves. It grows wild in Europe and the temperate parts of Asia, but became naturalized in the United States and Great Britain. The wild seed is smaller than the cultivated one, but delivers a stronger flavor.

Caraway seed was more important in English cooking in the Elizabethan era than it is now. William Shakespeare, the world's greatest playwright, frequently incorporated into many of his plays everyday customs and habits of his time. In Part 2 of *Henry IV,* he has Squire Shallow inviting the popular and vividly depicted character of Falstaff to "a pippin and a dish of caraways." The tradition of serving roast apples with a little saucerful of caraway is still maintained at Trinity College, Cambridge, and at a few of the old-fashioned restaurants in London.

In Britain, Germany, and the Scandinavian countries, caraway seed has been routinely used for many decades to flavor cakes, dark-grain breads, cheeses, cabbage dishes, and soups.

Village Remedy for Earache from Shakespeare's Birthplace

Shakespeare was born in 1564 in the English village of Stratford-on-Avon. An effective remedy for earache then utilizing caraway seed has been preserved in some of his writings.

A small amount of caraway seeds were lightly crushed in a stone mortar with a pestle; then some fresh crumbs from a hot loaf of newly baked bread were added and worked in the same way. A little ale, mead, or some other type of spirituous liquor was incorporated to moisten the pounded mixture just a little, after which everything was placed on a very thin cloth and gently laid over the sore ear with a heavier piece of cloth put on top of that to retain the heat. Shakespeare's mythical characters, who employed this remedy, claimed it "never faileth to drawe awaye the eare paine."

What Shakespeare Did for His Indigestion

In 1594, William Shakespeare became an actor and started his remarkable career as a playwright for the Lord Chamberlain's Men, the company that later became the King's Men under James I. He remained with that company until the end of his London stay. As an actor he played old men's roles, such as the ghost in *Hamlet* and Old Adam in *As You Like It.*

It was not uncommon for people in those times to get upset stomachs quite frequently. Sometimes it was due to the rich foods they consumed—much meat, few vegetables, a lot of pastries, and excess liquor; but on other occasions it was attributed to lack of adequate chewing. A popular cure for such widespread indigestion was caraway seed.

Preparation was quite simple: To 1 cup boiling water was added $1/4$ teaspoon caraway seeds, which were allowed to steep until the liquid was lukewarm. A lump of sugar was added for flavor, and the tea was consumed following a heavy or hurried meal. Relief was given within a matter of minutes, reported a very old cookbook used in the castle kitchen of King James I.

More information on caraway may be found in my other reference work, *Heinerman's Encyclopedia of Herbs and Spices.*

CARDAMOM SEED
(Elettaria Cardamomum)

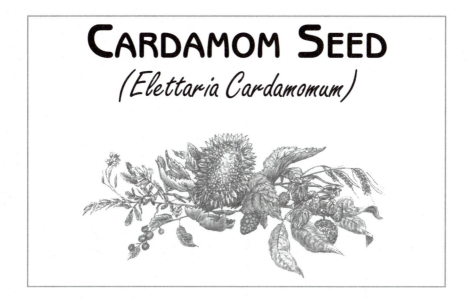

BRIEF DESCRIPTION

Cardamom is a spice that which came from the Orient into Europe by way of the ancient caravan routes. It is rumored to have been grown in the royal hanging gardens of Babylon by Nebuchadnezzar the Great over 700 years before the birth of the Messiah.

Cardamom is a perennial and belongs to the ginger family. It forms a bush with large lance-shaped leaves, somewhat like palm fronds (but no relative to them), and grows to about eight feet. It grows in wild abundance in the wet hill jungles of southern India, usually on the sides of ravines and under majestic tropical trees—just the sort of place one is apt to find deadly king cobras and pit vipers. Hence, gathering cardamom used to be a real "life-and-death" ordeal, but today there are cardamom plantations in many tropical countries, including Central America.

The cardamom stalks bearing the little seed pods (the part used) sprawl flat on the ground as they grow from the base of the plant in a rather unusual way. The seed pods appear over a long period and do not all ripen at the same time, so they are gathered every few weeks. They are dried in the sun or over heat and are sometimes bleached white, though their natural color is pale green or brown.

It is the dried seed pods that are bought in some specialty food stores and spice shops as cardamom. Though they vary in color and length, they all have a roughly triangular section. Good cardamom can be examined by pulling apart a pod and looking inside. The seeds ought to be slightly sticky, brown-black, and with a strong aromatic smell and taste. Cardamom is virtually worthless when bought as a ground up powder, since it quickly loses all of its warm and wonderful essential oils.

Cardamom for Celiac Disease

Celiac disease is a chronic diarrheal disease marked by intestinal malabsorption of virtually all nutrients and precipitated by eating gluten-containing foods, generally involving breads and cereals. The two peak periods of life in which it becomes manifested the most are very early childhood and the standard age for retirement (60–65).

I've worked with this problem a number of times in those who've sought out my counsel and advice with regard to folk remedies for their digestive discomforts. And they have found cardamom *in the pod* to be one of the very best things for it if they are unwilling to forego gluten-containing foods. When cooking any kind of whole-grain cereal, just throw in a teaspoon of sticky seeds. If baking bread, muffins, pies, or cakes in which regular flour is being used, just crush some seeds between two layers of wax paper with a rolling pin and work into the dough. Not only will cereals and bread-stuffs come out smelling and tasting great, but the digestive system will be able to tolerate the gluten without negative reactions. Actually, elimination of gluten entirely from the diet is the primary therapy for this disease among practicing physicians.

Help Keep Cholesterol Down

If you really want to spice up stews and soups, just add some crushed, fresh cardamom seeds to them. Not only is the flavor greatly improved, but the stews' and soups' high cholesterol content is also held in check within the body once they are fully digested. I had an Italian waiter in Naples tell me this some years ago.

He also told me this little tale about a very demanding, middle-aged, overweight, and apparently wealthy American woman who visited the same fancy restaurant the week before I got there. She insisted on having one of the made-to-order soup specialties of the house. The chef added a couple of cardamom seeds to impart a vague hint of eucalyptus. The waiter delivered it and left. But as she started stirring it around with her spoon, one of these seeds rose to the surface. She screamed and he quickly returned to her table, asking what the matter was. She loudly protested that there was a *cockroach* in her soup. The waiter fetched the manager, who, in turn, called the chef from the kitchen. He stood over her patiently listening to her complaints. After she stopped for a moment's breath, he very casually lifted both cardamom seeds out of the soup with her spoon, picked them up with his fingers, and popped both into his mouth, at the same time smacking his lips and exclaiming, "Why do you not like zis *wonderful* leetle fishes?" The sight of him gulping two large hairy cardamom seeds that resembled insects was almost too much for the poor woman, and she nearly fainted on the spot! But the chef got his revenge and returned to the kitchen with nary another word from his unhappy customer.

Cashew Nut
(Anacardium Occidentale)

Brief Description

The cashew belongs to the *Anacardiaceae* or cashew family. Other plants that belong to this family are mango fruit and the pistachio nut, as well as toxic plants that produce skin blistering, namely poison ivy, poison oak, and poison sumac. In fact, the double shell of a cashew nut contains the aracardic acid and cardol; both are very toxic and irritating to the skin if handled straight from the tree without gloves and before being heated in special liquid to detoxify the shells and make them brittle.

The cashew tree is a hardy, fast-growing evergreen perennial with a symmetrical, umbrellalike canopy. Under favorable conditions, it may reach a height of 40 to 50 feet. The stem tends to be gnarled and tortuous and the branches crooked, giving the tree a decidedly unkempt appearance. The lower branches frequently rest on the ground and strike root, thereby enhancing the spreading form. The leathery, oblong-oval leaves, four to eight inches long and two to three inches in width, are heavily veined. The aromatic five-petaled flowers are yellowish-pink and polygamous. The flower cluster is composed of both unisexual and bisexual types. The rough, resinous bark contains an acrid sap similar to what is in the nut shells.

The cashew is strange and versatile: It not only produces the edible nut but also a nutritious, edible "apple" and a valuable nut-shell oil used to make several types of resins that are used in the manufacture of clutch facings, foundry resins, waterproof paints, corrosion-resistant varnishes, insulating enamels, and special quality lacquers.

The highly unusual cashew fruit consists of two distinct parts. The first is the fleshy, pear-shaped stalk, known as the cashew "apple," which is rather juicy, thin-skinned, golden-yellow, red, or scarlet in color, and about 2 to $4\,^1/_2$ inches in length. It actually looks more like a pear than an apple. The second is the grayish-brown, kidney-shaped nut, which is about $1–1\,^1/_2$ inches long. It is attached to the lower end of the "apple." The cashew nut is the true "fruit," while the cashew "apple," about 8–10 times as heavy as the nut, is the swollen stalk, or *peduncle,* which supports the flower.

Possible Snakebite Antidote

The ayurvedic medicine of India, which is still very popular and routinely practiced after several thousand years, has relied upon various parts of the cashew nut as an antidote against poisonous snake bites. The fresh cashew shell, with its kernel still intact, is first roasted in a large frying pan over an open fire or on a metal sheet in an oven to remove most of the toxic material that causes skin irritations. The kernel is then removed from the shell and dried. After this its reddish-brown outer coating, the *testa,* is peeled off by gentle rubbing with the fingers.

Indian scientists over some 60 years ago carried out a series of extensive pharmacological and toxicological investigations on animals with these cashew materials as well as with numerous other medicinal plants. Healthy dogs weighing from 13 to 22 pounds were injected subcutaneously with venom from the king cobra, largest of all the venomous snakes found in southern Asia. They can reach a full length of 18 feet. The dogs were then given an internal administration of cashew nut, which consisted of a very concentrated tea solution made by boiling some of the roasted shells and testa together. For external application the roasted cashew shells, testa, and kernel were all ground into a fine powder and then applied directly over the site of inoculation of the venom. The internal administration seemed to be the most beneficial from the observations later recorded, although the external application, in some instances, did prevent localized swelling. Cashew nut, then, may be considered a possible folk antidote for poisonous snakebite, with some efficacious benefits (*Indian Medical Research Memoirs,* No. 19, January 1931).

Toothache and Sore Gums Relieved

Some years ago I spent a brief period of time with native witch doctors in several West African countries. In one folk healer's hut in the village of Badagry, Nigeria (near the frontier with Dahomey), I watched as an *ifa* treated toothaches and gum pain with great fanfare. With the aid of an interpreter hired for this occasion, I watched as this particular witch doctor held up a small wooden bowl containing an ointment preparation,

He began speaking in his native tongue, while my interpreter leaned close to my ear and whispered the translation of the same to me. The *ifa* declared that he had just discovered two things possessing stronger spirits than the disease spirits with which his patients were then afflicted. He said that in the bowl that he held up in his hand was a mixture of crushed cashew-nut kernel and honey. He claimed that "the souls of both medicines" would work only once he had said a magical incantation over them. But before doing so, he turned around and walked a short distance to a table in one corner of his rude clinic, on top of which stood a nine-inch high-carved wood figurine. He bowed himself down before this household god and implored it to help him make a suitable prayer offering over this remedy he continued to hold in one hand. All six of his patients in the room promptly bowed themselves low on the earthen floor as he did. My guide and interpreter gave me a poke in the ribs with his elbow, and I quickly followed his example by falling prostrate upon the ground. To have done otherwise would have greatly offended this witch doctor's gods, and I would have been chased from the village by an angry mob wielding long spears or sharp machetes or knives.

When the witch doctor finished his ritual, he got up and everyone followed suit. I brushed the dry clay dust from my forehead, face, neck, arms, hands, and clothing. He then walked over to his first patient and barked an order for the guy to open his mouth wide. Putting his forefinger and middle finger into the powdered cashew-nut-and-honey mixture, he scooped some of it up and then inserted both fingers into the patient's mouth. He carefully smeared the paste around two back molars, which the man had declared earlier were paining him terribly. He then proceeded on to the next patient dispensing more of this sticky medicine across the man's upper and lower gums.

I had a chance to question both patients after they left the *ifa*'s humble home clinic a few minutes later. I asked each of them how they felt now; both replied with absolute sincerity that their dental aches and pains had completely vanished! I made the appropriate notes in my little spiral notebook that I carried in my shirt pocket at all times and thanked them for their help. Some months later when I returned to the United States I had occasion to test this folk remedy with a friend's ten-year-old son. I had been invited over for a weekend barbecue and I noticed the youngster was moaning and groaning. I inquired of the father as to the problem and he told me it was a toothache.

"We've given him some children's aspirin, but it doesn't seem to have helped very much," the father said. I asked if he had any cashew-nut butter around; he said he didn't, so I drove to a nearby health-food store and bought a small jar. In his kitchen I made a small amount of paste using one teaspoonful of cashew butter and one-quarter teaspoonful of honey, which he already had on hand. I also added a pinch of alum to the mixture, which he also had in the cupboard. Using a wooden tongue depressor (his wife was a nurse and had access to them), I carefully smeared a tiny amount of this stuff around the kid's sore tooth, I had the father instruct his son to not drink or eat anything for an hour, so it would stay in place. To everyone's amazement the pain diminished within five minutes, again showing that the ways of the simple are often more efficacious than all the wisdom of the educated combined.

Terrific Treatment for Scurvy, Leprosy, Syphilis, Warts, Ringworm, Psoriasis, and Cracked Feet

During my short visit to the village of Badagry, Nigeria, some years ago, I watched this same *ifa* use cashew-nut-shell liquid for a number of skin problems common to tropical regions of the world. He boiled some *freshly picked* and broken cashew-nut shells in a little water. From what I could observe, it was 2 cups of broken shells to

1 $1/2$ cups boiling water. This mixture cooked in an old iron pot hung over a fire from the end of a black iron tripod for about 30 minutes, as best I could judge. The Yoruba witch doctor then carefully poured off what liquid remained, straining it through a dirty old burlap gunny sack of all things! The amount of liquid remaining was about $3/4$ of a cup.

With this in a wooden bowl, he took a well-used artist's paint brush made from camel hair and proceeded to dip it into the bowl and paint the liquid onto the skin injuries of different patients who sat inside or outside his hut. I discerned scurvy, leprosy, and syphilitic sores, warts, ringworm, a form of psoriasis, and the cracked soles of feet being treated with this mixture.

Scarification for Tattooing Purposes

I'll just mention here something else in passing that is still very popular in parts of West Africa with many of the natives; but I don't advocate the reader doing it. The acrid sap from the tree bark and the irritating oil from the nut shell is routinely rubbed on the surface of the skin to deliberately induce scars, often keloids, and tribal marks, which are highly prized and considered marks of great beauty by those cultures.

Cashew Oil May Conquer Cavities

Don't be surprised if a nut-flavored toothpaste someday makes its way to the drugstore or supermarket shelf. Increased consumer demand for all-natural products has revived interest in tapping foods—edible plants in particular—for useful chemicals. In this quest, two organic chemists have discovered, almost by accident, that the cashew nut could very well fight tooth decay and other bacterial infections, according to a report in the February 1991 *Journal of Agricultural and Food Chemistry*.

In their research, a pair of Japanese scientists tested various tropical fruits and vegetables for antimicrobial activity. The oil from the cashew-nut shell, normally a waste product of the food industry, seemed to hold some potential, so the researchers extracted and tested 16 compounds from it. The oil and some of the extracts worked well against gram-positive bacteria, in particular

Propionibacterium acnes, which produces acne vulgaris in teenagers, and *Streptococcus mutans,* which causes tooth decay in young and old alike.

When killing bacteria in the mouth, these compounds also appear to interfere with production of the microbes' enamel-eroding acids. "It has anti-plaque activity, too," noted Isao Kubo, one of the chemists. But the shell oil isn't edible, he continued. However, its bacteria-fighting compounds also exist in the nut and the juice of the surrounding fruit. Kubo believed that the cashew compounds may eventually prove safe when mixed into toothpaste or mouthwash.

CELERY SEED
(Apium Graveolens)

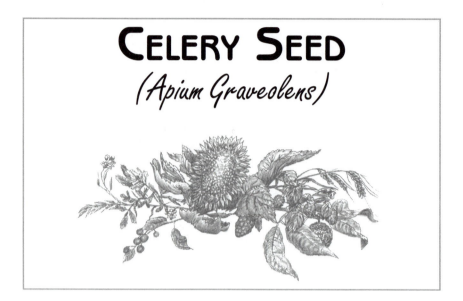

BRIEF DESCRIPTION

Garden celery is such a widely cultivated biennial plant that it virtually needs no introduction. The seeds are small, ribbed, and elliptic-ovate in shape. They yield a rather bitter flavor but have their place in the culinary arts.

Sedative for Nervousness

A tea made from the seeds helps calm stressed nerves. To 1 cup of boiling water, add $^1/_2$ teaspoon celery seeds. Steep 30 minutes, strain, and drink lukewarm on an empty stomach.

Heartburn and Gout Cured

Frank Mensch, a welder by trade, frequently sustained heartburn from eating chili dogs or hamburgers with "the works" included. And the fact that he loved soda pop only complicated his situation that much more. As if this wasn't bad enough, he also suffered from gout in his ankles, due to excessive meat intake.

His wife attended one of my health lectures in Youngstown, Ohio, some years ago and explained his physical dilemmas to me. Because her husband wasn't willing to make some reasonable adjustments in his eating habits, I was left only with providing a Band-Aid solution. I recommended that she make him some celery-seed tea as previously described and have him drink 1 to 2 cups of that every time he felt miserable.

I saw her some years later at another health conference in Chicago, where I inquired about her husband. "Oh, your remedy helped Frank with his heartburn and gout all right," she began enthusiastically enough. But then she dropped to a lower, more somber tone in the next breath: "Unfortunately, his chili dogs got the best of him—he eventually died of cancer!"

CHESTNUT
(Castanea Dentata)

HORSE CHESTNUT
(Aesculus Hippocastanum)

BRIEF DESCRIPTIONS

The first thing that needs to be established at the outset here is that the American chestnut (*C. dentata*) is botanically entirely distinct from and totally unrelated to the European horse chestnut. But because of a mistake long ago in the misnaming of the latter, many people have come to associate the horse chestnut with the true American chestnut; hence, both are included here for this reason. But just keep in mind that they are as different as night and day, scientifically speaking.

The American chestnut once covered more than 200 million acres from the Canadian border to the Gulf of Mexico in the eighteenth and nineteenth centuries. It was the preferred lumber by American and Canadian pioneers because of its durable, rot-resistant qualities. Chestnut lumber from majestic trees that towered upward to heights well over 100 feet and boasted trunk circumferences of up to 6 feet were utilized for farm fencing, furniture, ship masts, mine props, telephone poles, and railroad ties as both countries developed. Extracts from the bark and trunk of the chestnut provided a prime source of tannin for the leather industry. It was said that chestnut wood "carried man from cradle to grave, in crib

80

and coffin." The chestnut represented North America's most versatile and valuable tree.

The tree showed up in some of America's greatest literature, too. The nineteenth century naturalist Henry David Thoreau captured the enchanting nostalgia of this tree in his book *Walden, or Life in the Woods* (1854), an eloquent account of his experiment in near-solitary living in close harmony with nature and reflecting his transcendalist philosophy about life in general. Herewith are some brief excerpts:

When chestnuts were ripe I laid up half a bushel for winter. It was very exciting at that season to roam the then boundless chestnut woods of Lincoln...with a bag on my shoulder, and a stick to open burs with in my hand. For I did not always wait for the frost, amid the rustling of leaves and the loud reproofs of the red squirrels and the jays, whose half-consumed nuts I sometime stole, for the burs which they had selected were sure to contain sound ones...Behind my house [grew] one large tree which almost overshadowed it [and] was, when [in] flower, a bouquet which scented the whole neighborhood...These nuts, as far as they went, were a good substitute for bread."

Henry Wadsworth Longfellow wrote his well-known poem "The Village Blacksmith" in 1839 about a "spreading chestnut tree" that stood at the corner of Brattle and Story Streets in Cambridge, Massachusetts. The tree was chopped down in 1876 in order to widen Brattle Street. But strong evidence confirms that it wasn't the American chestnut, but rather something entirely different—the European horse chestnut.

Sadly enough, it wasn't the continuous cutting down of chestnut trees by frontier Americans that diminished the trees, but a canker-forming bark disease, caused by the fungus *Endothia parasitica*, which was introduced to New York City in the 1890s from the Orient with some Asiatic chestnut planting stock. Although the species from China and Japan were resistant to this destructive bark disease, their American cousin was highly susceptible. The chestnut blight on American chestnut trees was first reported in 1904 at the Bronx Zoological Park. Within half a century it destroyed virtually all large American chestnut trees from Maine to Alabama. Between 1904 and 1940 more than 3.5 billion American chestnut trees died as a result of this widespread tree epidemic.

The horse chestnut probably got its name originally from the many curious marks in the shape of minute horseshoes that appear all over its small branches. Actually they are leaf scars. A perfect facsimile of a horseshoe, right down to the seven nail markings, which are perfectly distinct, is traced on the bark wherever a bygone leaf has been. And among the twigs may be found some with an odd resemblance to a horse's foot and fetlock.

This ornamental tree is fast growing and erect and columnar. The bark is grayish-green and smooth. The sturdy, many-ribbed boughs and thick buds make it very conspicuous even in winter time. The buds are protected with a sticky substance; defended by 14 scales and gummed together, so no frost or dampness can harm the leaf and flower tucked safely away within each terminal bud, which develops quickly with the advent of spring.

The nuts it bears closely resemble those of the American chestnut, but are quite bitter, poisonous, and therefore unfit for food, whereas the former are of a mild, sweet taste and make a pleasant snack treat.

Ideal Food for Underweight

While many Americans suffer from the national disease of obesity, there are a fair number of individuals, both young and old, who have just the opposite problem. They are exceedingly thin, and no matter how much they eat, it just seems they can't put enough weight on their skinny frames. For older people this is especially a problem, because as the body ages muscle tissue tends to lose some of its fluid and elasticity, thereby shriveling a little.

My attention was first drawn to true chestnuts as a potential source of good food to correct this situation by reading different farm books and personal diaries of farmers written in the nineteenth century. Fresh, sweet chestnuts were highly prized by farmers in Missouri, Ohio, and all through the eastern United States. In the early fall, many of them fattened their hogs by letting them run loose in the woods to greedily devour chestnut mast.

My next few contacts with sweet chestnuts in reference to their being used as bulking agents turned up in several old animal husbandry books printed in England and Ireland. These works mentioned how farmers in that part of the world routinely chopped and mixed sweet chestnuts with beans to help fatten their sheep and cattle prior to slaughtering.

But in my mind the real convincing came from another book I once picked up for a few shillings in a small book shop in Piccadilly Square in London some years ago, Entitled *Britain's Wild Lader: Nuts* (London: Faber and Faber Ltd., 1957) and authored by Mrs. Claire Loewenfeld, it gave much valuable information concerning the nutritive benefits of chestnuts for weight gain. Roasted chestnuts, consumed while still warm, make a much healthier energy-giving snack than does a bag full of potato chips, *and* it helps one who is so underweight that it is a serious health issue to put additional bulk on his or her physical frame. Sweet chestnuts should *always* be cooked before being eaten, preferably roasted in the oven or steamed. Loewenfeld encouraged British housewives to "steam, roast, or boil" them in savory soups and stews with different root vegetables such as carrot, parsnip, potato, or turnip. She recommended cooked chestnuts being "combined with individual vegetables, such as spinach, cabbage and brussels sprouts." All these were good ways to utilize sweet chestnuts for the specific purpose of "bulking up," whether in skinny youth, emaciated elderly, or even underweight professional body builders.

Look in Appendix II for healthy recipes utilizing chestnuts and many other nuts mentioned in the text.

Convulsive Coughing and Spitting Blood Immediately Cured

Corsica lies just over 100 miles from southeast France, about half that distance westward from the mainland of Italy, and less than 10 miles from its southern neighbor, Sardinia. Oval-shaped, it comprises an area of 3,367 square miles, I was told by an old Roman Catholic priest in the town of Bastia in the northern part of this almost wholly mountainous territory.

The island language mix is an interesting blend of French, Italian, Arabian, Spanish, and Portuguese due to repeated invasions since prehistoric times. I found French to be the official language, but nearly everyone there speaks the Corsican dialect, which my host, Father René Pomponi declared in broken English to have evolved from Latin sometime in the Middle Ages. Although he himself was dark complexioned and of small build, I met enough fair-haired and tall people to remind me of the wide variety of physical types found in one place. For me, as an anthropologist, this was intriguing, even though my main purpose in going there was for folk remedies.

The priest and I went to an old woman residing some distance from his parish who was a reputed folk healer of extraordinary abilities. When we entered her neat little cottage she was in the act of having an older man drink a cup of some liquid for his convulsive coughing. In just a few minutes the gent's barking ceased and he went away very happy at being cured of his problem, taking with him the remainder of the liquid she had bottled for him. Another patient, a middle-aged woman sitting in one of the wooden chairs nearby, kept a crumpled up piece of cloth over her mouth. I noticed faint crimson stains on parts of it. The lady in charge bade the woman to come into another room, where she examined the contents of the rag. Shaking her head and telling the other woman in the native dialect that her spitting up blood wasn't good, she gave her some of the same liquid she had just given the former patient. After making some more verbal inquiries about her health, the folk healer handed her patient a similar small bottle of the same liquid and discharged her.

Being alone now without any more patients for awhile, the priest and I were able to converse with the folk healer. I learned from her that what she had just given the other two people to take was an extract of sweet chestnuts, fenugreek seed, and, curiously enough, *olive pits!* But she wasn't quite ready yet to surrender her folk cure until she knew something about the stranger full of questions who had disturbed her consultations. I let Father Pomponi do most of the talking, and instead assumed a very meek and contrite manner, keeping my eyes to the floor and answering only when spoken, and then in the most polite terms possible.

Her abrupt and unfeeling ways soon changed for the better after she became thoroughly satisfied in her own mind that I wasn't there to "steal" her "secret cure" and run off with it to America to "make a fortune from it." Both the priest and I reassured her that this wasn't my purpose; that I was just a scientist engaged in the gathering of medical folklore from around the world, which I some-day intended to use in books to help others. Convinced that my motives were pure enough, she confided to us the preparation of her formula.

To about a quart of water, she added $1\,^1/_2$ cups of crushed sweet chestnuts; these she boiled, uncovered, for approximately 40 minutes over a medium fire. After this she added 2 tablespoonfuls of fenugreek seed and 1 teaspoonful of crushed olive pits. She continued letting the mixture brew, uncovered, for another 25 minutes or so. By this time, the mixture had boiled down to about half of its original volume, or about a pint. She strained the liquid, added some honey, and bottled it. She would have her patients, who suffered from violent coughing spasms or bleeding lungs, take half-cup sips of this liquid every hour or as needed. She claimed that usually no more than two swigs were necessary to correct the problem.

We asked (at my gentle insistence) if we might interview both of her patients who had just left. She didn't seem to object to that. I gave her a little money and thanked her profusely for her kindness and willingness to volunteer the information she had. The man on whom we called an hour later wasn't coughing anymore. He spoke very highly of this woman's remedy. We were unable to question the woman, however, because she was very shy and spoke only through a crack in the door to her priest but not to the American stranger with him.

The old folk healer had asked only one favor of me in return for her help and that was not to publish her name in anything I wrote. Not that she objected to the recognition, but in her antiquated folk beliefs she imagined that her healing skills would be taken away from her by God if her name were ever associated with this cure in print. However odd her request seemed at the time, I have decided to still honor that promise after all these years, knowing full well that she might even be deceased.

Horse Chestnut for Fragile Capillaries and Varicose Veins

A woman in one of the New England states wrote me awhile back concerning some particular health problems. She sent her letter in care of my publisher, Simon & Schuster, who then forwarded it on to me in Salt Lake City, Utah, where I "hang my hat and call home." She suffered from fragile capillaries, varicose veins, and other circulatory disorders in both legs and wanted to know what I could recommend from my extensive repertoire of folk remedies.

I wrote back telling her to not smoke or breathe in second-hand smoke, as both are contributing factors to her kind of problems. I told her to not be on her feet so much. And that if she was, to try wearing elastic support stockings, and to try massaging her legs at least twice a day, soaking in a hot bath before bed, and taking 1,500 mg. of magnesium gluconate, 500 mg. calcium citrate, and bioflavonoids such as rutin (100 mg.) before going to sleep.

I also advised her on using a fluid extract of horse chestnut on her legs, by rubbing the calves of each with some of this solution morning and evening. Knowing that she couldn't buy such a thing here in the States as could be done in the herbal shops of Europe, I gave her simple instructions on how to make it.

I told her to strip some bark from a horse chestnut tree in the early spring and dry it in the sun. In a low-heat oven or a fruit dryer, then set it aside until the fall, at which time she was to collect some mature horse chestnuts. These were to be split open with a hammer or mallet and along with the pulverized bark soaked in a one-pint fruit jar of vodka for two weeks, shaking twice every day. Once the liquid was strained off and rebottled, she was to rub some of this on her legs as previously mentioned. I never heard from her again, but presume it must have helped, since this is a very popular remedy in Europe for the same health problems.

CHIA SEED
(Salvia Columbariae)

BRIEF DESCRIPTION

The chia is a distinctive annual springing up in the Southwest at the start of the late rains. It may also be found along roadsides below 4,000 feet. It is a rough sage with deeply incised, coarse, usually hairy, dark-green leaves that grow mostly close to the ground. Three or more whirls of small blue flowers are arrayed in a circle, similar to those for mint plants, in separated densities above prickly, dark-red, leafy bracts. These eventually mature into seed-filled pods that remain like skeletons when the rest of the plant has withered, not giving the winds enough room to blow them free and leaving them for various Native American tribes to harvest for food and medicine.

Chia seeds were harvested from June to September by women using a seedbeater. Stalks were bent and the seeds were beaten into a basket. It was reported on good authority by several ethnologists in the early part of this century that a woman could gather a couple of quarts of the tiny seeds in less than two hours. The seeds were hulled in several ways: (1) by rolling them in a metate and applying pressure with a mano, (2) by placing them on a hard surface and walking on them, and (3) by the use of flails in more recent times. Some years ago I saw some Pima Indian men gather, cut, and

87

bundle the dry stalks. The stalks were then walked upon to hull them, and the chaff was released to the four winds. After hulling, the seeds were winnowed in baskets. They were then parched either in the baskets or in clay trays with hot coals and pebbles.

The parched seeds were ground into a meal from which cakes or mush could be made. Unground seeds were stored for future use in ollas. Sometimes a beverage was made of unground seeds by soaking them in water. Ethnobotanist Edward K. Balls reported in his little work, *Early Uses of California Plants* (Berkeley and Los Angeles: University of California Press, Calif. Natural History Guide No. 10; 1965) that the nutritional value of chia seed is such that one teaspoon was sufficient to keep an individual going on a forced hike for up to 24 hours. I've had a lab analysis done on these seeds and discovered that they contain 24 percent protein, 36 percent oil, and 4.75 percent ash.

Easy Remedy for Flatulence

Ever bothered by intestinal gas in the most unlikely public places, such as sitting in church in the front row some Sunday morning when the minister is halfway through his "hellfire and damnation" sermon? Or in the center section of an opera house during the second act of Verdi's immortal *Aida,* when the pressing urge comes to "pass gas." Retain it for very long and your abdomen will ache like the dickens; but release it noisily and have a good part of the congregation or theater audience turn your way with disgusted looks on their faces.

Well, now there is something to take to save you such shame and embarrassment. It is *sprouted* chia seeds, grown in an easy and fun way. Go to any large department or discount store and ask a clerk where they keep those chia figurines you see advertised on television from time to time. They usually come in the form of an animal (like a sheep). All that is required is to water them frequently and within a matter of just a few days, sprouts will start appearing. They can be clipped with scissors after reaching an inch or more.

Merely chew a tablespoonful of them, slowly and methodically, making sure that plenty of saliva is mixed with them before being swallowed into the gut. The combination of the enzymes from the saliva and the chlorophyll and nutritional compounds in the seeds themselves produces an interaction that actually can *prevent* flatulence from occurring, due to hastily consumed food or poor food combining. Sometimes a couple of tablespoonsful may be necessary to get the job done. As long as the "chia pets" (as they are called) are constantly watered, they will keep on producing seeds. They are a delight and wonder for young children to behold, as it teaches them in a clever way the fascinating processes of life itself.

A Poultice for Infections

Some of the early Native American tribes that once inhabited parts of Southern California would make a mush out of some chia seeds for use as a drawing poultice on infections. Specific measurements for seeds and water are unknown, because of the amounts needed for intended areas to be covered. Suffice it to say, chia mush was made to the consistency of thick, hot cereal. Some of it would then be wrapped in a cloth or some other material and applied to the infected area.

Tea for Minor Eye Problems

A tea made from the seeds was an effective wash for removing foreign matter causing irritation from the eyes, as well as for inflammation, strain, and conjunctivitis. One tablespoon of seeds is simmered in 1 $1/_2$ cups boiling water for 15 minutes, allowed to cool, and then strained to make the tea for this purpose. A small eye cup should be used when washing out each eye.

Dual-Purpose Formula for Constipation and Diarrhea

Michael Tierra has been a practicing folk herbalist for a number of years in Santa Cruz, California. He spent almost six years studying herbal lore with the Karok Indians, about half that time learning additional things from the late Utah folk healer, John R. Christopher, and another six years acquiring an extensive knowledge in Oriental herbal folklore.

I've known Mike a number of years through several different herbal workshops and conferences that we've both been invited to as speakers, usually in wilderness settings. At one of these "back-to-nature" events, I remember him mentioning to the small crowd assembled outdoors, a good remedy for either diarrhea or constipation. He told us to take four parts Chinese turkey rhubarb root powder, two parts slippery elm bark powder, and two parts chia seed powder and add just enough liquid (preferably distilled water) to make a nice herbal dough, out of which can be made many little round pills the size of garden peas. These are then placed on a cookie sheet that has been covered with wax paper and dried out in the oven on low heat or in an electric fruit dryer. He suggested that they be dipped in a small amount of beeswax afterwards to help them enter the small intestines better. I've modified his amounts as well as the recommended dosage to four tiny pills twice daily; by making a few minor adjustments I discovered that the formula works equally well for both constipation and diarrhea.

Choke Cherry/ Wild Black Cherry
(Prunus Virginiana)

Brief Description

The mother of Captain Meriwether Lewis (of Lewis and Clark expedition fame) was a "yarb [herb] doctor" in her time. She taught her son the useful applications of many different types of medicinal plants with which she was very familiar. Upon one occasion in manhood, he became very ill with severe abdominal cramps and fever on the upper Missouri River. Remembering one of his mother's many remedies for such symptoms he picked a number of choke cherries from nearby bushy shrubs and consumed them throughout the day with great relish. By the next morning his condition had much improved and the symptoms were almost gone. This is according to Drake W. Will's article "The Medical and Surgical Practice of the Lewis and Clark Expedition," which appeared in the *Journal of the History of Medicine* (14:3:289, July 1959) some years ago.

Another common name for choke cherry is wild cherry or wild black cherry, which has been used as a principal ingredient in Smith Brothers' cough drops and other cough medications for many, many decades. In fact, long before the white man learned about its virtues, Native American tribes in the eastern United States and

Canada were employing the berries for food as well as medicine. The early Mohicans, for instance, placed the crushed, ripe berries in a bottle and permitted them to ferment in their own juice for a year, after which the mixture was used to treat everything from whooping cough to dysentery.

Choke cherry also grows on trees that can reach heights of 20 feet or more and that border on the edge of forests or cleared areas, seldom appearing in clusters. The branches sag with clusters of the pea-sized dark-red or blackish-purple berries, each pulpy berry encasing a single large stone. White flowers form in conelike spikes in May and June, and the berry ripens in August.

Besides being used in cough preparations, choke cherry has also been used to flavor various brands of rum, hence its other nickname of rum cherry.

The bark of the tree is glossy, rough, unevenly cracking, and scaly on regular, straight trunks. The bark is black on older trees, from which comes the wild cherry bark that has been extremely beneficial in all pulmonary disorders. On younger trees, though, the bark is reddish to olive-green. The cut wood smells like bitter almonds. Cabinetmakers value the dark red wood because it is hard, fine-grained, and can be easily polished to a glossy shine.

Eczema and Psoriasis Successfully Treated

Eczema is acute or inflammatory conditions of the skin, typically marked by redness, itching, blisterlike formations filled with fluid, and crusting. Psoriasis is a condition marked by reddish, silvery scaled lesions predominantly occurring on the elbows, knees, scalp, and trunk.

Some folk healers residing in the Appalachian mountains have relied upon choke cherry juice to relieve these symptoms. The afflicted parts of the body are liberally washed with the juice. This is usually accomplished by placing an empty pan beneath the area to be treated and a smaller receptacle filled with choke cherry juice beside it. Several cotton balls are wadded together, soaked in the liquid, and then slowly squeezed out over the afflicted skin. The juice can also be gently rubbed into the skin in a circular motion with the cotton balls. This helps to stop the terrible itching and reduce some of the swelling. The process is repeated several times a day.

A Sedative for the Nerves

I met Esther Henrickson at a church convalescent home in Chula Vista, California, back in 1991. At that time she was already pushing 105 years of age. She told me of her growing-up years in the farm country of Iowa. Being unable to go to a hospital for the proper training needed to become a full-fledged nurse, she ended up taking a correspondence course instead, before entering this noble profession.

She spent many years as a home nurse serving countless households in the Midwest and West. Most of her calls were in response to the birth of infants. She declared that the best sedative she ever administered to expectant moms to help them through the ordeal of delivery, including a few nervous fathers as well, was choke cherry juice. If the fresh berries were unavailable, she would make a tea from a supply of the dried berries that she always carried with her. The warm juice or tea never failed to calm even the most jittery case of "bad nerves," as she aptly put it.

Labor Pains Disappear

Esther informed me that when she moved west in her later years, she would travel across the border into Mexico once a week to assist impoverished Mexican women in taking better care of their children.

In using her choke cherry tea with some of them, she discovered how much their labor pains were relieved. Esther told me that the dried berry tea worked better than the fresh juice for this and that it showed a remarkable cessation of pain but only when slowly sipped while somewhat *hot*. For some reason, the cold tea never worked quite as well.

Making the tea was very simple, she said. To 1 $\frac{1}{2}$ cups boiling water, Esther would usually add a small handful of dried choke cherry, simmer for a couple of minutes, covered, and then let the contents steep for 30 minutes before straining and giving to her patients to drink. "But the tea always had to still be quite warm, otherwise it wouldn't work," she repeated.

CLOUDBERRY
(Rubus Chamaemorus)

BRIEF DESCRIPTION

The very name evokes an image of a delicate, fragile fruit. But nothing could be further from the truth, since the cloud berry is anything but a garden-nurtured wimp. This particular plant is rugged and solitary, thriving in the peat bogs of colder-climate countries. In Finland, cloudberry goes by the name of *lakka,* which signifies something tough and hardy.

Cloud berries found in a particular spot one year might be in an entirely different locale the next. To show you just how enduring this berry can be, consider that it thrives best at or near the Arctic Circle, where the nightless days of summer can last for a couple of months. There, showered with an inexhaustible supply of golden, growth-stimulating sunshine, the cloudberry literally glows in the boggy landscape making it almost too beautiful to pick.

In the Scandinavian countries, cloudberries are extremely popular. They are a delicacy that draws long lines at outdoor markets. The yellow berries give off a musky odor—admittedly a bit too strong for noses unfamiliar with their scent. When eaten raw, the cloudberry's seeds tend to make the berry rather chewy. Its complex bittersweet taste is a sharp contrast to the cloying sweetness of tropical fruits, indicating that this northern fruit is made of sterner, stiffer stuff than its fair-weather cousins in warmer climes.

Cloudberry's white flowers resemble those of the blackberry. Because of this, botanists can't agree on whether it is more closely related to the blackberry or the raspberry.

An Alaskan Dental Remedy

Cloudberries occur throughout much of our forty-ninth state. In fact, in some of the more remote parts of Alaska, they have been used to treat a variety of oral problems. Residents occupying the southern shore inlets of Cook and Prince William Sound have brushed their gums with the juice from crushed fresh cloudberries, to help tighten loose teeth and dissolve tartar.

Canker sores are effectively treated with the fresh juice, too. A single cotton ball is saturated with cloudberry juice and then placed in the mouth over the canker sore and kept there for awhile until another one is needed. This treatment usually lasts for an hour and can be repeated several times a day as needed.

In a land where many miles often separate isolated dwellings or distant villages from the medical services offered by larger metropolises, dentists are usually in short supply, which is why some of the Inuit and whites have resorted to something as simple as cloudberry to take care of their immediate health needs.

Dog Sledder Stops His Diarrhea

The 1,000-mile Iditarod sled-dog race from Anchorage to Nome is an annual attraction of major proportions. Every news organization in the United States and Canada has reported on some aspect of this historic celebration of Alaskan heritage.

"Mushers," as they are called by the locals, come from all over the world to enter this grueling race against each other, time, and the harsh environment around them. Some, such as Susan Butcher, who was the first female to win the race several years in succession, have become instant heroes or heroines to the millions who have followed this event with great interest.

One of the male participants with whom I spoke about this awhile back shared with me an interesting remedy. Although he didn't want his name used out of concern that others who knew him might make sport of his dilemma, he had no objection to my using his remedy. In the 1987 race, he said, he hadn't been careful with what he had eaten prior to its commencement.

"I found myself having to stop at different points along the way," he sheepishly admitted, "and,…well, you know…going off into the bushes to squat a spell before I made a mess of things." After several episodes of this, my informant realized that he would either fall way behind or else collapse from the sheer physical exhaustion that extreme diarrhea can produce.

"It soon ceased to be a laughing matter for me," he continued, "and became one of dire consequences if I didn't take care of it quickly." Along the route laid out for him and the other contestants he found some clumps of cloudberry growing and stopped long enough to pick adequate quantities of them. He filled the several outer pockets of his parka with these and then continued on his journey.

"I kept throwing occasional handfuls of them in my mouth and munching on them as I guided my dogs along. Within hours after this, my stool tightened up and I was able to finish the race without further mishaps," he concluded.

COCONUT
(Cocos Nucifera)

BRIEF DESCRIPTION

The coconut palm is one of the most important crops of the tropics. The slender, leaning, ringed trunk of the tree rises to a height of about 80 feet from a swollen base and is surmounted by a graceful crown of giant, featherlike leaves. Flowering begins in trees 5 years old and is continuous thereafter. Fruits require a year to ripen; the annual yield per tree can reach 100, but 50 is considered to be average.

The average coconut can be either oval or elliptical in shape, 1–1 $\frac{1}{2}$ feet in length and 6–8 inches in diameter. It has a thick, fibrous husk surrounding the familiar single-seed nut of commerce. A hard shell encloses the insignificant embryo with its abundant endosperm, composed of both meat and liquid.

Marco Polo (1254?–1324?), the famous Venetian traveler, dictated an account of his travels to much of Asia, including the Arab world, Persia, Japan, Sumatra, the Andaman Islands, and to East Africa as far as Zanzibar. He told of paper currency, asbestos coals and other phenomena virtually unknown to Europe. Marco Polo was the first European to describe coconuts in his thrilling narratives.

The harvested coconut yields *copra,* the dried extracted kernel, or meat, from which coconut oil, the world's ranking vegetable oil, is expressed. Recently, nutritionists have denounced coconut oil as being very unhealthy for the body, implicating it in arteriosclerosis and coronary heart disease. Many fast-food places still use coconut oil in their deep fryers to cook french fries, breaded shrimp and chickens and fruit pies.

Coconut "Cures" from the Philippines

During the week of July 16–24, 1994, I was in Manila conferring with a number of health-care providers in regard to the different natural remedies they use on many of their patients. Surprisingly enough, some of my best informants so far as coconut "cures" went turned out to be several medical doctors who work at Philippine General Hospital, Manila's largest health-care facility.

Earache Relief. Jesus Alvarez, M.D., a pediatrician, routinely uses warm liquid drops from coconut to relieve earache in many of his young patients. He instructs the mothers to grate some raw coconut meat (about 2 tablespoons) and then gently simmer it in one cup distilled water over medium heat for 45 minutes, uncovered. The remaining liquid is then strained, bottled, and refrigerated until needed. Half a dropper full is then placed into a large metal tablespoon and warmed by holding it over a candle, gas-stove pilot light, or cigarette lighter. Then it is put back into the dropper by squeezing the rubber top to pick it up again. Have the child tilt his or her head and squeeze only 5 drops into each ear, placing a little cotton in each afterwards to retain the warm liquid.

Urinary and Penile Inflammation. Nuño Lopez, M.D., a urologist, frequently turns to coconut milk for allaying urinary irritation and providing relief to ulcers of the penis in men caused by sexually transmissible diseases. The coconut milk is the product of the expressed juice of the grated endosperms and is found in many supermarkets. It is used as a topical lotion and sometimes injected through the vagina in the form of a douche. Prior to sexual intercourse, the infected partner has a moral responsibility to inform the other partner if he or she has such an infection.

Body Lotion For Sexually Transmissible Diseases. Ro Estrada, M.D., has come up with what I believe to be one of the more novel uses for coconut shell. Certain sexually transmissible diseases such as clamydia, genital herpes, gonorrhea, and syphilis do not always respond well to the standard topical ointments currently used by the medical profession. He began experimenting with an old folk remedy borrowed from his grandfather. Dr. Estrada cracks coconut shells into small pieces about the size of his hand and burns them to ashes in a metal barrel with the help of a little lighter fluid squirted over them.

Upon learning I would be using this remedy in my next health encyclopedia, he emphasized to me the importance of *safety* that "your readers need to carefully follow before undertaking this." In *no* way can it be done inside a house or an apartment, it must be done outside, away from anything flammable, and when there is no wind prevailing. Having a fire extinguisher or pail of water handy is a good idea.

Once the shells have completely burned, he gathers their ashes from the barrel into a container. To one cup of coconut ashes he adds three cups of red wine, puts the lid on, and shakes vigorously for about three minutes. This makes an excellent skin lotion to rub on different parts of the body covered with such disease sores and inflammation. It seems to help stop the itching, reduce the inflammation, and relieve some of the pain.

Sexually transmitted diseases are highly contagious and may not always respond favorably to natural treatments alone. Therefore, prescription antibiotics may be necessary in conjunction with alternative therapies.

CORIANDER SEED
(Coriandrum Sativum)

BRIEF DESCRIPTION

The word *coriander* has such a pleasant sound as it comes gently rolling off the tongue. Like a whiff of exotic perfume, it has a hint of romantic adventure to its sound. However, the origin of the word itself is anything but charming. It comes from the Greek *koris,* which means "a bug." This is because of a fancied likeness between the smell of the leaves and bedbugs.

A hardy annual, this plant grows up to two feet in height with white, pink, or pale-mauve flowers. For seed, it must be sown in spring and harvested immediately when it ripens (in the early fall), or the seed will drop.

The seed of this herb is spherical in shape, can be easily split in half, and varies when ripe from pale-green to cream or brown. The taste is sweet, aromatic, and vaguely like orange peel. The way that this is related to the "buglike" taste of the green plant is clear only if you taste the ripening seeds over a period of time.

Make Your Own Coriander Massage Oil for Relief of Neuralgia and Sciatica

Some time ago I was in Calcutta, India, attending a medicinal-plants symposium conference where I gave a scientific paper on the medical virtues of gotu kola (a prolific weed found throughout Southeast Asia in great abundance). An Ayurvedic physician who is a friend of mine and runs a large clinic there taught me some new uses for coriander seed that I never before imagined possible.

Dr. Vaidya Anandakumar Govindachari was his name, but I called him Vaid for short. I casually mentioned to him that his long name reminded me of the old American tongue-twister we used to try and say very fast in elementary-school years ago but without much success: "She sells seashells by the seashore." However, something got lost in the translation of humor from my Yankee upbringing to his more staid and solemn Hindu background. "Who sells seashells by the seashore?" he inquired with the utmost seriousness. "Forget it, Vaid," I mumbled to myself, and he got down to the business of showing me how he made coriander oil for treating cases of neuralgia and sciatica.

He poured approximately a pint of sesame-seed oil into a small stainless-steel skillet (about the size of those used by American chefs to make omelets in). He set this on top of a gas burner over a medium flame and gently heated the oil to lukewarm. Then he sprinkled into the pan about two tablespoonsful of coriander seeds and spread them evenly across the bottom of the pan with the back of the spoon. He lowered the gas flame a little more and permitted the contents to simmer in this fashion for one hour. He kept close watch on it, so that things didn't get too hot to cause the oil to smoke or the seeds to burn. He added a little more sesame oil as he saw fit during this interval.

Afterwards, he strained the oil through a fine wire-mesh sieve and bottled it. Though he didn't add any, I recommend putting in about one teaspoon of vitamin E oil to preserve the quality of the coriander oil. When a patient comes to him complaining of neuralgia or sciatica, he reheats a little of this oil in a large metal spoon by holding it over a gas flame or a lit candle until it is quite warm; then he pours it into his cupped hand and vigorously rubs it into the patient's muscles in a circular, clockwise motion for several minutes. Some additional stretching of the muscles in the area being massaged, by pushing them with the palms and pulling them with the fingers, is done in order to remove any stiffness or soreness remaining. I watched him as he applied this procedure to one middle-aged woman who claimed after he finished with her that she never felt better in her life. He, of course, provided a rough English translation since I didn't speak or understand Hindi.

Wonderful Tea for Abdominal Cramps

Cindy Lesure works for one of those huge telemarketing firms located in Omaha, Nebraska—the place you reach when you dial a toll-free 1-800 number to order something from a commercial you've just seen on television. Cindy told me that she frequently got abdominal cramps, had been to her doctor to have it checked out, but that nothing had turned up as a result of the exam he conducted.

I suggested a cup of warm coriander seed tea the next time this occurred. I explained how to make the tea:

1 teaspoonful of seeds in 1 $\frac{1}{2}$ cups boiling water; simmer, covered, for 15 minutes; strain and drink on an empty stomach.

We never made contact again by phone after that because I didn't call any more toll-free numbers in response to TV ads for several years. But knowing how well it has worked with others, I assumed it helped her, too.

CRANBERRY
(Vaccinium Macrocarpum)

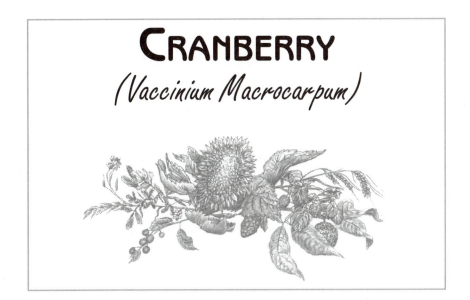

BRIEF DESCRIPTION

Cranberries were called "crane berries" originally by the Pilgrims and others who first settled the New England area. They did this because the flower stamens form a kind of "beak" resembling that of a crane. The early Native Americans, particularly the Wampanoag tribe, introduced the colonists to the berry, showing them how to use it for pemmican cakes. But the colonists soon Europeanized the cranberry, using it stewed and sweetened in puddings and tarts, for the unsugared cranberry will set your teeth on edge and grab your tongue with a mighty friendly "hello" shake on account of its tartness.

John Josselyn wrote *An Account of Two Voyages to New-England Made During the Years 1638, 1663* (Boston: William Veazie, 1865) in which he gave the cranberry considerable hype for his European readers: "At first they are a pale yellow Colour, afterwards Red, and as big as a Cherry; some perfectly round, others oval, all of the hollow, of a sower astringent taste… Furthermore," he enthused, they are "excellent against Scurvy." Europeans immediately warmed to cranberries and cooked them much as they would lingonberries, in sauces, pastries, and tarts, adding plenty of sugar, though, to make them more palatable.

Of all the berries with which I'm intimately familiar, I believe the cranberry is one of the most difficult to grow. First, you need a good bog, which requires five solid years of tending before the first cash crop is ever realized. The grower must clear the bog area of all plants, level the site, prepare the soil, plant the vines, and install a sophisticated watering system. It's also important for several bee-hives to be kept on the premises so that the cranberry flowers will be well pollinated. Therefore, the berry plants need to be pruned and the vines' runners have to be covered with sand to produce a more upright crop. Cranberries are so sensitive to weather changes that growers must stay constantly on guard. The spring growths are particularly susceptible to frost, so growers usually flood bogs to protect them. Today the berries are harvested by mechanical pick-ers or through flooding, which loosens them from the vines and causes the berries to float.

Preventing Urinary Tract Infections

Urinary tract infections occur with equal frequency in men and women alike, although uncircumcised men seem to have an increased incidence of it. However, women appear to be more prone to this problem as they get older, due to the fact that the female urethra (the tube through which urine flows out of the body is much shorter than that of men, thereby promoting greater bacte-rial invasion of the bladder.

Such infections usually affect the bladder and urethra. Occasionally, the infection can start in or spread to the kidneys. When symptoms do occur, they are generally nonspecific, such as fever, chills, irritability, and loss of appetite. More pronounced symptoms, though, would be indicative of something wrong in the genito-urinary area: pain and burning during urination; increased frequency of urination, pain in the lower abdomen; bloody, cloudy, or foul-smelling urine.

A growing body of medical literature has conclusively shown that cranberry juice can be very effective in eliminating this prob-lem. On the March 9, 1994, segment of "CBS This Morning," Dr. Howard Tormon presented clinical evidence to this effect.

Two months later in the *Tufts University Diet & Nutrition Letter* (12:3 1, May 1994) a new study by a group of Boston-based scientist provided the strongest evidence to date that the old folk wisdom of drinking cranberry juice therapy is grounded in sound scientific fact.

Researchers looked at two groups of elderly women who commonly have urine that contains bacteria and white blood cells—signs that an infection may be "taking hold" even if there are no symptoms indicating possible urinary tract infection. One group drank ten ounces of cranberry juice a day while the other consumed the same amount of a "placebo" beverage that looked and tasted the same but contained no cranberry juice.

After about six weeks, the percentage of juice drinkers who had bacteria and white blood cells in their urine dropped substantially—and remained low for the entire six-month study. Because the bacteria that cause the infections are unlikely to flourish in an acid environment, scientists theorized that drinking the acid-producing juice helped prevent the problem.

The latest theory on this, however, said Mark Monane, M.D., M.S., one of the scientists involved in the recent Boston study, is that a substance in cranberry juice keeps the problem bacteria from clinging to the wall of the urinary tract, where they can multiply and cause such symptoms as painful urination. It should also be pointed out that a few years ago a group of Israeli researchers tested seven juices and discovered that blueberry and cranberry juice contained a substance that seems to interfere with bacteria's ability to "stick."

Because antibiotics may not always be effective in getting rid of the problem entirely or because some people may develop allergic reactions to them, it seems reasonable to use cranberry juice as an alternative therapy. The Tuft University Letter advocates "cranberry juice…in conjunction with antibiotics to better fight occasional or chronic urinary tract infections."

Cranberry juice by itself may be too bitter for some people to drink. That is why cranberry juice *cocktail*—a mix of juice, water, and sweetener—is so popular with many consumers. Frozen juice concentrate may be more effective than the bottled juice cocktail in preventing and treating urinary tract infections. An eight-ounce glass every other day is recommended. There is also a powdered cranberry concentrate in gelatin capsule form from Nature's Way (two capsules daily) available in most health food stores.

Gout Cured with Cranberry Salad

Gout is a disorder or purine metabolism, occurring mostly in men. It is usually attributed to excessive consumption of red meat, but may also be genetically inherited. Gout is characterized by a raised but variable blood uric acid level and severe, recurrent, acute arthritis of sudden onset resulting from crystal deposits of sodium urate in connective tissues and particular cartilage. The wrists, elbows, knees, and ankles are the most tender parts of the body in someone suffering from this metabolic disorder.

Tony Arrellano is in his fifties and had suffered from gout for about nine years. He had tried many different medications, but without much success in relieving his situation. He informed me that the only times he experienced any kind of relief was on holidays. He said he could not figure out what he did differently then that he didn't do other times.

More careful interviewing on my part revealed that his greatest moments of freedom from pain were during Thanksgiving and Christmas. This prompted me to do a deeper probe into his dietary habits during those two times of the year. "Well, we all pile into the family station wagon and drive on over to my sister's place across town," this native-born Chicagoan said. "There we sit down to the biggest damn spread of food you've ever laid your eyes on."

I asked Tony what of everything put out on the table did he help himself to the most. His immediate response was, "Cranberries! Boy! do I love those suckers!" This was the important dietary clue I had been looking for.

I prescribed cranberry juice and cranberry sauce for him a couple of times a week. But since he loved gelatin salads, I gave his wife a recipe for cranberry gelatin salad that I used years ago when I worked in the food-service business as a chef in a fancy country club restaurant in Provo, Utah.

Needed are the following:

1 envelope of Knox unflavored gelatin (stay away from prepared mixes)
1 teaspoon lime juice
1 teaspoon lemon juice

1 teaspoon each grated lime and lemon rinds
1/4 cup cold tonic or spring water
1-pound can jellied cranberry sauce
1 medium-sized apple

Directions for making the gelatin salad are as follows:

Soften gelatin in cold water for a couple of minutes and dissolve over hot water. Next mash the canned jellied cranberry sauce with a fork and add the dissolved gelatin. Refrigerate for awhile. Coarsely grind lime and lemon juice and rinds and the entire apple in a grinder or Vita-Mix. Just as the gelatin mixture begins to gel, stir in the citrus and apple. Turn into salad molds and chill until firm.

Eat one helping twice daily for lunch and dinner. Within two weeks of this treatment, Tony's gout was gone for good!

CURRANT
(Ribes Species)

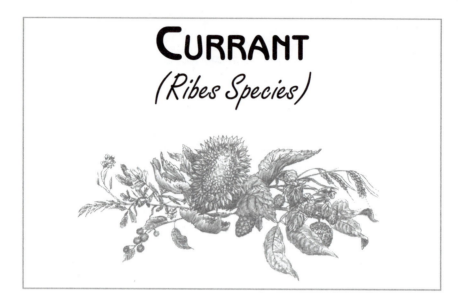

BRIEF DESCRIPTION

What is it about the currant that has inspired such affection and loyal cultivation in Europeans, and especially so with Britons? Perhaps, it's because the currant has been so intertwined with the customs of the British Isles. But what is unquestionably most inspiring about the currant is its taste. *Ribes*, the plant's genus name, is the Latinized version of an Arabic word describing a plant with an acid juice to it. Black currants are quite tart, while reds and whites tend more toward sweetness. All are pleasantly aromatic.

Currants are indigenous to cool, moist, northern regions and need to grow in places where there is plenty of summer rainfall. In some parts of the hot South and Southwest it can prove very challenging to grow them. The situation has improved markedly, however, since colonial times, and there are now varieties adapted to suit regions where currant production would have been unthinkable in bygone years.

Currants are esteemed for their culinary versatility: They can be used in summer soups and make succulent sauces for chicken, pork, duck, goose, deer, elk, moose, and buffalo. They are also outstanding as sorbets and preserves. Black currants are frequently employed in wine making in England and parts of France. In Finland, a vitamin-packed black currant-strawberry drink is extremely popular during the frigid winter months to keep the immune system in tip-top shape.

Food for Recuperation from Serious Illness

One of the problems that hospital patients face during their stay and after discharge is finding the right kinds of food for the excess nutritional needs their bodies demand while recuperating from lengthy illnesses or major surgeries. Such are not always easy things to locate. More often than not, patients find themselves eating things that barely meet the most minimal of vitamin, mineral, and protein requirements.

In the years I have spent among many different cultures worldwide, surveying the foods and medicines in each of them, I have found a particular Native American creation that is terrific for regenerating the body and giving it lots of energy. The food is called pemmican and was a travel staple of many North American tribes. Slices of lean venison or buffalo meat were sun dried, pounded to a paste, and packed with melted fat in rawhide bags. Dried currants were the favorite, but other berries such as choke cherry or cranberry were often included in the paste. Pacific Coast tribes use a similar fish compound out of which they made their own version of pemmican.

Almost two decades ago, I traveled to the Crow Indian Reservation in eastern Montana, where I spent time with Joy Yellowtail Toineeta. This older lady was gracious enough to show me the step-by-step process for making healthy pemmican that can revitalize frail bodies with dynamic health. I'm giving the complete instructions here for the first time just as I obtained them from her. The butchering part can be omitted, however, if you're able to obtain the preferred animal parts from your local supermarket.

"Take the tenderloin from deer, elk, or beef," she told me. "The tenderloin is the back strap, a long muscle on each side of the backbone.

"After the carcass has been skinned, use a sharp knife to cut through the tough gristlelike skin oven the backbone from the neck to the hip bone and to the ribs. Cut down next to the backbone to the ribs, the full length of the back and remove the long straps from each side of the backbone.

"The tough gristlelike skin on the tenderloin is the sinew used for sewing. To remove the sinew for sewing purposes, remove the outer skin and fat by hand or knife. Next to the tenderloin is a white gristle covering the meat. Use a thin sharp knife to peel this white gristlelike cover carefully, beginning from the wide end of the long tenderloin. Then soak the sinew in water until the meat and fat adhering to the sinew scrape off easily. Remove all trace of meat and fat, wash the sinew clean, and spread it out smoothly on a flat surface to dry. When dry it will become loose from the flat surface. Store until needed.

"After removing the sinew, the tenderloin is ready to be sliced and dried. Take the long tenderloin and cut down the center the full length to within one-half inch of cutting through. Then carefully slice the meat away from this center, cut one side at a time to make a thin sheet of meat, one inch thick. Handle carefully as this is very tender and will tear apart. Spread the sheet of meat on a drying rack or pole, or a window screen that permits the air to dry the meat from the underside. [**CAUTION**: Be sure that the metallic coating on the screening material doesn't seep into the meat where it can cause poisoning if consumed.] Turn the meat often to hasten drying. It is best to dry the meat on a breezy day. The meat must be quite dry. To make the best pemmican, use tenderloin. Other dried meat can be used, but be sure to remove all visible traces of gristle and connective tissues before roasting in the oven. This makes the pounding and pulverizing process easier.

"Fresh ground lean meat can be used by dry-roasting it. Put the ground meat in a roaster or shallow bread pan and roast in a hot oven. Stir often and pour off the drippings until the meat is brown and quite dry. Remove from pan and proceed with the pounding with hammer or hatchet or clean canvas until the hard kernels are mashed. Measure the pounded meat and place in a large mixing bowl or large dish pan; add stewed currants, fat, and sugar and mix well.

"To roast the dried tenderloin or other dried meat, place it in a flat sheet or a shallow pan and roast in a hot oven 425°F, 10 to 15 minutes. Watch closely, as the dried meat scorches easily. Turn once or twice then take out of the oven and sprinkle a little water on the meat on both sides; this makes a moist powder. Break up the larger pieces to convenient grinding size and put through a food grinder or chopper, using the fine blade.

"Thaw out enough frozen ground currants [or cranberries or choke cherries] to equal one half the amount of pounded meat. It is best to pour off excess liquid if the mixture is soupy. Then mix with melted marrow fat collected from cracked marrow bones and melt enough tallow fat or vegetable shortening or lard to equal the amount of currants. Mix the currants and fat with the pounded meat; add sugar to taste. Form into oblong balls to fit the palm of the hand. Place in a shallow pan to store in a cool place to set. Serve warm or cold.

"Pemmican is such a special dish that it is sometimes worth a horse in exchange or gifts of wearing apparel and money today. There is even a ceremony called the 'Cooked Meat Sing' that features the pemmican as a means of barter; this is a thanksgiving ceremony for our people [The Crow Indians].

"The medicine man begins the sing. After the opening prayer, burning the incense and smudging the medicine bundle, the bundle is passed to the guests. Each guest takes the bundle and holds it to his or her breast and offers a prayer for the sponsor or for the person for whom the ceremony is conducted until everyone has prayed. The bundle is then placed in the center of the circle. With a rattle to keep time, the sing begins. The medicine man sings first, and he gives each clan uncle and aunt a ball of pemmican for the privilege of singing. He sings at least four of his medicine and power songs and then any number of social or other songs that he particularly likes. The rattle is passed to the next guest and he does the same. If he wishes to buy very special prayers or blessings from an uncle, he speaks for his large portion of pemmican and gives him a horse for it. If he does not have a horse, he may give him a sum of money instead. The guests are required to give a gift to the sponsor, and this is placed near the medicine bundle. The length of the sing depends on the number of songs each one sings; sometimes it lasts all night.

"This is our culture. This is the Crow way of doing things," Joy reminded me. "Whites and other minorities cannot appreciate a ceremony like this. It is very different from your own customary way of celebrating Thanksgiving. The Crow thanksgiving ceremony is done whenever our tribe feels like doing it. There is much religious significance and socialization connected with it. It brings people together and unites their spirits. Thus united, we then become one with the Great Spirit himself."

Joy said that she has used pemmican on more than one occasion to help bring a seriously ill person or an enfeebled individual around to good health again. Pemmican, she asserted, contains all of the nourishment necessary for weak systems to fully recuperate by. "Pemmican isn't just an Indian thing," she said. "It's a 'health thing' for giving you more energy and stamina, more vim and vigor." Joy Yellowtail Toineeta believed very much in the revitalizing powers inherent within pemmican. And currants or choke cherries or cranberries are an integral part of this wonderful Native American food for recuperation.

DILL SEED
(Anethum Graveolens)

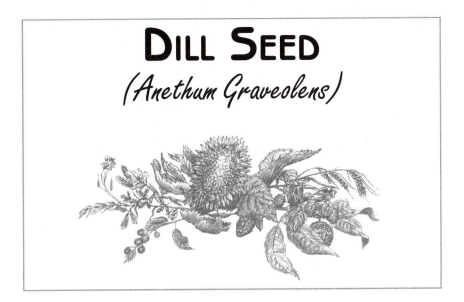

BRIEF DESCRIPTION

Dill is an annual, easily grown from seed sown in spring and thriving in almost any soil. It is hardy, but prefers a warm position out of the wind. If left alone, it will often self-seed.

The best known use of dill is in pickled cucumbers. These are soured by a lactic fermentation (as is sauerkraut or sour milk) and green dill—usually the entire plant together with the half-ripe seeds—is the dominant flavor. In the United States and Canada these are sold as dill pickles in all grocery stores and supermarkets.

Dill Tea for Bad Breath

Do you have a problem with "dragon's breath," as they call halitosis in the Orient? If so, then just gargle and rinse your mouth out every morning with some *warm* dill seed tea. It works better than commercial mouthwashes any day of the week. To make the tea, bring a pint of water to a boil and add 3/4 teaspoon dill seeds. Simmer, covered, for 15 minutes; strain and rinse the mouth while the tea is lukewarm.

Dill Tea for Baby Colic

Mothers who are faced with the dilemma of unhappy newborn babies screaming their lungs out due to the pains of colic can find immediate relief for their infants, not to mention their own nerves and ears as well. They should simply put $1/2$ cup of *lukewarm* dill and caraway seed tea in a feeding bottle and give it to the baby. The tea is made exactly as that for bad breath, except $1/2$ teaspoon each of dill and caraway seeds are used. It can be sweetened with pure maple syrup if necessary. Consult *Heinerman's Encyclopedia of Herbs and Spices* for more information on dill (Consult your pediatrician about the propriety of giving liquid sweets to children under two years of age).

DOGWOOD BERRY
(Cornus Species)

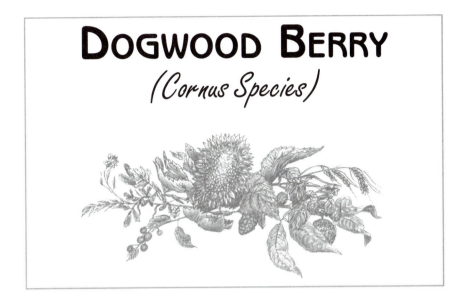

BRIEF DESCRIPTION

I've driven through parts of east Texas where hundreds of flowering dogwood trees (*C. floridia*) were in full bloom. As lovely a sight as they were, I also recall sneezing quite a bit from their allergy-inducing scent. But there is no denying the beauty of their blossoms—small, perfect clusters of flowers in hues of white, greenish-white, or yellow. They are a natural attraction for thousands of honeybees and other flying insects such as hornets and wasps.

The genus *Cornus* consists of about 40 species of shrubs or small trees native to the temperate region of the northern hemisphere, except for a single species found in Peru. Most species are deciduous and are used chiefly for their ornamental qualities: flowers, fruit, foliage, or color of twigs. The wood is hard and heavy; that of the tree species is used for turnery and charcoal. Some species produce edible berries, while the bark of others contains a substitute for quinine, the most important antimalarial alkaloid derived from cinchona bark.

The bark appears in short quilled pieces or irregularly curved chiplike fragments. Externally, it is a dirty-brown color, but if the corky layer has been removed, it changes to a dark reddish hue. In 1749 the Swedish naturalist Peter Kalm visited the first French fort,

Fort St. Frederic in Quebec, Canada, and observed how the Indians in the area utilized dogwood bark as a smoking agent. In the translated editions of his diaries, *Travels in North America (1748–51)* (New York: Wilson-Erickson, 1937), one finds this description: "On paring the bark from this branch people loosened it so that it remained attached at one end. Then they put the other end of the cutting in the ground a little distance from the fire and allowed the bark to dry a bit, whereupon they placed it in their tobacco pouch and smoked it mixed with their tobacco....I inquired why they smoked this bark and what benefits they derived therefrom. They replied that the tobacco was too strong to smoke alone and therefore was mixed [with dogwood bark]."

The so-called berries are really round or oval-shaped drupes with a thin, succulent, or mealy flesh containing a single or two small seeds. These "berries" tend to ripen in the late summer or fall and are usually bright red, or in some instances blue, as in the case of round-leaved dogwood fruit (*C. circinata*).

Leg Cramps Disappear

Kalm made the following entry in his diary on October 20, 1749, just before leaving Fort Nicholson, the last American fort north of Albany, New York: "The wife of Colonel Lydius told me that after she had arrived in Canada she had suffered from pain in her legs as the result of the cold. It became so severe that for a period of three months she could not use one leg and had to go about with a crutch. She tried various remedies without avail." Finally, according to his informant, a Native American woman from an unspecified tribe, upon learning of her condition, went into the woods and harvested some dogwood berries and twigs. These she brought back with her to the house, boiled them in water to made a strong tea with, and then "rubbed the legs with this water. The pain disappeared within two or three days and she regained her former health."

Nineteenth-Century Cure for Alcoholism

Constantine Samuel Rafinesque was a French naturalist, born in Constantinople in 1783. He made several trips to the United States

(1802–1804; 1815–1840) and traveled extensively to identify many new species of plants and fishes, In his book, *Medical flora or manual of medical botany of the United States* (Philadelphia: Atkinson and Alexander, 1828) he described how a very useful tincture of dogwood berries was helpful in getting alcoholics off the bottle permanently, not to mention its help in improving digestion.

Ironically, some alcohol has to be used in making a tincture from the berries. But the resulting product is so bitter that even with the tiny amount of alcohol present, it's pretty much guaranteed to discourage further drinking. Immerse 6 ounces of dried and finely chopped dogwood berries with equal parts of 12 ounces vodka, brandy, and rum and distilled water. Let stand for two weeks, shaking twice a day, once in the morning and again in the evening. Then strain and pour the liquid into a bottle suitable for storage. Apply 20–30 drops beneath the tongue whenever the craving for liquor ensues. Treatment generally takes 6–8 weeks to complete.

ELDERBERRY
(Sambucus Species)

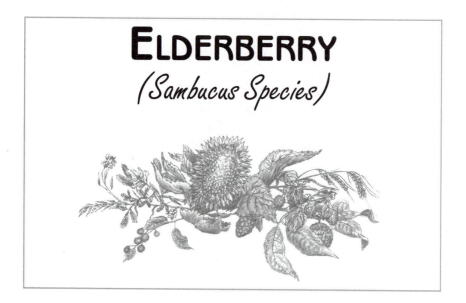

BRIEF DESCRIPTION

Elderberries differ considerably in form and taste, growing from bushy shrubs a few feet high to trees close to 50 feet in height. Their usual clusters of aromatic, star-shaped white flowers vary from flat-topped bunches to globular arrays, maturing to berrylike, limb-sagging fruits that differentiate in color from blue, amber, and red, to black and also changing considerably in taste.

Early Native American tribes employed the long, straight, hollow stems that became woodier with age for arrows and especially selected some in the springtime, dried them with their leaves on, pushed out all the soft and poisonous pith with hot sticks, and made either spouts for gathering maple and other sap or bored holes in them to fashion flutes, this gave the medicinal its added name of "tree of music." Some hunters who still use the old ways to track their game have bugled in elk with an elderberry whistle and have soon brought down a handsome buck.

Elderberries prefer rich, moist soil and are usually found in heavily forested areas, on rocky slopes, and in cool ravines. They are native to the temperate and subtropical regions of both hemispheres.

The fruit is a berrylike drupe, containing three to five one-seeded nutlets or stones. Wisdom dictates that only a few be eaten raw lest stomach upset occur. They are much better dried or cooked, but are more so when combined with tastier berries.

Mucus Accumulation Easily Discharged

Certain conditions bring about an excess of mucus accumulation in the lungs. Asthma, bronchitis, the common cold, influenza, and smoking or inhaling second-hand smoke can all result in a buildup of phlegm. A little bit of fresh elderberry juice, especially from the red drupes, is quite effective in promoting a discharge of such sticky yellow or green mucus from the body.

An old bachelor from the backwoods of Vermont once old me how he took elderberry juice to cough up "the stuff that rattles down below." His name was Zeke, and he thumped his chest with one hand to indicate where he meant they did the most good.

Zeke would put several handfuls of the ripe red berries through a coarse meat grinder clamped to one corner of his kitchen counter. He would then gather up the pulp and put it into a large piece of cheesecloth, draw the ends together and tie them, and then press out the remaining juice by pounding the packaged material with a wooden mallet. He claimed it only took two tablespoonsful on an empty stomach to get the phlegm out. He had a little rattle in his chest, probably due to his constant habit of pipe-smoking. He volunteered to show me just how quickly and effectively this worked, but I declined. I told him I believed the remedy worked without having to see actual slimy proof of the same, that would probably nauseate my senses for sure. He slapped his thigh, cackled a throaty laugh and took another puff. I gathered from this body English that he was probably having a good joke at my expense.

Quick Remedy for Constipation

In the August 1984 edition of *Natural Foods Merchandiser* (p. 54), a publication of the health-food industry, there was featured a survey of the best-selling herbal products in several thousand of America's leading health-food stores. Of those surveyed, it was found that 50 percent of all herb sales were for laxative products.

In my own formulating work that I've done over the years for a number of herb companies nationwide, I've discovered that my laxative formulas have always outsold every other product I've created, seven to one. It can truly be said that health-minded Americans have a real love affair with their colons and herbal laxatives.

Now, most of the herb books on the market will list a number of standard laxative agents: cascara sagrada, buckthorn bark, senna, turkey rhubarb, and psyllium seed. These are in addition to the much joked about old standby of prune juice. Granted that every one of them works within a few hours to produce the effects desired.

But what most people don't know is that a little bit of *fresh* elderberry juice will work like lightning to evacuate the bowels. Unfortunately for herbal manufacturers this isn't something you can capture and put into a bottle. It must be taken *fresh* in order to work as rapidly as it does. And amazingly enough, it's completely safe for everyone, from infants to the elderly. So says Varro E. Tyler, the retired dean of the Schools of Pharmacy, Nursing and Health Sciences at Purdue University in his book, *Hoosier Home Remedies* (West Lafayette, IN: Purdue University Press, 1985, p. 51).

Recommended intake is six tablespoonsful of *fresh* elderberry juice on an empty stomach for *quick* results. Because elderberries are *strongly purgative* they should be used infrequently.

Migraines Gone for Good

Recurring headaches of the specific type known as migraines, can be very troublesome for those who suffer from them. Not only do they interfere with the person's daily schedule of activities, often limiting what can be done, but they also create a deep sense of frustration in that nothing tried seems to work in helping them go away.

Many times the problem of repeated migraines is an internal signal that something isn't working right and needs prompt medical attention. It can be something as simple as a few chiropractic adjustments or new prescription lenses, or else something more complex in the way of surgery and specific medication before permanent relief is obtained.

An old Choctaw remedy of the early nineteenth century proved very efficacious in removing migraines from any white women who periodically suffered from them. The Choctaw formerly occupied central and southern Mississippi, with some outlying groups in Alabama, Georgia, and Louisiana. Their main economy was based on agriculture and they were perhaps the most competent farmers in the Southeast. After being forced to cede their lands in Alabama and Mississippi, they moved to the Indian Territory in Oklahoma in 1832, where they eventually became one of the Five Civilized Tribes to inhabit those parts. (The other four tribes were the Cherokee, the Chickasaw, the Creek, and the Seminole.) Here they lived for many years and peacefully practiced their way of life.

In 1889 the federal government opened up the first of several strips in the western section of territory to homesteaders. Prospective settlers lined up on the territorial border, and at high noon they were permitted to cross on a "run" to compete in finding and claiming the best lands. Those who illegally entered ahead of the set time were the sooners. This great colonizing event has been re-created in film and a Broadway musical, *Oklahoma*, by Richard Rogers and Oscar Hammerstein.

The influx of tens of thousands of white settlers brought them into constant contact with the Five Civilized Tribes. Some, like the Choctaw, were not adverse to sharing some of their remedies with their new neighbors. A few pioneer women who kept diaries of the period occasionally recorded some of these remedies. It was from one of these journals that I obtained this old Choctaw headache remedy. I've slightly revised it for twentieth century use, but it still works just as effectively as it did a hundred years ago.

One-half cup of ordinary table salt is poured into a heavy cast-iron skillet, evenly spread around with a wooden spoon, and heated on a medium-set stove burner. Or the same amount of salt can be evenly spread on a cookie sheet and warmed in an oven set at 345°F. Either way, the salt needs to be quite warm but not so hot as to scorch the skin in order for this remedy to work.

Next, thoroughly mash one-quarter cup of fresh elderberries. Then combine them with the hot salt in a large mixing bowl. This is best done by hand, stirring vigorously with a wooden spoon. It is important to get all of the berry juice mixed in with the salt so that none of it drips out.

Fill a clean white sock with the mixture until it is pretty evenly distributed three fourths to the top. Fold a little of the top edge over and tape it down with some masking tape to secure tightly, so the contents don't spill out. Remember that the salt must still be quite *hot* for this to work. The cotton material will allow the heat to penetrate through without burning the skin.

The headache sufferer should lie down on a bed or couch, place the sock over the forehead, making sure that the salt–berry mixture is evenly distributed around inside so it doesn't bunch up on one end to form a lump. Place a small, dry hand towel over the sock to retain the heat. Keep it on the forehead until it becomes cool. By then the migraine will have ceased and comfort will ensue. This same application can also be placed on the back of the neck if necessary. The sock mixture can be reheated several times and used this way to relieve backache, toothache, sore muscles, and pulled or sprained ligaments.

Eruptive Sores and Burns Completely Healed

The Choctaw also mixed some elderberry juice with a little boiled honey and used it as a wonderful topical application for skin eruptions and burns. The honey is primarily an adhesive agent to keep the juice from running off the skin.

One teaspoon of honey is used with two tablespoons of elderberry juice. An amount of liquid this small can be heated over a lit candle, gas burner, or cigarette lighter. The mixture is warmed only enough to loosen the honey so it can nicely blend in with the juice, which is more runny. After this, let the honey set up again before applying to the afflicted skin with a clean butter knife, popsicle stick or tongue depressor. This remedy should only be used for first-degree or minor burns. For advanced-degree burns, consult a physician in the emergency room of any hospital promptly.

FENNEL SEED
(Foeniculum Vulgare)

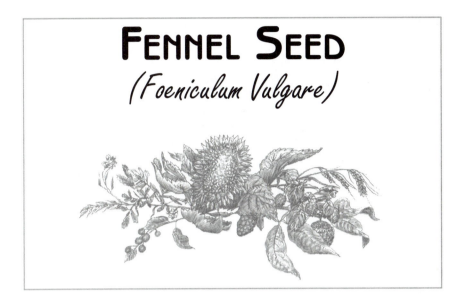

BRIEF DESCRIPTION

Fennel is a hardy perennial often found growing in home gardens as an annual. It is a large plant that can shoot up to over six feet in height. Fennel has pretty yellow flower heads and bright-green feathery leaves. It will come back every spring for several years as long as it isn't permitted to flower.

Fennel seeds are often distinguished in commercial markets into "shorts" and "longs"; the latter is the more greatly valued. The odor of the seed is fragrant, its taste rather warm, sweet, and deliciously aromatic. Alcohol and boiling water are the two mediums in which the seed best yields its virtues.

Fleas Flee from Fennel

Are you or your pet bothered with fleas? No problem. Just make some fennel seed tea and wash your pet and your own body with the same. And *voila,* no more fleas, g-u-a-r-a-n-t-e-e-d! In one quart of boiling water, cook 3 $\frac{1}{2}$ heaping tablespoons of fennel seed, covered, on medium heat for 25 minutes. Then steep for another 15 minutes. Strain and use warm or cold.

Nifty Eye Remedy

Are your eyes tired, sore, and bloodshot? Then bathe them with some fennel seed tea and they'll be as good as new. So said Dr. Henry Lloyd, a London-based eye surgeon, in *The London Times* several years ago. One-eighth teaspoon of seeds simmered in $1/2$ cup boiling water for 10 minutes, then strained and cooled, makes a "nifty eye remedy" the good doctor was quoted as saying. For more on fennel consult *Heinerman's Encyclopedia of Herbs and Spices*.

FENUGREEK SEED
(Trigonella Foenum-Graecum)

BRIEF DESCRIPTION

The appearance of fenugreek somewhat resembles that of clover in that it has a tiny pealike flower. The seeds are bitter with a faint but characteristic smell, and they contain a yellow coloring. They are used as a spice in all countries surrounding the Mediterranean Sea. Fenugreek is the second most important ingredient in Indian curries, with turmeric being the principal one.

Further information on the description of fenugreek may be found in my other reference work, *Heinerman's Encyclopedia of Herbs and Spices*.

An Egyptian "Milkshake" for Diabetes, Hypertension, Fever, and Heart Problems

In modern-day Cairo, Egypt, many of the common poor make a thick "milkshake" from *hilba* seeds. The green seeds are soaked in warm water until they swell in size to the consistency of a thick mush. Sometimes they are soaked in warm beer, which gives them a frothy or "milkshake" appearance. This thick paste is then diluted a bit by adding $1/2$ cup water or some other liquid to $1/2$ cup of this

125

paste. The flavor can be improved by adding a pinch of powdered cinnamon, nutmeg, or cloves and $1/2$ teaspoon honey or date sugar. The "milkshake" is routinely prescribed for diabetes, hypertension, fever, and heart problems.

A Treatment for Tinnitis (Ear Ringing)

Noises in the ear may be effectively treated by drinking a cup of warm fenugreek seed tea twice daily, Simmer 1 tablespoonful seeds in 2 cups water on low heat for 5 minutes, then cover and steep for 30 minutes; strain and drink. Fenugreek seed contains lecithin, which is good for the nerves. *Hilba* may be used for the same purposes mentioned for flax seed.

FLAX SEED
(Linum Usitatissimum)

BRIEF DESCRIPTION

The history of the flax plant reaches all the way back into antiquity. It was grown in Palestine before the arrival of the Israelites, for Rahab the harlot (Joshua 2:1,6) hid the two spies under the stems of flax she had drying on the flat roof of her brothel. The cloth, made from locally grown flax, would have been much welcomed by the Jews, whose clothes after such a long trek through the wilderness might have been showing signs of considerable wear.

Solomon congratulates a good wife who separates the fibers of the flax and makes fine linen (Proverbs 31:13). Fine flax is mentioned in Isaiah 19:9, when it is obvious that white cloth and thin white linen were made.

It is obvious that the Egyptians knew about growing and using flax. Making linen for Pharoah gave Joseph of Egypt fine linen clothes himself. And after the Israelites had escaped from Egypt and had "spoiled the Egyptians" under the capable direction of Moses, they were able to make fine linen priestly garments for Aaron and his sons (Exodus 28:3).

Solomon knew the value of flax linen and seems to have made it a state monopoly. Linen was used also as sails for yachts (Ezekiel

27:7). In the New Testament linen towels and napkins are mentioned (John 11:44; 13:4). Linen also was used for the wrappings of dead bodies (Mark 15:46).

The flax of which we speak grows two to four feet in height and bears beautiful blue flowers (there are occasionally white varieties). The plants were grown until they were fully matured, at which time they were pulled up whole and laid out to dry. To lose a crop of flax was serious business and was thought to be one of God's punishments (Hosea 2:9).

The capsules of flax are called "bols." and the bolled flax is the mature flax, ready for harvesting and drying. Bundles of flax are soaked in water for three to four weeks. This causes what is called "retting" (i.e., the fibers separate, and it is only then that the threads can be combed).

Of course, the best linen was used for wrapping the body of Jesus Christ, just before it was interred in an empty tomb provided by one Joseph of Arimathaea: "Then they took the body of Jesus, and wound it in *linen* clothes with the spices..." (John 19:40). This same Apostle John also recorded some years later in a grand vision he had while banished to the Isle of Patmos that the true Christian Church (likened unto the bride of the risen Lord) would someday be "arrayed in fine linen" (Revelation 19:8), not to mention the angels themselves being robed in pure white flax linen (Revelation 15:6).

Flax linen is the oldest of textile fibers and was apparently graded into three types—(a) coarse (Ezekiel 9:2); (b) better texture (Exodus 26:1); and (c) really fine and expensive (Esther 8:15). By the way, the Talmud gives full instructions as to how orthodox Jews should harvest, bleach, and prepare flax linen used by the rabbis.

The fruit of the plant is a globular capsule, about the size of a tiny pea, containing in separate cells ten seeds. These seeds are brown (but white within), oval to oblong in shape, and flattened, pointed at one end, shining and polished on the surface, and between one-sixth to one-quarter inch long. The seeds are without odor except when rendered to powder. But their flavor is slightly unpleasant and quite mucilaginous (in other words, having a somewhat slick or slimy taste to them).

Oil is obtained by crushing flax seeds; in this form it is referred to as linseed oil, which, when laid onto wood in thin layers forms a hard, transparent varnish. It has been chiefly used in the arts for its remarkable properties as a drying oil. It is a viscid, yellow liquid in appearance.

Boiled linseed oil is produced by heating raw flax seeds to a temperature of 302°F and including a small amount of a metallic drier; this process enhances its drying properties to a much higher degree. On our family ranch in the painted desert wilderness of southern Utah, we have used boiled linseed oil through the years as the only exterior cover for all of our wood-framed buildings. Over one and a half decades the many buildings have acquired somewhat of a bronze hue to them, so that when the sun slowly sets in the western sky in the early evening, it gives everything a burnished gold appearance. And with the copper-colored rocks and soil in the background, the entire place takes on a "golden look" somewhat reminiscent of what one might expect to find in a celestial city seen in a heavenly vision.

Wonderful Drawing Poultice for Boils, Abscesses, Open Sores and Wounds, and Breast Tumors

Flax seed is one of my favorite remedies. In previous trips to the Middle East, I've observed with considerable interest how the residents in that region of the world utilize its wonderful healing properties. I've watched folk healers in the slums of Cairo make a simple poultice by combining one-quarter part ginger root powder with three-quarter parts flax seed powder and adding just enough hot water or hot herb tea of some kind to moisten. This mixture was then applied directly to the skin and left there for some time (between six to eight hours) in order to draw out any purulent matter close to the surface. This remedy is wonderful for boils and abscesses, provided they are first lanced with a sewing needle that has been sterilized over an open flame. It also works very well for any runny sores or open wounds.

Local folk healers in Damascus, Syria, have been known to gently lance the swollen breasts of women afflicted with tumors and then apply this poultice with some good success. In my own personal experiences with this remedy for breast cancer, I've modified it slightly by adding a pinch of cayenne pepper and lobelia powders to triple the amount of flax seed powder, and have then moistened it with a small amount of hot comfrey root tea. Talk about a tremendous drawing poultice! Of course due to the seriousness of breast cancer, it is advisable that treatment be obtained from licensed health professionals. The above folk remedy is merely cited from a cultural perspective.

This method, of course, often works better in rural or primitive settings where medical help may not be readily available for such things. The more sensible approach would certainly be for a woman to avail herself of every medical opportunity at her disposal if she lives in a large metropolitan area where hospitals and clinics abound.

Snakebite, Insect Bites, and Stings Easily Treated with Flax Seed

I recall some years ago having to use a flax seed poultice myself while in India. I had been accidentally stung by a very angry hornet when one of my bare, sandaled feet invaded his ground domain. The moment his stinger penetrated my flesh, it felt like a bolt of electricity whizzing to my brain and setting off all my pain alarm to the tune of a most incredibly loud "Y-E-O-O-W-W!" quickly followed by other superlatives that can't be printed here.

I hobbled inside the residence of my host where I had been staying at the time, and one of his house servants—an older Hindu woman of a lower caste—quickly attended to my injury. As I sat in a chair trying not to concentrate on the terrible heat or pounding that my foot was experiencing, I looked with respectful fascination at what she did. After removing my sandal, she first soaked my foot in a pan of cool water. That was like instant salvation from my excruciating agony; the relief it afforded felt great.

Next she took what I judged to have been about three level tablespoons of flax seed powder and mixed it with one tablespoon of powdered turmeric (the principal ingredient in curry powder). Then she moistened both with some hot *lemon juice*, of all things! This paste was then spread over the afflicted area and left there for the next few hours, while I kept my foot propped up on a small wooden stool. After the dried poultice had been scraped and washed away, my foot felt fine.

I've recommended this same treatment for snakebites and other insect bites and stings with great success. If using for a more serious condition like snakebite, there are several very important steps to follow if medical help isn't readily available. First, and most important, is to keep the snakebite victim from moving around a lot or becoming hysterical. Such agitation only works the poison into the system more quickly. Secondly, the victim should be given adequate water to help dilute the toxin in the circulating blood plasma. Thirdly, a flaxseed poultice can be made according to the previous instructions for purposes of drawing out whatever poison remains at the site of the injury. This ought to be done as quickly as possible. Finally, the victim should be transported to a hospital emergency room as soon as circumstances permit.

Marvelous Tea for Asthma, Bronchitis, Colds, Coughs, Gallstones, Kidney Stones, and Urinary Tract Infections

A marvelous tea made by some folk healers in Israel works incredible healing wonders for any kind of lung or throat disturbance in which there is an accumulation of unwanted mucus or inflammation or both. Hacking coughs also benefit from this treatment. And stones formed in the gall bladder or kidneys are easily evacuated with this tea, provided a tablespoon of olive oil is taken an hour *before and after* 1 $1/_2$ cups of this *warm* tea are consumed. The same thing holds true for urinary tract infections, only without the olive oil. Because of the seriousness of the foregoing problems, medical assistance should be sought in addition to self-treatment.

Bring one pint of water to a boil; add 1 $1/_2$ level teaspoons of flax seed, reduce the heat, and permit to simmer, uncovered, for about 7 minutes, stirring occasionally. Then cover with a lid and steep for another 35 minutes. Strain and drink while still rather warm. The addition of 1 teaspoon of lemon or lime juice seems to make this tea more effective for the conditions just mentioned. However, if the taste is more than you can bear, just sweeten with a little pure maple syrup or blackstrap molasses to improve the flavor.

Lower Back Pain or Sciatica Relieved

A fellow, whom I'll call George, was working on the local dock of a local trucking firm, moving many heavy items around by hand one day. When he got home that night he complained to his wife of having a terrific pain in the lower part of his back, which radiated out across the buttocks and down the backs of his thighs and calves.

She called me and asked what to do, saying in a teasing way within earshot of her husband in pain: "My p-o-o-r baby isn't feeling t-o-o good right now, and I want to make him better!"

I advised her to boil one quart of water and add to it 1 $\frac{1}{2}$ tablespoons of flax seed and cook on low heat, uncovered, until about half the liquid remained. I told her to give him one cup of this *warm* tea every 3–4 hours on an empty stomach. I further instructed her to take the boiled seeds (which by now were very soft) and put them in a muslin or cloth bag and apply this poultice as hot as her husband could bear it to the lower portion of his back where the pain was greatest. I suggested she cover the bag with a heavy bath towel to help retain the heat longer.

By the next morning his pain was gone and he was able to resume work again, only being more careful in how much he lifted and in how many times he bent over.

I might add that when some flax seed powder is combined with powdered mustard seed, it definitely improves the therapeutic benefits expected from a classic "mustard plaster" (see under Mustard Seed for making this).

GINKGO NUT
(Ginkgo Biloba)

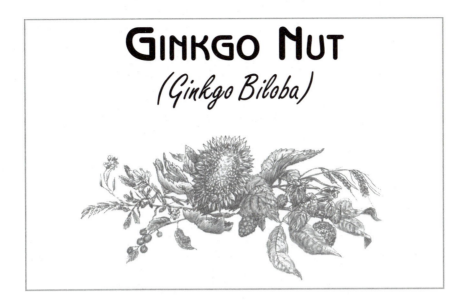

BRIEF DESCRIPTION

The ginkgo is one of the few plants that has survived from the age of the dinosaurs. Along with the horse tails and certain ferns, it enjoys the distinction of being classed with some of this planet's oldest medicinal herbs. The order to which the ginkgo tree belongs, *Ginkgoales*, can be traced back through fossil remains to the Permian era (250 million years ago). During this time period the plants were widely distributed throughout the northern hemisphere and parts of the southern hemisphere.

As a genus, *Ginkgo* appeared approximately 180 million years ago during the lower Jurassic period, existing as 4 distinct species by the time of the dinosaurs in the lower Cretaceous period (80 million years ago). Film producer Steven Spielberg went to great lengths to include several ginkgo trees in his $1 billion epic motion picture *Jurassic Park,* about an island amusement park with live, huge dinosaurs that eventually run amok and cause much destruction and death. (The trees were nearby the sick Triceratops in case you missed them.)

One of these species, the now extinct *Ginkgo adiantoides,* appeared to have nuts and leaves nearly identical to those of the surviving *Ginkgo biloba.* The cold weather and physical action of the glaciers at the end of the Tertiary period (two million years ago) caused the extinction of many plant species, including most types of ginkgo. Only the *Ginkgo biloba* escaped complete extinction when the southward progression of ice stopped in eastern Asia, becoming the sole survivor of the family *Ginkgoaceae.* The remaining trees apparently did not flourish, however, and with the coming of modern history, the number of wild ginkgo trees was limited.

Convincing evidence has been presented that a few *wild* ginkgo trees existed as late as 1933 in southeastern China. But the plant was considered sufficiently rare and precious before the time of the Sung dynasty (late tenth century) that seeds from native regions were sent as a yearly tribute to the emperor, who then had them planted in Kaifeng, the capital city of the Sung dynasty. In time, seedlings from cultivated ginkgos were introduced into Japan, Korea, Holland, England, and eventually America, in 1784. From these humble beginnings, the ginkgo is now extensively cultivated in Asia, Europe, North America, and the temperature regions of New Zealand and Argentina.

This "living fossil" (as it has been rightly called by some plant scientists) is incredibly resistant to all types of pollution, viruses, and fungi. Several individual trees in China have been scientifically dated to be between 3,000 and 4,000 years old! It truly is "the doyen of trees" on account of its great antiquity.

The ginkgo tree has a gray-colored bark, can exceed 100 feet in height and can reach a fat girth of 23 feet. The tree exhibits an odd branching stem dimorphism, resulting in long and short shoots. Leaves appear along the length of the long shoot and as clusters at the end of both the long and short shoots each spring. The leaves turn from a light-green color when young to a deep-green color when mature and to a golden-yellow color during senescence in the fall. The species name "*biloba*" was added in recognition of the frequently notched, leathery, fan-shaped leaves.

Ginkgo trees have imperfect flowers, with male and female reproductive organs on different trees. Ginkgos do not begin to reproduce until they are more than 20 years old, after which they can continue reproducing for the next several *millennium!* Only the female ginkgo which bears an inedible fruit with an edible nut inside, which is extremely popular in Oriental cuisine and medicine.

The fruit containing the nut falls to the ground and soon emits a volatile, foul odor. The smell, believed to contain butyric acid along with other compounds, is reminiscent of a dead corpse in the first few hours of decomposition. (I ought to know because I once worked in the funeral business as an apprentice mortician and have smelled enough ginkgo fruits during my visits to China, Korea, and Japan to quickly draw the connection between the two.)

Japanese "Secret" to Avoid Getting Drunk While Imbibing Alcohol

A while back I went to Japan in company with Earl Mindell, the noted pharmacologist and author of several best-selling nutrition books, Dr. Morton Walker, a podiatrist and author of many health books, and other equally eminent figures. We were the special guests of the Wakunaga Pharmaceutical Company of Hiroshima, makers of the world's most popular and best-researched odorless garlic product (marketed under the brand name of Kyolic). During the nearly two-week visit, we saw and learned much about Japanese culture, diet, medicine, and industry. It was "a trip of a lifetime," well worth remembering.

I had an opportunity to meet with some doctors there who practice something else besides their own orthodox hospital medicine replete with its potent prescription drugs, nuclear radiation, and surgery. It is an alternative system of health care known collectively as *kampo* (or *kanpō*). The main focus is on diet adjustment, exercise, herbal therapy, vitamin supplements, acupuncture, moxibustion, massage, and a modified form of psychotherapy. They practice this brand of noninvasive medicine when they're not working at their regular medical practices. In my opinion, it is the *best* blend of both worlds—thoroughly trained physicians in all the rigors of modern medicine and anatomy, but tempered with an equal understanding of those things in alternative health that work. In the event something goes wrong in the latter, there is the medical expertise of the former to immediately implement it if necessary. Now what could be a finer balance than this?

Several of these kampo doctors informed me that they routinely prescribe the gingko nut to help fight drunkenness. They encourage many of their male patients, who are aggressive corporate executives and heavy drinkers, to consume ginkgoes *with* their cocktails. They told me that their own research has shown that the ginkgo nut contains unique compounds that actually can speed up the metabolism of alcohol. This means that no matter how much is consumed, as long as they take plenty of ginkgo *with* their drinks, there is little chance of them going into a drunken stupor.

The World's Best-Researched Herb

Tolerant to the common urban stresses of insects, diseases, and air pollution, the ginkgo has become a favorite ornamental tree for landscaping and adorns several parks and streets in Europe and America. Cultures throughout Southeast Asia have employed the nut of ginkgo medicinally and for culinary purposes for some centuries. In fact, the body of folklore surrounding this practice is quite extensive, I've discovered.

However, it has only been in the last couple of decades that this plant from the dinosaur era has become a very promising herbal drug agent. I did a computer check in June 1994 through the National Library of Medicine's information retrieval systems (MEDLINE and MEDLARS) and received a very generous printout on *Ginkgo biloba* that was three quarters of an inch *thick* and contained over 300 different clinical studies that have been conducted on it. Little wonder then that it has earned the distinctive moniker of "the world's best researched herb!" Not bad for a nut that has somehow managed to survive global catastrophes over many aeons.

The Ultimate Antidote for Aging

Let me set the record straight here with regard to this very, very ancient nut. Ginkgo will *not* reverse the aging process; it is *not* a miracle "potion" for lost youth. But it will help you in many ways to age more gracefully with only minimal physical discomforts if you start taking it now. Rob McCaleb of the Herbal Research Foundation in Boulder, Colorado, put it best of all, when he said: "Gingko successfully addresses many of the conditions that afflict the elderly, one of the most powerful and fastest growing political constituents in the country today." Throughout Europe, he notes,

"Tens of millions of folks have already benefited from its effects on memory, cognitive function and conditions of the eyes, ears. heart and peripheral circulation. However, the irony to all of this, he adds, is that "the young in the United States seem to be discovering the herb more rapidly than the elderly are."

Because space is limited I'm unable to present dozens of clinical cases to support every single thing for which *Ginkgo biloba* is good. Therefore, I've elected to briefly summarize what the extract powder in capsule form can do in several important health categories that especially affect the middle-aged and elderly. The single product I most recommend, based on numerous testimonies given to me from many doctors in America, Europe, and Asia who routinely recommend it to their patients, is something called Ginkolic. It is a special high-potency preparation containing ginkgo and isolated ginkgo compounds (called ginkoflavonglycosides), Japanese aged garlic extract (Kyolic), and Siberian ginseng. This unique formula is manufactured by the Wakunaga Pharmaceutical Company of Hiroshima and distributed through health-food stores in the United States and Canada by Wakunaga of America in Mission Viejo, California. The suggested number of capsules per day is given after each health entry. Because this product has been formulated and tested by a pharmaceutical firm in Japan, it is completely safe to use for preventive as well as treatment purposes. However, a program of three weeks on and one week off of this product is a good idea to follow so the body doesn't become entirely dependent on any one thing. (See the Appendix for the complete address and phone number of Wakunaga of America.)

Cerebral Impairment (Memory Loss, Dizziness, Tinnitus, Impaired Intellect and Concentration, and Neurological Disturbances). Between two to four capsules daily is strongly advisable. Age-related impairment of cerebral function can result from organic degeneration of the cortex, multiple vascular infarcts, or a combination of both causes. As the World War II "baby boomer" generation continues to age, these conditions will increase and become even more of a therapeutic challenge than they currently are. The effects of ginkgo nut and leaf extract in ameliorating the signs and symptoms of cerebral impairment have been thoroughly assessed by scientists all over the world.

Vascular Impairment (Arteriosclerosis, Venuous Insufficiency, Hypertension, Migraine Headache, Stroke, Heart Attack, Peripheral Vascular Disease, Varicose Veins, Blood Clot, and Diabetes). An average of three capsules daily is highly recommended. Oral administration of Ginkolic for several months has shown to be substantially more effective than placebos in placebo-controlled clinical evaluations in adults suffering from a number of blood-circulation disorders. Ginkgo acts as a blood thinner, lowers blood pressure, and expands peripheral blood vessels, including the capillaries, which often become reduced in size due to stress, bad diet, and disease.

Macular Degeneration (Loss of Vision). Up to four capsules each day is believed to be of some therapeutic value. Senile macular degeneration is an aging disease that involves gradual and irreversible loss of visual acuity and for which *no* medical treatment has yet proven effective. Elderly patients placed on *Ginkgo biloba* extracts were found to have consistent increases in capillary and venous blood flow to their heads resulting from decreased resistance to circulation.

Help for Degenerative Diseases

Alzheimer's, atherosclerosis, cancer, Crohn's disease, free radical impairment, multiple sclerosis, muscle atrophy, muscular dystrophy, nerve deterioration, Parkinson's, rheumatoid arthritis, and system lupu erythematosus are all benefitted to varying degrees with three natural supplements. Equal amounts of four capsules each of Ginkolic and evening primrose oil accompanied by one tablespoonful of Rex's Wheat Germ Oil. (NOTE: Rex's Wheat Germ Oil is *the* strongest, most pure and unrefined vitamin E oil on the market, but is available only to veterinarians and livestock breeders for animal use. However, I have been recommending it for many years as well as taking it myself without any problems. See Appendix XII for cost and ordering.) Free radicals may be compared to molecular sharks zipping around in our cellular seas, doing great damage to body tissue. There is more than adequate information to show that ginkgo nut and leaf extract definitely inhibit free radical activity. A good textbook that I recommend for readers who are interested in doing more research on their own is C. Ferrandi's, M. T. Dory-Lefaix's, and Y. Christen's (eds.) *Ginkgo Biloba Extract (EGb 761) as a Free Radical Scavenger* (Amsterdam: Elsevier, 1993). The addition of evening primrose oil and Rex's Wheat Germ Oil are based on my own independent trials and research.

Nerve System Dysfunction (Nervousness, Senile Dementia, Depression, and Prevention of Suicide). Between three to six Ginkolic capsules daily. I recommend another very good textbook by Y. Christen, I. Costentin, and M. Lacour (eds.) entitled *Effects of Ginkgo Biloba Extract (EGb 761) on the Central Nervous System* (Amsterdam: Elsevier, 1992). It provides all the necessary clinical and scientific data to show that this prehistoric herbal nut merits use as an anti-aging tool for the central nervous system.

Proctological Problems (Acute and Chronic Hemorrhoids). An average of three capsules daily. Several clinical studies reported good or very good results in 86 percent of several dozen patients with hemorrhoids in a more or less advanced stage. The compound was particularly effective in individuals with congestive conditions and bleeding. Ginkgo nut and leaf extract appears to have less effect on fissures, but is very good at relieving pain and stopping rectal bleeding and itching. (See E. Parnaud's "Ginkor en proctologie courant; a promos de 36 observations" in the French medical journal *Therapeutique* 47:483 [1971] for his clinical observations on ginkgo for various proctological problems.)

The range of beneficial pharmacological activity of *Ginkgo biloba* extract has been amply demonstrated in noncomparative and, more important, well-designed comparative trials in numerous patients with a wide variety of health problems that fit into one of the previously mentioned categories. The overwhelming abundance of data suggests that cerebral, vascular, and free radical impairments are the main indications for this wonderful herbal nut. It appears to be well tolerated. Only 33 of a total of 8,505 recipients involved in a retrospective analysis reported any side effects; the most frequent, reported by 9 patients, were gastrointestinal in origin. Symptoms of heartburn, nausea, and vomiting were mild and transient in these few people. It's concluded that ginkgo is very safe for most human biological systems.

GOOSEBERRY
(Ribes Grossularia)

BRIEF DESCRIPTION

Gooseberry has had to struggle for recognition over many centuries of time. The Normans first introduced it to France from the Scandinavian countries somewhere around the tenth century. But this plump, tasty berry failed to inspire gardeners there. This was probably due, in part, to its culinary association with cooked mackerel, a fish enjoyed by the peasant population. This unfortunate linking earned it the unlikely sobriquet of *groseille à maquereau*. Because gooseberry failed to inspire the French, the British ignored it too; it wasn't until the early sixteenth century that it began to be widely cultivated in English gardens.

Another mistaken identity for this three-to-four-foot-high shrub with the lovely fruit was its association with the Devil. The moniker "Old Scratch" has been applied to the Prince of Darkness for centuries in Europe. Because of the thorns that are present on gooseberry bushes and can cause nasty scratches on the skin if not carefully picked, it was naturally assumed by superstitious peasants that

Satan himself frequently snacked on this fruit. Hence, the name of "Old Gooseberry" was often given to his evil majesty in medieval times.

But the present name for this delicious fruit is derived from the old British culinary practice of serving roast goose stuffed with gooseberries and a nice gooseberry sauce served alongside it. There is also told the tale of long ago about a British peasant in the countryside who was fermenting a crockery jar of the berries for a little "midnight nip" now and then. His wife, upon discovering his secret brew and being disgusted with her husband's drunkenness anyway, threw the entire batch out in the yard. A gaggle of dignified geese walking by stopped long enough to greedily devour the discarded contents. Within a few minutes, the high amount of alcohol in those sour berries finally connected from stomach to brain, and the entire bunch of birds were bumping into and falling over each other in such ludicrous fashion that those who saw the scene couldn't help but laugh themselves silly at such a spectacle.

The American gooseberry is no match in terms of size and flavor for the European variety. In her eponymous cookbook, *The Alice B. Toklas Cook Book* (New York: Harper & Row, 1954), the author got to the point in a hurry without wasting words: "The gooseberries in France are four or five times larger than those grown in the United States, and very much sweeter." Gooseberries are usually a bit bristly and generally greenish in color but sometimes can also be yellow or even red.

Serum Cholesterol Levels Lowered

Gooseberries have about them certain nutritional properties that help to lower serum cholesterol in the circulating blood plasma by assisting fat metabolism within the liver. The following nutritional analysis for gooseberries came from an article entitled, "Mineral element composition in Finnish foods," which appeared in *Acta Agriculturae Scandinavica* (Supplement 22:102, 1980). Scandinavian scientists who've studied the effects of gooseberries on blood cholesterol and triglyceride levels think that the rich array of trace elements may account for their medical benefits in this regard.

One kilogram (about 2 lbs. 2 oz.) of gooseberries contains the following rich array of vital nutrients:

Nitrogen	1.4 grams
Potassium	2.5 grams
Calcium	0.36 grams
Magnesium	0.10 grams
Phosphorus	0.25 grams
Sulfur	0.11 grams
Iron	3.7 milligrams
Copper	0.49 milligrams
Manganese	1.7 milligrams
Zinc	1.4 milligrams
Molybdenum	0.1 milligrams
Cobalt	5.0 micrograms
Nickel	0.03 milligrams
Chromium	10 micrograms
Fluorine	0.1 milligrams
Selenium	2.0 micrograms
Silicon	5.0 milligrams
Rubidium	1.3 milligrams
Aluminum	4.0 milligrams
Boron	1.2 milligrams
Bromine	1.0 milligrams
Mercury	0.2 micrograms
Arsenic	0.01 milligrams
Cadmium	2.0 micrograms
Lead	10 micrograms

Gooseberries make an excellent accompaniment to just about any type of meat dish that is traditionally heavy in fat content. Not only does it add considerable flavor to them, but it also lowers the cholesterol found in items such as duck, goose, turkey, lamb, mutton, beef, and pork. In such instances, it is best to serve this tart fruit as a stew, jelly, or jam, but without the white sugar (use honey instead to sweeten). Try cooking gooseberries with sweet corn sometime for a real taste treat that's also very good for you.

Relief Obtained for Erysipelas

Medically speaking, erysipelas is defined as a type of cellulitis, which is a potentially dangerous skin infection. It can spread deeply into and throughout the body and, if left untreated, could eventually cause death. This disease begins most often on the face, or on an arm or a leg. The characteristic lesion is shiny-red with well-defined margins. It is swollen and tender, and nearby lymph nodes may also be enlarged and sore. As the infection progresses, the sore becomes larger and turns purplish.

Erysipelas is caused by bacteria. The most common culprit is a bacterium called Group A beta hemolytic streptococcus. But other "strep" bacteria can also be found in the raised, spreading, purplish lesion that is a hallmark of this disease. A fungal foot infection can also be a source of erysipelas.

The young, the old, and the weak are the most common victims of this painful skin infection. Erysipelas often arises soon after one has had a bad cold, strep throat, or other respiratory illness. Regardless of origin, the bacteria probably enter the skin through a cut, scratch, or sore. They take up residence in the lymph glands, where they multiply and then spread through the lymphatic channels. Later, the bacteria spread through the bloodstream and pose a threat to the kidneys and other organs.

Latona Old Elk, a Crow medicine woman from the Crow Agency in eastern Montana has used the juice of green gooseberries to bring relief to those patients she treats, both Indian and non-Indian, who suffer from erysipelas. The first thing, she told me some years ago when I visited the reservation was to be adequately protected when going out to gather them. I accompanied her to a nearby creek where there were stands of the shrubs lining either side of it. We put on heavy work gloves and used a couple of sharp hatchets to trim several fully loaded shrubs with. Prior to this we had spread out on the ground a large canvas tarp. Over this we held the sagging limbs and knocked the berries off with a couple of hickory sticks. Afterwards, the ends of the tarp were folded together and tied. Upon returning to her house, we washed the gooseberries in a large iron kettle of water, removing debris such as leaves, stickers, and dirt.

Next, Latona put the cleaned berries in some other water and boiled them until their skin broke. This probably took 30 minutes to do. She then poured the berries into a large aluminum colander (sievelike pan) that was set inside a larger round enamel pan. Holding a small block of wood in one hand, she rubbed this over and around the gooseberries in a circular motion until they had been thoroughly mashed. The resulting juice dripped through to the bottom pan.

This she strained and bottled. Sometime later on when a patient came to see her about a condition of erysipelas, she would give the individual some of this gooseberry juice, instructing the person to dip a four- or six-inch length of gauze strip in the juice and then to lay it over the skin and leave it there for a while until it dried out. She also said to spray the juice on using a clean, empty spray bottle with a squirt applicator to it. This remedy never fails to work, she said.

Treatment for Rosenbach's Disease

Also called Heberden's nodosities, Rosenbach's disease are cartilage-capped bony projections arising from bones that develop from cartilage. Such projections (called exostoses) are about the size of a pea or smaller. They are found on the bones between the two joints of the thumbs and fingers in osteoarthritis.

While this particular malady is one of those that only a very small percentage of the population may have, it nevertheless deserves mention here because of what my Crow Indian informant used for it. Latona Old Elk had a couple of her white patients with this disease soak strips of cotton cloth in gooseberry juice and then wrap them around their fingers. Over them were loosely wound other strips of dry cloth and pinned with safety pins to hold them in place. She said that this afforded some relief for Rosenbach's disease.

Remedies for Erythema and Lupus Erythematosus

I learned a lot from the time I spent with both my informants on the Crow Reservation years ago. Joy Yellowtail Toineeta and Latona Old Elk taught me that the Crow ways are sometimes better than the white man's ways. For example, money and material wealth is not as meaningful to them as kin ties and clan relationships are. This fact was evident in Crow celebrations I witnessed where individuals living on federal subsidies gave away armloads of clothes, blankets, or tools to friends and relatives.

Joy pointed out to me that "the Crow Indian child is taught that he or she is a part of a harmonious circle of kin relations, clans, and nature. But the white boy or girl is taught that he or she is the center of the circle." Similarly, she added, "The Crow believe in sharing wealth, and whites believe in accumulating it."

To which Latona contributed: "We are willing to share our remedies with you, because we know that you will, in turn, eventually share them with others who will benefit from our medical wisdom and skills. But you couldn't very well get that from a white doctor, who might be jealous of his position and unwilling to give out information that might be beneficial to others later on."

They both told me how they have used fresh gooseberry juice to successfully treat two inflammatory skin diseases, namely erythema and systemic lupus erythematosus. But first a brief explanation about each disease.

Erythema is an inflammation reaction of the skin. Symptoms manifested by this disease are several in number. Red weals or blisters can suddenly appear in a symmetrical pattern usually on the hands, feet, and face. Itching can be moderate to severe. Joint pain and fever are generally present. Lesions can occur in the mouth and throat, causing drooling and making chewing and swallowing very difficult. Painful swelling and the appearance of pus in the eyes is common. Also, there is the appearance of painful red nodules that gradually turn blue and then brown.

Systemic lupus erythematosus is an inflammatory disease that can damage connective tissue throughout the body, including tissue in the joints, muscles, skin, kidneys, heart, lungs, and nervous system. It is actually an unusual form of arthritis that afflicts mostly women. In fact, women outnumber men almost nine to one with this disease. For some unknown reasons, lupus is also more common in African Americans, Native Americans, and some Asian groups than in Caucasians.

The name lupus is derived from the Greek word for wolf, and it is believed that the disease is so named because of the persistent or tenacious way in which it often attacks various organs. Also, one of the most characteristic symptoms is a butterfly-shaped rash that develops over the face, which sometimes is described as giving lupus patients a wolflike appearance.

Besides this butterfly rash on the face, skin on other parts of the body may also develop reddish, weeping, and scaling rashes; the medical term for this type of skin lesion is erythematosus. And since lupus tends to be a systemic disease, affecting organs throughout the body, its full medical name is systemic lupus erythematosus, or SLE for short. Like rheumatoid arthritis itself, lupus is an autoimmune disorder, wherein the body's immune defenses run amok and turn upon themselves.

Joy and Latona have incorporated gooseberries several different ways for each malady. The usual course of treatment for erythema has been to bathe the skin frequently with some of the juice as well as to apply poultice of the crushed berries on the forming nodules, forehead, and throat. Some of the juice is also gargled, if necessary.

For SLE, however the juice is diluted with an equal part of water and taken internally as a tonic tea several times daily (2 cups on an empty stomach). Gooseberries are also set out on a screen and dried, from which a tea is then made and drunk twice daily (2 cups). One-half cup of dried berries is added to a pint of boiling water, simmered for 10 minutes and allowed to steep another 45 minutes before being strained and drunk. Afflicted portions of the body are also periodically bathed with some of the juice or tea.

The frequent use of gooseberry jam or jelly (made without sugar) is encouraged. Between these various forms of internal consumption, much relief has been obtained from SLE symptoms by those few Native American patients whom they've treated in the past for it.

GRAPE (see Wild Grape)

HACKBERRY
(Celtis Occidentalis)

BRIEF DESCRIPTION

The hackberries comprise a large, widespread genus that includes about 70 species of shrubs and trees in the northern hemisphere. The small, greenish flowers appear in the spring as the new leaves emerge. Hackberry fruits are unevenly circular drapes with a thin pulp enclosing a single bony nutlet. Good seed crops are borne practically every year, and the fruits persist on the branches well into the winter time.

Paleoindians from prehistoric times picked the berries by hand from trees between October and December. Collection was always made easier after the leaves had dropped off. For several decades now archaeologists have placed a major focus of their efforts on the southernmost 70 miles of the Illinois River Valley, a few miles north of St. Louis. Here it is believed was a major concentration of several different early paleoindian cultures that had time to develop over a few thousands years. Today, however, this archaeologically rich region is sparsely populated farmland.

The period of time that archaeologists have assigned to a specific phase of their research is called the Woodland period (600 B.C. to A.D. 900). During those many centuries, paleoindians subsisted on

147

a number of edible plants, nuts, berries, and seeds, which they gathered from the wild. These were in addition to their usual meat sources of bison, deer, small game, and fish. More detailed data about this prehistoric food use of hackberry appears in A. A. Zawacki's and G. Hausfater's monograph, *Early Vegetation of the Lower Illinois Valley* (Springfield, IL: Illinois State Museum, 1969; Investigative Report #17).

Like the butternut and the black walnut, hackberries have the unusual distinguishing trait of having their pith divided into naturally enclosed cavities. Splitting a twig longitudinally, you'll see the soft spongy interior as a series of white dividing walls, separating empty chambers.

Odd, too, is the fact that the generally even, grayish bark sometimes roughens with dark, hardening, wartlike protuberances that resemble bumps and raised corklike strips. Just as the human body can sometimes develop warts, moles, and other growths quite mysteriously, the same is true for some species of trees such as the hackberry.

Seasoning Replacement for Black Pepper

The early Omaha and Ponca nations ate hackberries only occasionally. But the Dakota Indians utilized them more frequently as a wonderful flavoring for roast bison, deer, elk, rabbit, and other wild game. For this purpose they pounded the hackberries very fine, seeds and all. When they first sag the peppercorns of black pepper and their use as a condiment when ground by white men, the Dakotas likened them to their own *yamnumnugapi*. They called black pepper *yamnumnugapi washichu* or "white man's *yamnumnugapi*." However, when some of them tasted the ground black pepper of the whites, they spat it out in disgust, preferring their own pounded hackberry condiment instead.

An Old Pawnee Remedy for Kidney Stones

In the Pawnee language, *kaapsit* was the word for hackberry. An effective food remedy frequently employed for the relief of kidney stones and urinary tract infections in Indians and non-Indians alike called for a handful of hackberries to be pounded very fine with a little bit of bear or buffalo fat rubbed in and then mixed with some parched corn. Lumps of this would then be dropped into some boiling water for a few minutes and cooked much as dumplings might be. The Pawnee described this combination as being a very good dish and remedy besides, according to Melvin R. Gilmore in his report, *Uses of Plants by the Indians of the Missouri River Region* (Washington, DC: U.S. Government Printing Office, 1919; Thirty-third Annual Report of the Bureau of American Ethnology).

If you intend to make this, the hackberries can be crushed on a countertop with a heavy rolling pin or else placed on a wooden cutting board and pounded with a hammer. Shortening can be substituted for animal fat, and cornmeal will nicely substitute for parched corn. A pinch of salt in the boiling water will add a little more flavor. I've had five different people try this peculiar "food medicine" for kidney stones. Four of them said it worked and only one complained that he couldn't tell any difference, although he freely admitted the dish tasted pretty good "for Indian food."

What the Omaha Indians Did for Wounds and Sores

Wounds and sores were pretty common among the early Native American tribes, who at one time freely roamed this continent. Frequent engagements between hostile tribes often resulted in injuries being incurred with arrows, tomahawks, knives, and other weapons of war. Also, the lack of adequate hygiene by many tribes could result in serious infections developing in these wounds, not to mention eruptive sores appearing from time to time on other tribal members.

Although the Omaha nation were quite unlearned in the ways of the white man and didn't know anything about the growth of microorganisms in attended wounds and sores, they did have enough understanding with regard to plants in their surrounding environment to use these in times of medical need.

A handful of hackberries were crushed and put into some boiling water. Also, the inner bark of the shrub or tree was stripped off, shredded into pieces, and thrown in. After cooking awhile on an open fire, the resulting tea was used to bathe wounds and sores many times each day until the sores healed. I've used a simpler version of the same thing, incorporating both ingredients (2 table-spoons) in a quart of boiling water. I've let them simmer on low heat for 5 minutes, then removed them and continued to let them steep, covered, for another 25 minutes. After this I strained the contents into a clean fruit jar and refrigerated it.

Festering wounds, diabetic ulcers, syphilitic lesions, and bed-sores can be frequently washed with this solution with amazing results. You can almost see the rapid healing ensue within a matter of days.

HAWTHORN BERRY
(Crataegus Oxyacantha)

BRIEF DESCRIPTION

Hawthorns in North America consist of 100 to 200 species of small trees and shrubs, mostly in the eastern half of the United States. Their taxonomy is difficult and confusing; some 1,100 specific names have been published, but most are no longer accepted. Hybrids no doubt exist, and many varieties are recognized.

Hawthorns furnish food and cover for wildlife; species with fruits that persist over winter are especially valuable. Many species are useful for environmental plantings. Because they tolerate a wide variety of sites, hawthorns have also been planted to stabilize banks, for shelter belts, and for erosion control.

The hawthorns have thorny twigs and branches, although a few species are spineless. The leaves are single and what is known as simple, growing alternately in varying shapes and different degrees of lobing and serration. The conspicuous flowers have five creamy and sometimes pinkish blossoms and loom up importantly in this nation's history, as they gave the Pilgrims' ship the *Mayflower* its name. Growing in ordinarily fragrant clusters in midsummer, they usually thrive in flatish, terminal groups.

151

The small applelike fruit, characteristically tipped with the remnants of the outer floral leaves, are really pomes, a fleshy reproductive entity with five seeds enclosed in a capsule and an outer more or less thick, fleshy layer that differs markedly in taste on each shrub or tree, especially when it is raw. They are generally less than one-half inch in diameter and are mostly reddish, sometimes yellow and rarely bluish, purplish, or black, often with a high-sugar- and low-protein- and fat-content pulp.

Exellent Remedy for Hypertension

Hawthorn berry has been a very popular treatment for many heart-related problems throughout the British Isles. *The Sunday Times* magazine (a London-based paper) for May 24, 1981, cited the amazing work of a Scottish doctor some 42 years ago and the incredible results he obtained with it for hypertension.

In 1939, Dr. James Graham of Glasgow University showed that a fluid extract of hawthorn berries was very effective in the treatment of 10 patients confined to bed with high blood pressure. He made his extract by combining 4 tablespoons of dried and crushed berries with 1 pint of dark mead (any dark English ale or dark German beer will do). He shook the flask that the mixture was kept in daily and did so for 15 days. He then strained the liquid into another flask and gave his hypertensive patients 25 drops of it beneath their tongues twice daily. Within a week, full recovery was evident for all 10 of them.

Wonderful Tonic for Coronary Problems

The same British newspaper also reported that in 1969, medical doctors in Bulgaria were treating scores of patients suffering from coronary problems with a fluid extract of hawthorn. After 6 weeks of treatment, consisting of 15 drops beneath the tongue twice daily, three quarters of a group of 62 patients fully recovered.

The fluid extract was made pretty much the same way that Dr. Graham made his preparation, with the sole exception of vodka being used as the medium of extraction for the berries. *The Sunday Times* also explained how hawthorn berries were active in the treatment of heart palpitations, angina, and stroke. This action was attributed, in part, on the bioflavonoids such as rutin and hesperidin and vitamin C present in the berries.

A clinical report on the use of freeze-dried hawthorn berries for the treatment of heart and menopause problems in an elderly woman was given to me a few years ago by Scott Tyler, an internist then working at the Portland Naturopathic Clinic in Oregon. John Collins, M. D. was the supervising physician; I am grateful to both of them for this case study and for their letting me use it in this book.

> Mrs. S. is a 67-year-old woman with right shoulder pain, irregular heart rhythm, mild hypertension and persisting symptoms of menopause. She had been taking Premarin for the past 15 years, on her doctor's recommendation. We felt she was experiencing multiple side effects from the Premarin and explained this to her. She decided to wean herself from this drug. Her menopause symptoms worsened almost immediately. We began a course of treatment with botanical tinctures containing female hormone precursors. The symptoms abated. The patient's shoulder pain was discovered to be due to thoracic outlet syndrome. Appropriate therapy was undertaken and the problem resolved.
>
> The patient's cardiovascular complaints were treated also botanically. It seemed to us that we could address both the mild hypertension and the cardiac dysrhythmia (palpitations and paroxysms of tachycardia) with one botanical. [Hawthorn] solid extract was given, $1/4$ tsp. each day in divided doses. The patient responded to the therapy well, but the expense of the product was substantial for her. When we learned that [hawthorn] was to be made available in freeze-dried form, we considered substituting it. The patient began taking 2 capsules a day of freeze-dried hawthorn berries—the equivalent of the solid extract dosage. The patient's palpitations and tachycardia were entirely eliminated by use of the freeze-dried hawthorn berries, and her blood pressure reverted to within normal limits.
>
> We conclude[d] that freeze-dried [hawthorn] berries provided the same non-toxic therapeutic action as the [hawthorn] solid extract, but at a significantly reduced cost.

HAZELNUT/FILBERT
(Corylus Americana)

HICKORY NUT
(Carya Species)

BRIEF DESCRIPTIONS

There are two species of hazelnuts indigenous to North America—the American hazelnut, located principally in the East; and *C. cornuta*, the beaked filbert, which ranges from the Atlantic to the Pacific. Both are small, hardy, shrubby trees or bushes. Nuts of these American species are small, with thick shells. They were a valuable source of food, along with hickory nuts, for many paleoindians inhabiting the continent. In the western United States these nuts are called filberts, while in the East the term hazel is still commonly used. About 70 percent of the world's filbert production comes from small Turkish farms bordering the southern coast of the Black Sea, another 20 percent originates in the coastal regions of Italy, 7 percent in Spain's Mediterranean coastal areas, and the remaining 3 percent is produced in the Pacific northwest of the United States.

The hickories are members of the walnut family. They are widespread throughout the temperate regions of eastern and central North America from the Canadian border to northern Mexico. The only commercially important hickory is the pecan, which is covered in a separate section of this book. There are several other American hickories worthy of mention that produce edible nuts: the shagbark

154

(*C. ovata*); the shellbark (*C. lacinosa*); the mockernut (*C. tomentosa*), the pignut (*C. glabra*); and the butternut (*C. cordiformis*).

The most abundant and popular of these is the shagbark hickory, so named because of the peculiar, shaggy, unkempt appearance of the bark of mature trees of this species. The trees are moderately tall, reaching 60 to 80 feet in height, with trunks 1 to 2 feet in diameter. The crowns are open, and the branches large. The glossy, dark-green leaves are deciduous, 8 to 14 inches in length, and are usually made up of 5 leaflets. Shagbark nut yields are much less than that of pecans. The shagbark fruits, commonly about 1 $^1/_2$ inches long, contain a single, compressed, creamy-white kernel, resembling that of the Persian walnut in its shape, with a sweet flavor similar to the pecan.

High-Energy Foods for Chronic Fatigue Syndrome, Hypoglycemia, and Yeast Infection

Around 1970 important archeological work was begun in the cornfields of the farm of the late Theodore Koster, located in Greene County, Illinois, about 50 miles northwest of St. Louis, Missouri, and about 270 miles southwest of Chicago. In the beginning the excavations were conducted by Dr. Stuart Struever, former chairman of the department of Anthropology at Northwestern University in Evanston, Illinois.

From one of North America's most important archaeological treasures, now known as the Koster Site, has come a wealth of information about how the peaceful, sophisticated inhabitants of the lower Illinois River valley lived around 6400 *b.c.* For one thing, they balanced their diets with *two* types of protein usually consumed in the same meal. Abundant evidence existed to show they consumed hazel and hickory nuts along with lots of freshwater fish. The nuts are easily digestible and have a high protein content that resembles the meat of large mammals. The fish, on the other hand, are very lean and tasty.

Now let's fast-forward this scene by some eight millenniums to the mid-seventeenth century and the Algonquin Indians of Virginia. They pounded hazel and hickory kernels and shells in a mortar until they were finely powdered; water was added, the mixture passed through fine strainers, and the process continued until a nourishing milky drink called *pawcohiccora* or "nut milks" was produced. This rich, creamy concoction was then added to venison broth, or used to prepare hot cornmeal cakes, hominy, and roasted sweet potatoes.

What we have here are two examples of protein always being used together in conjunction with carbohydrates to produce *two* different forms of energy. The *high*-protein nuts yield a *sustained* energy with a *gradual* release to it, while the *leaner* fish and wild deer meat provide more *immediate* energy with *quicker* release value. In working with diets fashioned after these findings, I've discovered that *the* single best way to get energy is to *always* eat a combination of high- and low-protein foods in the same meals. This virtually guarantees a reservoir of energy that should last a minimum of six hours and a maximum of eight hours.

For those suffering from energy-draining diseases that require them to eat every few hours, this comes as welcome news. Data have been collected on volunteers suffering from chronic fatigue syndrome, hypoglycemia, and yeast infection and who have been placed on nut-fish or nut-wild game meals with very positive, if not somewhat astonishing results. It's amazing what we can learn from prehistoric peoples to improve our own health. More can be read about these paleoindians in the fascinating book *Koster: Americans in Search of Their Prehistoric Past* by Stuart Struever and Felicia Antonelli Holton (Garden City, NY: Anchor Press/Doubleday, 1979).

"The Caveman Diet Program" for Obesity, Diabetes, Hypertension, and Constipation

To my esteemed colleague Dr. Vaughn M. Bryant must go ultimate credit for laying the foundations of our famous "Caveman Diet Program." This department head and professor of Anthropology at Texas A&M University in College Station first introduced the concepts of it way back in the winter of 1979. There he was, in the February 19 issue of *People* magazine, sitting crosslegged on an untanned animal hide, wearing nothing but a leopard skin slung across one shoulder, and nibbling away on a wild persimmon. Conveniently scattered around him was a paleolithic feast of yucca plant, fox grapes, cactus pads, nuts, and sunflowers.

By training, Vaughn is a botanist, anthropologist, and palynologist. He had to go home and look that last word up in his dictionary to even know what in the heck it meant. (Palynology is the study of individual grains of pollen, ancient or modern, visible only through powerful light and electron microscopes.) He met a Canadian botanist by the name of Eric O. Callen, who had pioneered the field of coprolite research. During the three smelly days Vaughn spent with him, this somewhat eccentric scholar taught him how to restore fossilized feces to their original moist, pliable state so that they could be teased apart and their delicate plant and animal material, as well as pollen grains, thoroughly evaluated.

Vaughn confesses with something of a mischievous smile that he reluctantly became one of the world's foremost experts on excrement. "I am to poop what Einstein was to physics," he teases. And what are the requirements for evaluating prehistoric human turds, he is asked? "A well-ventilated laboratory and vivid imagination of scented roses," he opines rather dryly. Replacing Callen after he suddenly died, Vaughn went to Peru and took an active part in a major archaeological excavation there. From that and numerous other digs thereafter, he became the first American scientist to study all aspects of coprolites—their pollen, seed, bones, hair, feathers, parasites, and other constituents.

He became so engrossed in his work that somewhere along the way he neglected his diet and body. Too much junk food and lack of adequate exercise made him look like a short and pudgy "Pillsbury dough-boy." "My biggest fear," he admits, "was becoming a fat professor. When I went swimming, I had to wear a T-shirt to hide my big gut." Determined to not stay that way, he took some drastic steps to immediately correct the situation.

Becoming his own guinea pig, Vaughn forced himself for months to consume nothing but a high-roughage diet consisting of cactus pads, acorns, nuts, berries, yucca, and mesquite seeds. For high protein he ate fish and lean meat, but drew the line at prehistoric delicacies like mice, snakes, and lizards. For exercise, he walked, hiked, jogged, swam, and played tennis. In a very short time, he shed 30 ugly pounds and ever since has managed to hold his weight at an athletic 165, his former high school football-playing weight.

Recently he has condensed much of his research with coprolites into a lengthy and informative article entitled, "The Paleolithic Health Club," which appeared in the *1995 Yearbook of Science and the Future* (published annually by Encyclopedia Britannica, Inc., Chicago, pp. 114–133). He calculates that "our foraging ancestors probably consumed about 150 grams (a third of a pound) of fiber each day," compared with a daily average intake of just 20 grams for the majority of us.

But most of this fiber, he insists, as revealed in ancient coprolites from preagricultural groups residing in North and South America, was *indigestible* fiber—in most samples analyzed it was as much as one half to three quarters of the total weight of an individual fecal sample. He calculates that our foraging ancestors consumed approximately 150 grams (a third of a pound) of fiber each day, compared with a daily average intake of just 20 grams for the majority of us.

Because so much of the food we consume today has been highly refined, we don't get anywhere near the fiber we need. Fiber is essential to speed the passage of food through the small intestine. Indigestible roughage adds needed bulk to the large intestine and stimulates waves of muscular contraction there (known as peristalsis), which are necessary for normal bowel movements. Fiber also helps in the excretion of fat, which would otherwise accumulate in the body. Additionally, roughage helps to maintain a delicate balance in blood-sugar levels. Finally, fiber keeps the body's sodium levels to a minimum, maintains good kidney function, and improves overall blood circulation.

But the most important function of fiber is to promote *a feeling of fullness!* The indigestible fiber of nuts, whole grains, seeds, and root vegetables creates a sense of hunger satisfaction that can last for hours. This is good because one then isn't tempted to snack so often on those types of junk foods that are sugary, salty, and fatty, which contribute to disgusting obesity.

Major sources of protein for these preagricultural groups were fresh- and saltwater fish and lean venison. They did without dairy products such as milk, butter, and cheese, simply because they had no access to them. Poultry and eggs were seldom consumed. High-carbohydrate tubers such as yams, sweet potato, parsnip, and regular potato were eaten occasionally. Berries and certain fresh fruits in season were always gathered for meals. Some use of leafy greens was made, but the archeological evidence indicates such salad items were not as popular as they are for us today.

I've expanded beyond Vaughn's work to include spices in our famous "Caveman Diet Program." Spices such as cayenne, garlic, turmeric, rosemary, sage, and thyme seem to "turn up" the body's "fat thermostat" a few extra degrees, thereby allowing for the internal combustion of more stored fat, which can then be quickly converted to energy.

Certain nuts and seeds also work well with these spices. Not only do hazel, hickory, pine, and pistachio nuts add a creamy richness to the foods they're cooked in, but they also somehow work synergistically with the spices to expedite weight loss more quickly *and to keep it off permanently*. I've been intrigued with the possible mechanisms by which this can be accomplished.

I believe I've found at least part of the answer. Spices contain volatile oils that account for their sharp, pungent smells and flavors. "Nuts generally contain relatively large concentrations of most trace elements," say the editors of *The Analysis of Prehistoric Diets* (Orlando, FL: Academic Press, Inc., 1985; pp. 347–350). Hazel and hickory nuts, for example, are fairly typical of what you might find in the way of nutrients in nuts. They usually have *double* the value of manganese, copper, zinc, and magnesium over mineral values for cereal grains, vegetables, and meats. But it is in the area of a relatively little known nutrient, *strontium*, that such nuts are particularity rich. Levels in hazel and hickory nuts exceed by 20 to 30 times the amount of this trace element that which is found in other basic foods; the same high concentration holds true for other nuts as well.

The combination of certain volatile oil compounds from some spices and the strontium from nuts in general work in an aggressive chemical manner to enhance specific biological functions that can cause the body to convert or "burn" more stored fat into productive energy. Spices alone will do some of this; nuts by themselves will do a little. But when they're put together in the same meals, the body's "fat thermostat" is nudged up a bit and "melting" environment is soon created that actively deals with stored fat, the hardest thing to get rid of and keep off permanently. This is the essence of a proven diet program that works.

HIGH BUSH CRANBERRY
(Viburnum Americanum)

BRIEF DESCRIPTION

There are roughly 120 different species of *Viburnum* that occur in the northern hemisphere. Many species are important for environmental plantings and for ornamentals. The viburnums are part of the honeysuckle family.

V. americanum also goes by several other common names: Squaw bush and cramp bark are the most frequently used. Once you've smelled this sweetish-sour viburnum, you'll forever after recognize the presence of this food-medicine, especially valuable since it remains usable all year round.

The distinctive reddish-orange berries, growing at the ends of the limbs, expand from usually white flowers in the spring into flat clusters, shriveling but clinging throughout the nearly barren woodlands throughout the wintertime. As with any other established gourmet treat, getting to like the berries is definitely an acquired taste. But just let a few of the frozen, juicy fruits melt in your parched mouth like flavored ice as I did one year in Montana's Glacier National Park and you'll become a convert for life as I did.

The fruit is a one-seeded drupe with a soft pulp and a thin stone. During the ripening process, berries of most species change in color from green to various shades of red, with orange red being the most common.

The generally maple-shaped leaves, becoming beautifully spectacular like those of that tree in the autumn, have coarsely irregular teeth and about three to five major veins culminating near the base.

Reducing Glandular Swelling in Measles, Mumps, and Chickenpox

The Penobscot and Malecite Indians (tribes of the Algonquian nation) formerly utilized the fresh or dried berries both as a tea and poultice for reducing swollen glands due to measles, mumps, chicken pox, and smallpox. The details of their use for these different maladies were given in detail by Frank G. Speck in his article, "Medicine practices of the Northeastern Algonquians," which appeared in the *Proceedings of the XIXth International Congress of Americanists* (Washington, DC: 1915 [published in 1917]; p. 310).

I had a chance to put this particular Native American remedy into actual use some time ago, but in an ironic way. About seven years ago I was in Shannon County, South Dakota, doing some ethnological research among the Oglala Sioux on the Pine Ridge Indian Reservation. Shannon County has the dubious distinction of having the nation's highest rate of poverty; more than 63 percent of the residents there live in poverty. (The next poorest county in America is Starr, Texas, with 60 percent poverty.) Economic decay is everywhere among the county's population, which is 95 percent Sioux. It is the *worst* poverty I've ever witnessed in my life.

I was interviewing Tom True Elk in his tar-paper shack with the rusting corrugated metal roofing. Some of his eight children were at that time sleeping in several abandoned cars parked indiscriminately around his house. An assortment of dogs, cats, and pet squirrels and raccoons shared the same sleeping quarters with the kids.

Two of his children, a boy aged 7 and a girl aged 9, were down with the measles. Their mother had been giving them aspirin, which I advised might do more harm than good. They were desperately strapped for cash and couldn't afford the necessary medicine they needed. In a stand of trees about 150 yards from the shack, I discovered some high bush cranberry growing. Remembering what the Algonquian had previously used it for, I obtained permission from the parents, who knew absolutely nothing about its medicinal properties, to treat their sick kids with this.

I heated up a quart of water in an old aluminum pan on a kerosene stove inside their hut. When the water started to boil, I added a full handful of the fresh berries. I reduced the heat and let the berries simmer for about five minutes, then covered the pot with a lid and removed it from the stove to steep an hour. I then strained some of the liquid, which by now was lukewarm, and went out to the abandoned car, where the boy lay on the front seat and the girl on the back seat, both covered with blankets. I gave them each half a cup to sip slowly. I instructed the mother to repeat this treatment every two hours until they went to sleep. I strained some more liquid into a separate pot and reheated it until it was rather warm, but not intensely hot. I then took an old rag lying around the place (there was nothing else cleaner to use) and tore it into a piece about the size of an average wash cloth. This I soaked in the strained tea, wrung it out, and went out and placed it across the throat and up under each ear of the girl, and left it there until it had cooled down. Then I repeated the same process with the boy. I alternated this treatment between them for up to two hours. I found an old, dry towel that wasn't too filthy and used this to cover up the hot rag in order to keep the heat in as long as possible.

By the afternoon of the following day, both children showed remarkable improvement, could swallow more easily, and were being fed, if you can imagine this, ice cream, of all things, by their mother! Needless to say, the treatment worked in spite of the dietary ignorance I had to cope with.

Wonderful Pain Reliever for Cramps

Although most of the younger generation of Oglala Sioux have completely lost touch with their ancestral traditions, there are still a few of the older folks who remember some of the healing ways of long ago. Agnes Many Teats (her real name, by the way), who was then somewhere in her seventies, recalled for me how her own mother used high bush cranberry when she was a girl.

"I'm so old, I can't remember just *how* old," she joked with a toothless grin. She then proceeded to explain how her mother had made a tea of the fresh berries similar to what I had made for True Elk's sick children. "She'd give us as much of this as we could drink," Agnes stated, "whenever we had cramps in our legs or stomach or just 'hurt all over.'" Agnes said she never found anything better. "I used to use it a lot myself, but now that I'm getting older, I can't get around like I used to, do the things I did before."

Oh, by the way, Agnes said that the tea needs to be taken *cold* for cramping and body pain.

Prevents Miscarriages

Rachel Her Many Horses, an old Pawnee medicine woman living in Manitoba, Canada, informed me some years ago, that *akiwasas* had been used a lot in the past by members of her tribe to prevent miscarriages. This is the name they give high bush cranberry.

In going back over my notes made at the time of my visit with her, I discovered the following hand scribbled instructions hastily jotted down as I watched her make the tea for this condition.

"Informant [meaning Mrs. Her Many Horses] brings 1 $\frac{1}{2}$ pints water to boil. Add two-thirds cupped hand of shriveled berries. Simmers 5 [minutes]. Steep c/[overed], no heat, [for] $\frac{1}{2}$ hr. [or 30 minutes]. Strain/female patient drinks 1 cup 2xd [two times a day]."

Rachel permitted me to interview four local women to whom she had given this tea to prevent miscarriages. One of them, a white lady in her mid-thirties by the name of Sandra Leontin, told me she had had two previous miscarriages, but stated quite emphatically that her third attempt was a "total success." She had given birth to an 8 pound, 7 ounce daughter, whom she and her husband had named Rachel in honor of the medicine woman whose tea had made the girl's birth possible.

What better tribute than this could one hope for in a remedy that seems to work for a very disheartening medical condition to many expectant mothers.

HUCKLEBERRY
(Gaylussacia Baccata)

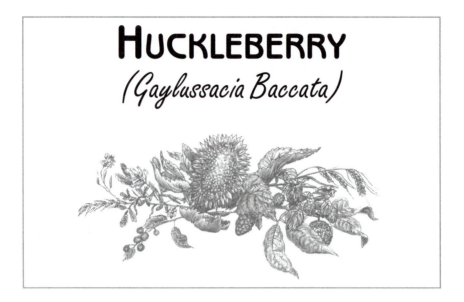

BRIEF DESCRIPTION

There is a certain mystique to the huckleberry. Wily as a fox, yet beloved as an infant, the huckleberry balks at growing in the backyard garden, preferring instead to "rough it" in the wild, which probably prompted Samuel Clemens (aka Mark Twain) to name his famous character in literature, Huckleberry Finn, after it.

If you're the frail, delicate type or were referred to do being a "pantywaist" in school when you were younger, then I *do not* recommend huckleberry hunting for you. The plants grow like mad at high elevations and deep in the woods of North America. A search for these elusive berries is pretty much like deer hunting—an adventure in exercise your body soon won't let you forget if you're not in shape physically. A lot—and I mean A LOT—of hiking and climbing is involved in their procurement.

It's also questionable whether you'll find the berries in the same remote location come next season. Although huckleberries are notoriously unreliable, they're likely to pop up in burned-out areas where the ground has been well nourished by a fire's ashes. As with blueberries, their distant cousins, huckleberries thrive in acidic soil.

Henry David Thoreau, a New England schoolteacher, transcendentalist, naturalist, and author, mentioned in his writings that the taste of huckleberries was like "ambrosia" in flavor, but added that the only real way to experience them unsullied was to devour them fresh, right off the bush.

There has always been a great deal of confusion over the botanical differences between the huckleberry and the blueberry. In his classic forager's tome, *Stalking the Wild Asparagus* (New York: David McKay Co., 1962), the late Euell Gibbons wrote, "If you really want to know whether the berries you are picking are [huckleberry] or [blueberry], examine the seeds. [Huckleberry] has ten hard, seed like nuts inside, while the [blueberry] has many softer seeds."

In addition to this, the huckleberry has tiny quantities of wax on its foliage and new shoots. The berries, when ripe, range in color from jet black to maroon and are great favorites of black bears, moose, elk, skunk, wolverine, mountain sheep, and other wildlife.

Frontier Remedy for Bacteria-Induced Diarrhea

Here is an old Mormon pioneer remedy for effectively treating diarrhea caused by bad food or unclean water. Laboratory tests in modern times with the extracts of the bark and berries has shown them to be quite effectual against disease organisms and germs.

To 1 quart of writer add 6 heaping tablespoonsful of huckleberries. Gently boil down, uncovered, on low heat for 45 minutes or longer until just a pint of liquid remains. Strain this into another container while still hot and add 4 tablespoons of honey and 2 tablespoons of glycerine (obtainable from any pharmacy). Cool, seal tightly, and store in a cool, dry place.

When diarrhea becomes a problem, take half-cup amounts every hour on an empty stomach until the problem is corrected.

JAPANESE WINEBERRY
(Rubus Phoenicolasius)

BRIEF DESCRIPTION

The taste of Japanese wineberries always takes me back mentally to the mysterious Orient: a musky, provocative, almost sensual quality and an air of intrigue characterize this succulent delicacy. People who've come to regard any of the pink-toned, luminous fruits with the honeyed sweetness of a raspberry will be somewhat disappointed in the wineberry, with its low sugar content, but time and patience, not to mention a small dollop of honey, will bring them in line with more well-known Rubus fruits. However, if you like the taste of your berries with a little more complexity and haunting features, then the wineberry is surely for your palate.

Besides its obvious presence in Southeast Asia, the wineberry also grows in the southern Appalachian regions, where mountain folk there occasionally nickname it "strawberry-raspberry" and transform it into beautiful coral-colored condiments, such as jellies and jams.

When left to its own devices, the Japanese wineberry will form dense thickets, its canes arching over and rooting themselves at the tip. The canes themselves are downy with orange-reddish hairs and sport a few prickles, but nothing quite so tenacious as those of its relative, the blackberry.

Aesthetically, the wineberry is a boon to the berry garden. Its leaves have beautiful purple veining and are dusted on their underside with a white felt. The tiny pink or white flowers sport a bristly red calyx. These give way to the pleasingly round berries, which literally shine and appear to be illuminated from within.

In terms of medicinal or culinary usages, the wineberry is to the raspberry as the huckleberry is to the blueberry. In plain talk, you can switch Japanese wineberry in any formula or dish that calls for raspberry; however, there will be a more exquisite, very subtle difference emerging in the taste of the remedy or recipe to be consumed.

The name wineberry would seem to hint at wine making, but this isn't at all the case. The name was appropriated to the berry because of its complex taste and fragrant bouquet, vintage year unknown but no doubt dating back to the ancient Samurai, who, it is said, drank the juice with great pleasure.

Childbirth with No Pain

As I mentioned earlier, throughout Japan there is a system of alternative medicine practiced called *kampo*. Its practitioners are usually full-time medical doctors who work on both sides of health care in the same day—alternative healers by day and hospital physicians by night, or vice-versa.

When I was in Japan several years ago, courtesy of Wakunaga of America, distributors of the world's premier-selling Kyolic garlic, I spoke with a number of these kampo doctors. Some of them, who are obstetricians, routinely employ *warm tea* made of the fruit and leaves of Japanese wineberry for all their female patients during pregnancy, parturition, and the puerperinum.

They reported to me that there was seldom a case of morning sickness, difficult delivery, or difficult expulsion of the afterbirth when wineberry tea was consumed regularly.

Here's how they recommended the tea be made by their patients: Bring one quart of water to a boil. Add two tablespoons of fresh or dried wineberries and an equal amount of chopped or cut leaves. Stir, cover, remove from the heat and steep until tolerably warm to drink. Strain and drink one cup on an empty stomach twice daily during the first eight months of pregnancy.

In the last month prior to parturition the intake should be doubled to four cups daily. One handy recommendation I learned from some of my kampo informants was that expectant mothers are encouraged to make some of this tea in a coffee thermos and carry it around with them. Then they can drink it warm whenever they like without any problems. The index finger can be placed across part of the thermos opening to hold back the berries and leaves as some of the liquid contents are poured into the top cap. They insist that their patients bring a thermos with them when being admitted to the hospital prior to parturition.

In the event Japanese wineberries are unavailable in your area, the same amount of red or black raspberries and their leaves may be substituted. This is a wonderful remedy for women to take if they want childbearing to be a pleasant experience and not a painful nightmare.

JOJOBA NUT
(Simmondsia Chinensis)

BRIEF DESCRIPTION

Jojoba is a bush of low to medium height, complex branched and broadly dense, with thick and leathery round leaves bluish-green in color. These are paired and form a distinctive glandular swelling around the stems. The plants are different sexes; females, bearing hundreds of acorn-sized nut fruit, are usually in the more sheltered and moister sides of the colonies. The leaves persist year round, and the whole plant resembles manzanita or silk tassel, except for the opposite leaves, blue-green foliage, and overall environment. Jojoba is a handsome, distinctive, and frequently dominant plant wherever it grows.

Jojoba (pronounced *hoh-hoh'bah*) is native to the highlands of the Arizona Sonora desert and is especially cultivated in Yuma County for its valuable nut oil. Wild jojoba also thrives in Baja California and northward through San Diego to Riverside and Imperial counties in southern California. It seeks protection of mountain slopes and hillsides where warm winds save the seedlings from frost. It grows in many well-drained and well-aerated soil types, at sea level on the Mexican coast to more than 4,500 feet in southern Arizona.

The peanut-sized beans yield an oily wax that has been used in the last several decades on a very selected basis to produce a high-grade motor oil for gasoline engines that require an oil change only about every 19,840 miles. This is because the nut oil doesn't break down with frequent reheating to high temperatures, making it an ideal lubricant for automatic transmissions, power tools, and in a couple of instances, artificial heart pumps designed by the Westinghouse Corporation. The oil produced by the jojoba nut isn't even a common nut or vegetable oil at all, but rather a liquid *wax;* for this reason has it been successfully used in auto wax and floor polishes, here it nearly equals the shining performance of carnauba wax. In fact, jojoba is the only plant in the world whose seed oil is *not* a triglyceride.

Jojoba nut oil also has many wonderful medicinal applications, but it is quite unsuitable for food preparation without considerable chemical processing. This is due to every bitter tannin that combines with the straight-chain monoethylene acids and alcohols as esters to form the liquid wax for which it is so renowned.

Clearing Up Acne Vulgaris

In 1965 the research and development division of the Purex Corporation published a significant medical paper entitled, "A Different Approach to the Treatment of Acne Vulgaris." The paper stated: "Jojoba is a therapeutic agent for excessive secretions from sebaceous glands. Serum exertion sets in rapidly when layers of serum fat reach a certain thickness. There is a rapid excretion when fat layers are removed again. Instead of removing self-limiting sebum layers as quickly as it forms and encouraging replacement, the purposeful application of fat layer resembling sebum might aid in developing a critical thickness."

Jojoba also Tested for Dry Skin

In a separate research project the Purex Corporation tested the benefits of the effects of jojoba on a number of high school and college volunteers who suffered from dry skin. It was discovered that when jojoba was used on a regular basis it kept the epidermis or surface layer quite moist, even when exposed to periods of sunlight and hot, dry temperatures.

Now, in both tests, involving scores of young people, the jojoba was applied externally to acne and dry skin in the form of a cream. Students were instructed to thoroughly cleanse, rinse, and dry their faces first of all. Then they were told to apply some of the special jojoba cream with their fingers in a circular motion into the skin until all of it had been absorbed. It never left an oily or greasy feeling. Eighty-seven percent of those using jojoba noticed definite improvement in their skin conditions.

Jojoba oil, creams, and lotions are available from most health food stores, drug stores, and supermarkets. Based on the evidence presented, it seems to be a wonderful agent for improving the texture, look, and health of the skin. The only other thing that comes anywhere close to what jojoba oil is capable of doing for your skin is sperm whale oil, and that is nearly impossible to obtain because of the international ban placed on the hunting of these great ocean behemoths.

Treat Your Hair to Some Jojoba Nut Oil and Prevent Dandruff, Scaliness, Baldness

The average consumer can obtain a wide range of jojoba oil products, shampoos and moisturizers sold in any health food stores, drug stores, and supermarkets. The jojoba oils in such shampoos help to dissolve sebum—fatty lubricant on the scalp—make the scalp less acidic, and control the sebum discharge itself. This incredible nut oil is the most effective scalp cleanser around.

Nonhereditary hair loss can be caused by dandruff and scaliness. Abnormal cells may renew from horny scales attached to the skin surface and delay new cell maturation. The scales may become encrusted by more sebum and inhibit normal sebaceous glandular activity retarding the hair-growth cycle. When this occurs, the cycle of glandular activity is inhibited and the hair-growth phase slows down. The hair follicles enter a resting stage resulting in baldness and excessive thinning.

But jojoba nut oil retards the production of new sebum, cleans debris from the hair follicles, and stimulates germinating cells in the epidermis, thus accelerating hair growth. It energizes the hair and scalp, giving more bounce, body, and volume to the hair. Other conditions—itchy scalp, overporous and dry, brittle hair, as well as split ends are greatly benefited.

Using jojoba oil in different hair-care preparations improves the overall condition of your scalp. A definite difference is noticed in hair texture and skin tone after only a few days use. About ten drops of jojoba oil by itself can also be gently massaged into the scalp for added benefit.

Healing Salve for Cuts, Scratches, and Sores

The Mescalero and White Mountain Apache of southern Arizona were masters at using the jojoba plant. They would build a small fire and let it burn down to embers. Then they would rake the ashes away and put a few nuts on the embers, covering them with ashes. As soon as the oil started oozing out of the nuts, they rubbed the nuts against a rock or in a stone metate with a mano to grind them into a salvelike substance. This salve was then applied to cuts, scratches, sores, insect bites and arrow wounds with great success. Rapid healing of the injured sites soon ensued.

Jojoba is found in a few ointments and lotions in most health-food stores or drug stores. There is also the jojoba oil by itself. Both can be used for minor skin problems, including diaper rash on infants and bedsores on those confined to long periods of rest due to age or illness.

A Native American Coffee Substitute with a Very Distinctive Bite for Gout

The Cahuilla Indians are a Shoshonean-speaking people whose historical relationships connect them with the well-known Hopi of Arizona and the Paiute of Nevada, Utah, and Arizona. Before contact with the Spaniards several centuries ago, the Cahuilla population was estimated to be about 6,000 people spread over 2,400 square miles and divided into 7 or more politically autonomous groups. Now there are less than 700, occupying an area no bigger than the land extending from San Bernardino to Palm Springs, California, and flanked on both sides by the San Bernardino and the San Jacinto mountain ranges.

Rodney Goatshett is a noble Native American with a very problematic surname. "I changed one vowel," he told me with a laugh, "to minimize the ridicule, but it still sounds terrible when pronounced." Here was a man who had managed to retain his family's last name over many generations without dropping it altogether in preference for something better sounding. "Why should I dishonor my ancestors this way or offend the Great Spirit?" he asked me, "just to please the White Man? It may be a problem for *others,* but I carry it with all of the dignity that my forefathers did."

He gave me some real food for thought in the years that have since intervened. Here was one who overcame an obvious obstacle, not by removing it but by accepting and making the most of it by how he lived. He made these remarks many years ago when he showed me how he made jojoba coffee. We went out into the southern foothills at the base of the Eagle and Cottonwood mountains, which separate the Mojave Desert from the Colorado Desert. We were at about the 4,700-foot level sweltering like dogs in the scorching July sun, gathering these inch-long, brown-to-black-colored seeds the size of acorns, most of which had already dropped to the ground. These were preferred over those still on the female plants, Rodney informed me, because the husks had already come off most of them.

We returned to his house some miles away and I watched as he spread them on an old cookie sheet and stuck them into the oven. He set the temperature at 250°F and left them to roast for about 6 hours or until they were thoroughly darkened. Removing them from the oven, he let them cool down awhile before grinding them up in a manual food grinder that he had clamped to the edge of a table. He took 2 heaping tablespoons of these ground jojoba nuts and added them to $2\,^1/_2$ cups of water and boiled the strange mixture for 5 minutes. He then poured the liquid into two large ceramic mugs using a fine-mesh wire strainer.

"Do you like yours pale, like the Pale-Face you are?" he inquired with a grin, meaning did I want any cream or sugar?

I met his witty challenge with one of my own. "No, Rodney, I'll take mine as dark and savage as the host who is serving it up."

He pointed his forefinger in my direction, saying, "You're pretty quick with the wit."

I muttered back, "You're not too shabby yourself either."

Well, I drank his jojoba coffee just as I said I would. My tongue stood at attention and my Adam's apple did a couple of quick salutes as I swallowed this real he-man beverage. Rodney kept searching my face for signs of disgust, but I am happy to say that I took my medicine very bravely.

"What do you think of it?" he asked with impish curiosity.

"It has a most *distinctive* taste," I soberly replied.

That night in his bathroom, with the door closed, I vigorously brushed my tongue, the insides of my cheeks and the roof of my mouth *several times!* I don't ever remember brushing my teeth for that matter. After that I slowly sucked on a sugar cube as I lay in my bed, to get rid of the powerful YECCCH! YECCCH! YECCCH! taste image that still pounded in my brain incessantly. Eventually, I fell asleep with sweeter dreams in mind.

Come morning my well-intentioned host was intent on making me some more of his delightful brew, but I earnestly declined with all of the politeness at my disposal. However, Rodney informed me that this coffee substitute had some medicinal merit to it. "In all the years I have drunk it," he said, "I have never once been bothered with gout. I know friends of mine, who are of my tribe, who also drink the stuff just to keep from getting gout in their legs, ankles, and wrists. Maybe if more of your people drank our jojoba coffee, there would be less aches and pains," he conjectured sympathetically.

An old gent named Ed Harris (long since deceased) from Kingman, Arizona, told me some years ago that he himself drank this same jojoba nut coffee and "*never once* got gout." He claimed it was unbeatable for this problem. So, I guess something good does come out after all from an item that tastes perfectly *h-o-r-r-i-b-l-e!*

JUNIPER BERRY
(Juniperus Communis)

BRIEF DESCRIPTION

Those who imbibe gin have only to take a whiff or sip of it to be able to discern the scent and taste of juniper berry. Although it also grows as a tree, one usually thinks of the juniper as a low, scraggly, creeping, prostrate evergreen with miniature vinelike needles instead of leaves and fragrant blue berries that provide a nourishing and pleasant nibble.

Our family owns a large ranch in the Painted Desert wilderness of southern Utah, just below and east of Bryce Canyon, a world-famous national park noted for its beautiful towering sandstone formations. Juniper trees, wild Oregon grape shrubs, and sagebrush dot the landscape everywhere. It is a tree we have come to love and respect.

The common juniper is a low evergreen shrub between 12 and 30 feet high, growing low rind spreading upright. The bark of the trunk is reddish-brown and shreddy. The pine-family needles are straight, sharply tipped, ridged, and nearly at right angles to the branchlets.

The male flowers are yellow rind form a short catkin; the greenish female flowers are composed of three to eight pointed scales, some or all of which bear one or two ovules.

Scales of the female flowers become fleshy and fuse to form small, indehiscent strobili commonly called berries, which ripen the first, second, or occasionally the third year, depending upon the species involved. When I was in the former Soviet Union in 1979, various plant scientists with whom discussed juniper used the term *aril* instead of berry for these fruits. They informed me that the immature berries are generally greenish; ripe berries are blue-black to red-brown, and are usually covered with a conspicuous white, waxy bloom. I've discovered in my own investigative work with juniper berries that the fruit coat may be thin and resinous as in eastern red cedar, Rocky Mountain, and one-seed juniper, or nearly leathery or mealy as in the Utah juniper, which grows abundantly on our ranch.

There are usually one to four brownish seeds per fruit; rarely will you find as many as a dozen seeds. The seeds are rounded or angled, often with longitudinal pits. The seed coat has two layers— the outer layer is thick and hard, the inner thin and mebranous. Embedded within the fleshy, white-to-creamy-colored endosperm is a straight embryo with two to six cotyledons. However, many seeds from a given tree may lack endosperm or embryo.

Sometimes berry crops will be heavy throughout a woodland, but at times there are years when few berries are ever produced throughout a large geographic region. Almost every year a tree can be found in a stand that is so loaded with berries it appears covered with wax; such trees are popularly known as candle trees.

Antiseptic Aerosol for Lung Disorders

I'm intimately acquainted with juniper berries. I've used them for many years in treating a wide range of health problems in folks who've sought out my herbal wisdom. But they are particularly efficacious in certain lung disorders.

An elderly lady residing in Hurricane, Utah (about a two-hour drive from our family ranch), was suffering from bronchial asthma a while back. She had been under doctors' care for some time with her problem. Just about every medication commonly employed for this situation had been used, but with little relief or benefit being obtained. Both she and her family were getting very discouraged with her lack of progress.

The matter was referred to me by one of her daughters. I recommended the use of juniper berry oil in an electric vaporizer. I instructed the daughter to have her aged mother mix 15 drops of juniper berry oil with 3/4 cup distilled water and then put this in a vaporized setting on a nightstand by her bed and turn it on. Her mom was then to lay down on the bed and inhale the antiseptic aerosol given off for a period of 1 hour. This treatment would enable her to breathe better for up to 4 hours, after which time the process would need to be repeated again.

I explained to her how to make the juniper berry oil as well. One full cup of ripe juniper berries are lacerated and pounded in a stone mortar and pestle. (If such items aren't handy, then use a cutting board and wooden mallet for this procedure.) Add the pulpy mixture to two pints of pure virgin olive oil and allow the entire solution to set in a glass mason jar in a warm place, with the lid lightly screwed on for three days. After that the oil is strained, bottled, and labeled.

It was reported to me sometime after this by the daughter that her mother's condition had vastly improved by weeks of this treatment. The treatment is also recommended for asthma, emphysema, sinusitis, head cold, and influenza. The use of juniper berry incense or the aerosol oil also helps to disinfect a room previously contaminated by germs emitted from a sick person's breathing, coughing, nose blowing, talking or laughing.

I probably should mention in passing that in the preparation of juniper oil, some of the needles can be crushed with the berries to increase its strength.

Knocks the Flu for a Loop

When influenza hits a person, it usually spells a long period of aggravating miseries, which seem to change with the infection going through its several different stages of activity. The worst part about the flu, however, is that it usually tends to linger for days, even weeks, after the worst symptoms have past.

There are a number of herbal remedies for coping with the flu. But none of the herbalists I know or the books they write have ever suggested hot juniper tea for this problem. In fact, I didn't even know myself just how good it was until an old Navajo shaman years ago acquainted me with it when I was staying as an invited guest in his hogan, located out in the middle of nowhere.

I somehow picked up the flu "bug" before I got there, and it didn't take very many hours to aggressively dominate my body. In plain words, I felt like hell! But my friend, Ned Many Sheeps boiled me up some tea by throwing a handful (probably one-half cup) of juniper berries into an old coffee pot sitting on top of an old iron stove situated in the center of the dirt floor and filled with one quart boiling water. A series of black stove pipes snaked their way up through a hole in the rounded clay roof firmly packed down on top of sawed juniper planks laid next to each other in a circular fashion and expertly supported together in the middle without the benefit of a center column.

Between the strong juniper scent and the hot tea he kept pouring down me every couple of hours, I got better in a big hurry, I can assure you. The warmth of the tea felt good going down and induced the perspiration I probably needed to throw off the excess poisons within me. The strong disinfectant properties in the berries themselves went a long way in killing the viruses responsible for my miseries.

Not only did I quickly recover, but I fully recuperated. I'm not being redundant with this statement. Remember earlier how I said that remnants of the flu usually tend to hang on for days or weeks after most people have gotten over the worst parts of their infections? Well, in my case, there was *no* additional evidence of anything lingering; when I got well, that was it, *period*.

Stops Internal Hemorrhaging Quickly

Here's an herbal math equation for emergency situations: juniper astringency times internal bleeding equals first aid *coup d'etat*. You see, when juniper berries ($^1/_2$ cup) are simmered in hot water (1 $^1/_2$ pints) for awhile (25 minutes), certain important constituents from their oils are extracted that help to hasten the coagulation process when taken internally.

The tea must be warm, however, for this to work. Half-cup amounts should be slowly sipped every 1 $^1/_2$ hours when the stomach is empty to do the most good.

CAUTION: Juniper berry is contraindicated in pregnancy and in cases of kidney inflammations.

KOLA NUT
(Cola Acuminata)

BRIEF DESCRIPTION

The kola (also spelled "cola") tree is indigenous to Sierra Leone, North Ashanti, near the tributary sources that comprise the mighty Nile River, and is cultivated extensively in tropical western Africa, the West Indies, Brazil, and in Indonesia on the main island of Java. The tree grows about 40 feet high and sometimes has a few short spines. Its leaves are evergreen, alternate, oblong to ovate, pointed at both ends, somewhat leathery in texture, and between six to eight inches long. The lovely flowers are clustered in leaf axils, whitish or pale yellow with a red or purple center to them. They are without any petals, however. All in all, kola makes for a good-sized and rather attractive tree, found mostly near the sea coast in Ghana and Nigeria.

The fruit of the kola tree is a very large, rough, and woody, mostly five-celled dehiscent capsule. Each cell can contain up to three seeds, but the best varieties from the West Indies contain but one kernel per capsule. The seed coats are thick and rather soft. The seeds are left for several days, when their coats partly decay or soften, and then are removed and the nuts washed. When fresh, the seeds are either white or purplish-red. The native use of these ker-

179

nels is almost wholly in the fresh state and usually after they have been caused to germinate. By then they are sweeter in taste, as I discovered for myself some years ago when visiting West Africa.

They do not keep their bright colors for very long, but soon change to a dull and rather ugly purplish-brown. For drying, their cotyledons are separated and exposed to the sun for several days. When thoroughly dried, they can be easily and perfectly kept for any desired length of time.

An Effective Jamaican Remedy for Severe Diarrhea

The voodoo practitioners of Jamaica routinely prescribe a decoction of the grated nut for diarrhea. At other times the nut kernel is thoroughly pounded to a fine powder. Either way, the kola nut is mixed with a little brandy or rum and taken one cupful at a time. One voodoo high priest informed me that it always took care of even the *worst* case of loose bowels.

Some years later I happened to mention this to an ultra-conservative religious group, many of whom were distributors for a multi-level herb company out of Hobe Sound, Florida. But knowing how opposed to any type of liquor they were, I omitted mentioning the alcohol and instead suggested taking three capsules of powdered kola nut with one glass of water for this aggravation.

When someone from the audience raised his hand and asked for the source of my remedy, I casually mentioned my witch-doctor friend from Kingston, Jamaica, as the reference for this. This set up quite a hullabaloo later on, with some of the more narrow-minded people rejecting this very effective remedy simply because it had come from someone they considered to be "an absolute, unsaved heathen and tool of the Devil." Faced with that kind of thinking, I wasn't about to defend the cultural merits of the voodoo religion.

An Incredible Cure for Indigestion from the Cayman Islands

The Caymans are situated between Cuba and Jamaica. They comprise three islands: George Town (the capitol and chief port) is on Grand Cayman; the other pair are Little Cayman and Cayman Brac. The islands have a rather dubious reputation for offshore banking for clients from America who don't want the Internal Revenue Service poking into their private financial affairs.

Maurice Coutoubou, the great-great-grandson of Jamaican slaves who once labored on a Colonel Bourder's cotton plantation beyond Guanoboa well over a century ago, emigrated to Grand Cayman Island many years ago. He brought with him not only the rich history of his people, but also a number of their natural remedies.

We met through a mutual friend, one Lord Sylvester Whitehall, a British nobleman who had taken up residence in George Town and showed a keen interest in the local medical folklore. Maurice showed me a weathered, yellow parchment of some considerable age. Though the ink was somewhat faint, he read to me the medical prescription for *any* kind of stomach problems, written out by one of his great-grandfathers, and then translated it into English for me.

"If your belly swells up from eating too much cooked pork and taro [an edible starchy rootstock of the arum family], then take some bichy or cocu [kola nut] in this formulation: Mix a pinch of the powdered bichy with an equal measure of dago-peepee [cayenne pepper]. Stir them into some rum [probably one-half cup] with the finger, then drink all at once. Soon you will notice the fire and pain go away."

I thanked him for this most unusual remedy and filed it away for future reference as I've done with hundreds of others collected through the years from folk healers all over the globe. I had occasion, while in New Orleans one time with several other friends, to put it to the test. One of our group named Paul pigged out on a local favorite, shrimp jambalaya, which was seasoned to the hilt with every pungent herb imaginable.

He moaned and groaned until the rest of us became very wearied by his incessant noises. I happened to have a bottle of kola nut capsules back in my hotel room. I retrieved five of them, opened the ends, and emptied their contents into an empty dinner plate. I then added an equal amount of red cayenne pepper powder from a glass shaker sitting on the restaurant table at which I was working. Stirring everything with my forefinger, I then refilled each capsule and put the ends back together; the tiny residue of leftover powder I discarded. I then handed these 5 capsules to Paul with a glass of milk and told him to take them. He did and within 30 minutes *all* of his gastrointestinal miseries had *totally* disappeared.

"Super Energy" and "Pep" for Chronic Fatigue Syndrome, Hypoglycemia, and Yeast Infection

A great amount of information could be written about the use of kola nut in herbal formulas for energy and stamina. I dubbed them "herbal uppers" years ago in an article I did for *East/West Journal*, wondering aloud in the title if they weren't really "herbal downers." I noted that occasional use was perhaps justifiable for when an extra surge of adrenaline and burst of clarity were absolutely needed. But I warned that indiscriminate an excessive consumption of such formulas could lead to an unhealthy dependence on them and could create havoc with the brain and nervous system.

This position won me few friends in the powerful health-food industry at the time. But my views came in light of my contact with other companies that vigorously pushed such products as near "miracle" supplements. One of them launched its business with N-R-G (the acronym for "en-er-gy"). And Orion Herbs, the company I became associated with for several years as chief educator for their thousands of distributors on botanical medicine, started outright sampling of consumers on the street with something called "Super Energy."

This particular product was formulated by the late Lyle Harrison of Wheatridge, Colorado, whom everybody later called "Liar" Harrison. Orion eventually went bankrupt due to greed and dishonesty and Lyle hung himself when all of his corruption finally came to a head.

Now this isn't an indictment against kola nut per se, because when used responsibly, it *does* help to boost energy levels when they're at their lowest ebb. And unlike coffee, which requires a number of strong cups to be drunk before any noticeable stimulation occurs, just a couple of kola nut capsules with a glass of water will suffice. In fact, I've known kola nut not only to add pep to an exhausted system, but also to allay occasional migraine headaches.

Today most herbal manufacturers like to combine kola nut and other caffeinated herbs, such as guarana and yerba maté, with Chinese ephedra or mahuang. The two together really add "snap, crackle and pop" to the brain and the nerves. But again, as I once did in that magazine article of a decade ago, I must pose the question, "Aren't such herbal 'uppers,' really 'downers' when you get around to it?" I'm afraid the answer to that is a most resounding response in the affirmative.

There is certainly something to be said for the health codes of the Mormons and Seventh-Day Adventists. Both religions ban the consumption of caffeine in *any* form—and this includes kola nut and its equally addictive herbal cousins. I remember Mark Owens, a former co-owner of Orion Herbs and the inventor of the tremendously popular "Pep" and "Lady Pep," remarking to me some years ago while we were debating the pros and cons of kola nut: "Heinerman, nobody's going to notice the difference as long as they keep on taking it" [meaning the Orion "Super Energy"]. But that *is* just the problem—when the consumer ceases to take it, the body desperately cries out for more kola nut. And *that,* dear friend, is very bad for the body!

LINGONBERRY
(Vaccinium Vitis-Idaea)

BRIEF DESCRIPTION

When cool breezes of late summer ruffle the leaves of the forests covering major portions of Sweden, Finland, and Norway, the lingonberry season is in full splendor. Amid mushrooms of every size, shape, and hue, the forager will find the wild berries thickly covering the ground, glittering in the sporadic play of forest sunlight. Lingonberries grow so abundantly in Scandinavia and other northern climes that they are not cultivated by farmers at all, but simply reaped from the wild as they appear.

Lingonberry is native to the northern areas of Europe and Asia and North America, although it is more prolific in Scandinavian countries and the new nation republics of the former U.S.S.R. A relative of the cranberry, it is a creeping evergreen plant and has attractive glossy oval leaves. In springtime, the lingonberry decorates the forest floor with delicate, nodding pink urn-shaped flowers.

In Scandinavia, the lingonberry is as common and sought after a fruit as the strawberry is in America or the currant is in England. Every effort is made to reap the wonderful berries from the wild, and berry picking there is an everyday activity. This is why, carefree as berry picking may seem, it is taken so seriously in Scandinavia—

to the extent that the berry-picking theme has found its way into folklore and ancient rituals.

The lingonberry is a significant fruit in the life of northern peoples simply because it is so delicious. It is not really a sweet berry, but not as tart as its relative the cranberry. A favorite Finnish dish is *pronkäryistys,* or sautéed reindeer, which is often garnished with lingonberries. Lingonberry preserves are also a common Scandinavian food—a welcome treat in the dark depths of winter, the fresh taste capturing the summer rays of the nightless day. A traditional Swedish dish is called *fyllda strutar,* or pastry cones filled with lingonberries and whipped cream. It is traditionally served by placing a drinking glass in the center of a shallow glass bowl and placing a cone in the glass. Other cones are leaned up against the glass, and more cones are leaned against these until the bowl is filled.

Nerve Inflammation Removed

In 1979 I went to the Soviet Union with a group of American scientists. We were guests of the Soviet Academy of Sciences and had been invited there to study the famous centenarians or people of incredibly long-lived years. But before we landed in Moscow, our plane touched down in Helsinki, Finland, next door, where we were able to spend a couple of days getting to know the people and the country better.

Some Finnish doctors, who believed in natural healing, told me through an interpreter that they routinely prescribed lingonberry tea for neuritis commonly associated with neuralgia, sciatica, hyperesthesia (abnormal acuteness of sensitivity to touch or pain), anesthesia, paresthesia (an abnormal sensation, such as burning, pricking, tickling, or tingling on the skin surface), paralysis, and muscular wasting in the region supplied by the affected nerve.

They said that there are in lingonberries certain trace elements that can effectively do away with nerve inflammation. By what process this is accomplished isn't as yet known. But they showed me patient records to verify their claims for the tea they use. Two tablespoons of lingonberries are added to 1 pint of boiling water, covered, and allowed to steep away from the stove for approximately 35 minutes. The tea is then strained, sweetened with a little honey, and given to the patients to drink 4 times a day in between meals or snacks. They said improvement was generally observed within 5 days of treatment.

While in the capitol, I visited the Department of Food Chemistry and Technology at the University of Helsinki. There I met M. Lahelma, N. Nurrtamo, and P. Koivistoinen. They shared with me important nutritional data relative to lingonberries. It seems the fruit is particularly high in these several trace elements—all figured on one kilogram (2.2 pounds) of fruit: manganese, 38 milligrams; zinc, 2.1 milligrams; chromium, 20 micrograms; cobalt, 5 micrograms; and silicon, 20 milligrams.

I asked them if they thought any or all of these nutrients might have something to do with removing inflammation of the nerves, but none of them would hazard a guess in this direction, since they were research scientists and not health-care specialists. From the scientific literature I've read in relation to silicon, I know that it is an important cross-linking agent for muscle tissue and is critical to the production of synovial fluid, which serves as a lubricant in a joint, tendon sheath, or bursa. Perhaps the silicon in lingonberries may also benefit injured nerves in some way.

LITCHI "NUT"
(Litchi Chinensis)

BRIEF DESCRIPTION

The tree that produces the litchi or lychee "nut" is a native to southern China. It is a member of the Soapberry family (*Sapindaceae*). A handsome, medium-sized, tropical or subtropical tree that grows to a height of 50 feet, the litchi is very sensitive to frost, drought, and wind. It has glossy, evergreen, feather-shaped leaves, 3–4 inches in length. The delicate flowers are small and greenish-white in appearance.

After a decade of maturity, the tree starts to bear loose clusters of 2 to 20 fruits that, on ripening, assume a pinkish-crimson tint that turns to a dull brown as the fruit commences to dry. The ripe fruits are nearly round, about 1 inch in diameter, have a warty rind, and resemble strawberries to some extent. The peeled skin reveals a white, juicy, bitter-sweet, jellylike pulp or aril. This is surrounded by a single, small, smooth, dark-brown seed. The seed and skin are inedible, although the former has reputed medicinal value in China for intestinal maladies. Only the rich pulp is edible; its texture is somewhat suggestive of grapes.

Litchis are fruits, not nuts, but when they first became available in this country many years ago it was in dried form only. The dry

187

peel was a fragile nutlike shell that caused the fruits to look like nuts—an illusion that brought about the confusion in nomenclature. Now the taste of dried litchis, similar to raisins, I think, bears no resemblance to the fresh fruit. Canned litchis, with rind and seed removed, do manage to at least retain some of the flavor of the fresh fruit.

Chinese Prescription for Hernias, Gastritis, Heartburn, and Testicular Swelling

In 1980 I accompanied a delegation of medical students and physicians from the American Medical Students' Association (part of the regular A.M.A.) to the People's Republic of China. We were invited by the government in Beijing to view their peculiar system of medicine—a unique blend of alternative measures such as herbal therapy, acupuncture, and moxibustion with orthodox medicine that includes regular prescription drugs, radiation, and surgery.

We spent some time at the Shanghai Second Medical College as well as the Soochow Chinese Traditional Medical Hospital. At both facilities we had the benefit of interpreters to assist us as we interviewed many doctors about their particular therapies. Dr. Xiao Li-Xiang told some of us about how he used litchi nuts in his practice.

He said that Lì Zhī Hé helped to alleviate heartburn, gastritis, and other stomach and epigastric pains in the upper part of the abdomen caused by a dysfunction of the liver and stomach. He attributed these several problems to "the stagnation of Liver Channel Qi," according to what our interpreter gave us. Dr. Xiao also spoke at some length on how he utilized Lì Zhī Hé for those of his male patients who suffered from hernias and other hernialike conditions and from testicular pain and swelling. He said that the "nut" worked best when it was combined with Xiao Hui Xiang (fenugreek seed).

A decoction was the standard form in which he prescribed both items for his patients. To 1 pint of boiling water should be added 1 level tablespoon of fenugreek seeds. Simmer, uncovered, for 20 minutes. Remove and allow to cool. Strain and pour liquid into a blender. (Use a Vita-Mix Nutrition Center or equivalent food machine for this.) Then add 6 tablespoons of litchee nuts (these can be canned if fresh aren't available) and blend for 1 minute. Have the patient drink 1 cup of this every 4 hours with a meal.

He also demonstrated to us in one hospital ward with some male volunteer patients how he gave litchee fluid extract intramuscularly with the aid of a large hypodermic needle. But that part I will omit, because for the average lay person it isn't practical to try at home.

Dr. Xiao seemed to place great faith in the litchee. Several patients with whom we spoke reported substantial improvements in their conditions of hernias, testicular inflammation, and gastrointestinal disturbances.

LOGANBERRY
(Rubus Ursinus Loganobaccus)

BRIEF DESCRIPTION

While most Victorian-era plant breeders were fussing with the strawberry, Judge James H. Logan, who was especially fond of bramble berries, let his thoughts drift into thornier pastures. In the warmth of his backyard berry garden in Santa Cruz, California, the visionary Judge Logan dreamed of introducing an entirely new plant to the Rubus genus.

After much experimentation, he succeeded in raising a new kind of berry from seed in 1881. It was introduced commercially the following year. The new fruit was a red-berried, upright-growing bramble whose parentage is still open to argument. Some botanists believe it is a hybrid of the western dewberry and the red raspberry, while others maintain that it is a variety of the dewberry. The difference, for those who can appreciate berry esoterica, is that a hybrid is the result of a cross between two species or subspecies, while a variety is a plant with a species that differs from the norm in some way. Some loganberry fanciers suspect that the native California blackberry *R. vitifolius* is somehow involved in the parentage of this fruit.

The loganberry, a vigorous grower, became a favorite soon after it was introduced. It seems that Judge Logan wasn't too concerned about Easterners being able to grow his berry, because it has a limited range. This berry is ideally suited for the Pacific Northwest and the California coasts, although it can be grown in other places if heroic measures are taken to protect the trailing, prickly fruit from winter kill—generally by burying the canes in burlap and straw in cold weather.

Judge Logan lived to be an octogenarian and always admired the wonderful display that his creation put on in his garden. The charming white flowers are followed by pendulous groups of large conical fruits. These alluring berries ripen in August on peacock-blue stalks reminiscent of grapevines when they are trained in meandering loops on trellises. They have a distinctive, slightly acidic taste agreeable to all palates and should be used as you would a blackberry or a raspberry—whichever of the two you judge to be the dominant parent.

Canker Sores Can't Come Back

Judge Logan lived another 46 years after his berry made its public debut. He passed away in his sleep in 1928, undoubtedly dreaming about glorious gardens filled with his lovely creation.

Sometime in 1919 one of his grandchildren developed canker sores in her mouth. As to how they got there was never mentioned in the family history, only that several doctors and dentists in the area weren't successful in getting rid of them. The high-school-age girl was beside herself as to what to do. Her grandfather advised eating some of his famous berries. She did and within days *every single canker sore had vanished!*

After reading this in the family papers of Judge Logan, I started recommending it to everyone who approached me with problems about canker sores inside the mouth or around the lips. Those who ate loganberries or drank the juice couldn't believe how quickly their cankers disappeared, almost overnight, in some instances.

MACADAMIA NUT
(Macadamia Integrifolia)

BRIEF DESCRIPTION

The macadamia is an evergreen tree and indigenous to the coastal, subtropical rain forests of southeast Queensland and northern New South Wales in eastern Australia. Before the middle of the nineteenth century the nut was known only to aboriginal tribes, who since prehistoric times gathered the nuts each autumn, but in all probability hardly ever cultivated the trees. Heaps of macadamia nut shells were found by the early white settlers in Australia near aboriginal feasting grounds. The aborigines had several different common names for it such as gyndl, kindal kindal, boombera, and burrawang.

The nut received its name from Baron Ferdinand van Mueller, who has been called Australia's foremost botanist. During the 1850s he traveled incessantly, over 15,000 miles on foot and horseback, methodically collecting 45,000 Australian botanical specimens. In early 1857 he was in the "bush" near the Pine River in the Moreton Bay District of Queensland when he discovered an unfamiliar species of tree. Consequently, he described it botanically for the first time and named it Macadamia in honor of his good friend John Macadam, M.D., who was at the time secretary of the Philosophical

Institute of Victoria. Ironically enough, Dr. Macadam never saw a macadamia tree nor tasted one of its nuts; he died at sea at age 37.

The edible nuts are produced by two species of the genus Macadamia: the smooth-shell type and the rough-shell type. The fruit consists of a fleshy husk that encloses a spherical seed $1/2$ to $1 \, 1/4$ inches in diameter with a very hard, durable shell. Inside the shell is the kernel or macadamia nut, whose distinctive flavor has been compared to that of a super-fine filbert. I've sampled macadamias for myself at one of the world's largest macadamia plantations, beautifully situated on the slopes of Mauna Loa Volcano at Keaau, near Hilo on the Big Island of Hawaii. And I can tell you from that enjoyable snacking experience that they have the most "luscious flavor" in the entire nut kingdom: crunchy, yet delicate, with a distinctive light oil that fills the mouth with every bite.

At present, the macadamia is considered a gourmet delicacy, ranking with pine nuts and pistachios as one of the world's most expensive nuts.

Soothes Sunburn and Chapped Lips

Diana Hurd of Sandy Bay, Tasmania, wrote to me some time ago to inform me of some wonderful uses that she had found for macadamia nut oil. "When I detect a place on my skin that has received a bit too much sun," she declared, "then I immediately rub some macadamia nut oil on the surface. I repeat this procedure at least twice a day, I find it doesn't peel or itch as bad by doing so." And she said that "when my lips or those of my children become chapped because of too much wind and sun, then I just rub some macadamia nut oil over them, and they quickly seem to heal. The nut oil softens and gives them a silky feeling."

Macadamia Improves the Health of the Heart

Olive oil, which cardiovascular physicians agree is beneficial to our health, is low in omega 6 fatty acids (8 percent). But macadamia nut oil is even lower (3 percent), while most of the other common vegetable oils such as corn, soy and safflower have a much higher level—20 percent to over 50 percent. Even canola oil (which is second to olive oil at 58 percent monounsaturated), with a high omega

6 content of 26 percent, has only a 1 to 2.6 ratio of omega 3 to omega 6. High levels of omega 6 fatty acids counteract the beneficial effects of omega 3 fatty acids, such as those found in fish.

Olive oil has a 1 to 8 ratio of omega 3 to omega 6 fatty acids. But macadamia nut oil has a 1 to 1 ratio. For those concerned about heart disease and high blood pressure, as most of us living a Western lifestyle should be, countering the difficult-to-avoid omega 6 fats in our standard diets by adding or replacing them with healthy amounts of omega 3 fats can dramatically improve our chances of avoiding the dietary reasons for heart disease, colon cancer, and arthritis. Hence, macadamia nut oil is ideal for preventing these problems.

A Potential Weight Loss Aid for Obesity

A preliminary study conducted some time ago by scientists at the University of Hawaii in Honolulu discovered that macadamia nuts can improve fat metabolism efficiently. Roughly 400 subjects were measured for a variety of dietary conditions. It was discovered that those who abundantly consumed macadamia nuts actually lost *more* weight than other subjects placed on a limited weight-loss diet. It is believed that these nuts "set" the "fat thermostat" (or "brown fat") in each person a little higher so that consumed fat was oxidized or converted into energy instead of stored flab.

Also, I might point out that the silky, "luscious" taste that well-chewed macadamias or nut oil leaves in the mouth certainly has a direct effect on obesity. Lining either side of the tongue are many tiny "taste buds," which send chemical signals to the brain all the time of whatever enters the mouth. Since fat tastes good, it has an appealing lure to the brain; hence, the body craves more of it. By substituting healthful macadamia nut oil for other notorious weight-gaining fatty foods, the taste buds are gently caressed with something that feels good and is flavorful. The septum pellucidum, the brain's pleasure center located just above the limbic system, is immediately notified that something delicious is coming into the body, which satisfies any cravings one may have for fatty foods.

Stores Longer and Cooks Better

Most oils in time become rancid, that is, they reach a state of deterioration wherein they smell bad or taste bad or both. But numerous tests with macadamia nut oil has repeatedly shown that once the container it comes in is opened, it can sit on the shelf for many months without ever going bad.

One important characteristic of a good-quality cooking oil is for it to have a high smoking point if the oil is intended for sautéing. But in order for this point to be reached, the oil must be highly refined; once this is done, however, the oil's free fatty acids, which account for its distinctive flavor, are greatly diminished.

Some oil, such as canola, which has a high smoking point of 400°F is virtually tasteless at the level of refinement at which it's sold commercially; therefore its use is merely to lubricate or coat the surfaces of the food in which it's being used. Extra virgin olive oil, though, which has a hearty, distinctive flavor, highly desirable for certain dishes, owes its flavor to its low level of refinement and its high retention of free fatty acids. However, this extra virgin olive oil's smoke point is just under 200°F; this means it will smoke very quickly and is therefore quite unsuitable for cooking at higher temperatures.

But with macadamia nut we find that its oil can be refined to a sufficiently high degree to achieve a favorably high smoking point (389°F) without sacrificing its appealing flavor in the process. In fact, some chefs with whom I have spoken in the past regarding macadamia nut oil have sworn that its unique nutty flavor is even *enhanced* at *higher* cooking temperatures.

For those wanting to attain some macadamia nut oil for themselves, call 1-800-367-6010 or 1-808-637-5620 or write to: Oils of Aloha, 66-935 Kaukonahua Road, P.O. Box 685, Waialua, Oahu, Hawaii 96791.

MILK THISTLE SEED
(Silybum Marianum)

BRIEF DESCRIPTION

One of my many duties as a scientist who studies medicinal plants in their cultural environments is to prepare papers on different herbs and read them before distinguished gatherings at various scientific symposiums held all over the world. I did a paper on milk thistle seed that was presented before the American Society of Pharmacognosy, Twenty-eighth Annual Meeting, held at the University of Rhode Island in Kingston, Rhode Island, on Monday, July 20, 1987. It is from that original, award-winning paper, supported by scientific grants from two different companies, that the material here comes.

Milk thistle is a member of the daisy family (*Composite*). It is closely allied to other thistles, including common thistle, star thistle, and edible artichoke (which is a thistle, believe it or not). However, only milk thistle, particularly the seed, contains the liver protectant silymarin.

Tremendous Liver Protectant

Work done by several German scientists in the last few decades has demonstrated the remarkable effectiveness of a curious flavonol isolated from milk thistle seeds, called silymarin. The scientific literature on this compound and various German (Legalon) and American (Livercare, Thisilyn) proprietary herbal preparations has already reached legendary proportions.

The liver-protective effect has been demonstrated on a number of models in many animal experiments. Carbon tetrachlorides will cause severe necrosis of liver parenchyma in rats. But silymarin will prevent this. It has necrotropic action in that it antagonizes hydropic cellular changes and also lipotropic action, reducing toxic fatty degeneration in the liver. Even more profound were the results seen with alpha-amanitine and phalloidin, dangerously toxic constituents of the death cap mushroom that cause severe damage to the liver, damage for which there has been no effective treatment until now. Preventive use of silymarin given by mouth significantly reduced the mortality rate in the experimental animals. This preventive effect was reproducible. Furthermore, it has been discovered that silymarin given by intravenous injection had curative action on even the severe liver damage caused by phalloidin. It may therefore be assumed that silymarin acts directly on the cell membranes in the liver parenchyma and can thus both prevent and cure liver damage.

Extensive clinical data have since confirmed the efficacy of silymarin found in German pharmaceutical and American herbal preparations. In cases of chronic hepatitis of all types there is an improvement noticed in the first couple of weeks of treatment, particularly where gastrointestinal symptoms are concerned. At the same time there as a remarkable improvement in appetite, and in almost all cases a feeling of well-being and improved physical performance. Apart from chronic hepatitis and the post-acute stages of acute hepatitis, the drug is also particularly suitable for the treatment of fatty liver degeneration, especially in alcoholics, and good results have been reported even with cirrhosis of the liver.

In most cases the bilirubin level rapidly returned to normal, an effect that persisted, and serum tolerance and transaminase activities became normal. These tests are known to provide effective monitoring of progress in all cases of hepatitis. Bromsulfalein retention tests also showed definite improvement, with a return to normal much more frequent than in patients not given silymarin preparations, especially those with fatty livers. Fatty liver may therefore be regarded as a particular indication requiring silymarin extracts.

German doctors have usually administered Legalon tablets, containing 35 milligrams of silymarin each, in proportions of 3 tablets 3 times daily following meals, for a period of 1–2 months. After this, the dose is usually reduced to just 1 tablet 3 times daily. Treatments are often lengthy, as a rule. It is recommended that when taking any American herbal preparation containing silymarin, that a *minimum* of 10 capsules twice daily be taken for up to 5 months. This is because the silymarin content isn't as concentrated as it is in the German product.

A final note about silymarin: It cannot be obtained from the seeds of milk thistle simply by boiling them into a tea. They must be submitted to a lengthy and sophisticated extraction process in order to get adequate amounts of silymarin in the final product to do the best job possible. I believe that hypodermic ejections or pharmaceutical herb preparations of silymarin from Europe are a lot more effective for liver damage than any American products are, although the latter can be used with modest expectations.

MULBERRY
(Morus Nigra)

BRIEF DESCRIPTION

The mulberries consist of about a dozen species of deciduous trees and shrubs native to temperate and subtropical regions of Asia, Europe, and North America. Russian mulberry was introduced into the United States by Russian Mennonites in 1875 and is probably the most widely planted mulberry. The Prairie States Forestry Project planted more than a million seedlings per year from 1937 to 1942 to serve as windbreaks on the Great Plains from Nebraska to Texas.

All mulberries are valuable food sources for birds and other wildlife and hold important medicinal benefits for humans. The seven or more varieties or forms of Russian mulberry differ in their relative drought resistance and chromosome number. Its high drought resistance makes Russian mulberry well suited for shelterbelt plantings.

The Russian mulberry is usually 20–30 feet high, but can sometimes reach upward of more than 70 feet. The leaves are simple, alternate, shiny, and broadly egg-shaped to irregularly lobed. They are distinguished by fine, short, closely spaced, more or less blunt teeth along their edges and by being often hairy on their tops, which are darker than their undersides. When broken off, the leaf

199

stems have a sweetish, milky sap that is also found in the twigs. The thin bark of the trunks, which are tough and rot-resistant, tends to flake and is a grayish to reddish brown.

The small, greenish-white flowers of the red mulberry blossom in springtime in dense, pendant spikes suspended by short stems that hang between the individual leaves and the branches. Male and female blossoms often grow on the same tree. The juicy, pleasantly sweet berries, about an inch long, are made up of densely clustered, one-seeded drupes, like those of the blackberry, and darken to a deep purple when ripe, during which time they drop from the trees, usually between the months of June and August.

The fruits of the white mulberry, while similarly shaped, often take on a more pinkish hue and do not have the same pungent flavor but are rather insipidly sweet.

Outstanding Burn Remedy from Thailand

The Hmong are the second largest hill tribes of Northern Thailand, numbering more than 82,000. Their population swelled rapidly at the end of the Vietnam conflict when many fled Laos because of terrible retribution by the Communist regime. But their roots are clearly in China, where there are an estimated four million members of this ethnic minority.

The Hmong are the only tribal people who make clothing from hemp cloth upon which they dye intricate batik patterns. They use mulberry juice as one of their primary colors for this. Many of them still grow hemp (better known as marijuana) for its strong fibers, which are stripped from the stem of the plant. Besides growing marijuana, they are also big producers of opium poppy, which is an important cash crop for them.

I spent some time in a few Hmong villages years ago. These people prefer to live in the higher mountains and tend to isolate themselves from other tribes. Rarely did I find fences in such villages, so livestock and kids wander everywhere. A typical item in the center of the villages I stayed in was a communal corn grinder.

Open fires in Hmong houses, village areas, and fields pose constant threats of burns, and these highlanders use several plants to effectively treat them. I found the introduced leaf succulent *Aloe vera* planted in most household gardens or in pots in the villages where I stayed. The ripe fruit of mulberry, which is quite common in the forest surrounding their villages, was used in conjunction with aloe.

First, some mulberries were crushed to extract their juice. Both juice and the pulverized flesh and skin were mixed together. The amount used is determined by how big the burn itself is. Generally speaking, about 1 cup will cover a burn size that is 3 inches in circumference. A 4-inch-long by 1-inch-wide piece of succulent aloe leaf is cut with a sharp knife and also thoroughly mashed. Then the pulverized contents of mulberry and aloe are mixed together by hand in a kneading action and spread over the afflicted part gently and carefully. This poultice is left in place by the tribal doctor for 12 to 14 hours before it is scraped away and another batch put in its place.

I saw one village healer treat a seven-year-old boy who had accidentally burned his right foot just below the ankle in the fire; from all appearances it looked to be second-degree in nature. After three applications of mulberry-aloe combination, the child was much better, free from most pain, and the injured epidermal layer seemed to be healing quite nicely. I returned to this village ten days later and was astonished to see the same lad up and about as if nothing had ever happened. A white piece of loom-woven cloth of the villagers' own making was loosely bound around his right foot. I asked for permission to examine it and, in company with the native healer, did so. I was amazed to see how rapidly the healing process had set in on such damaged tissue; the effects were nothing short of miraculous! Then and there I became a solid convert to mulberry and aloe as a most effective burn dressing. However, due to the serious nature of burns themselves, it is always recommended that medical services in the emergency ward of larger hospitals be quickly consulted for prompt treatment.

Help for Edema and Gout

Both the Hmong in Thailand and the Chinese in mainland China routinely employ mulberries in liquid forms to reduce swelling of the joints and extremities in cases of gout. Abdominal and facial edema are greatly facilitated too, because urination is increased. Mulberry tea, juice, and soup are the forms in which this medicinal fruit is consumed.

Skin Treatment for Ringworm and Lice

Parasitic afflictions such as ringworm and lice usually occur because of lack of adequate personal hygiene or by coming in contact with others who have them. Mulberry juice is rubbed on the skin and massaged into the scalp by the Hmong to clean up these troublesome conditions. Also clothing, bedding, and rooms should be fumigated to permanently get rid of lice. Household pets such as cats and dogs should be treated by a local veterinarian for such vermin. And young children should be properly educated in good hygiene to prevent getting lice.

MUSTARD SEED

(Brassica Nigra, B. Juncea, B. Alba or B. Hirta)

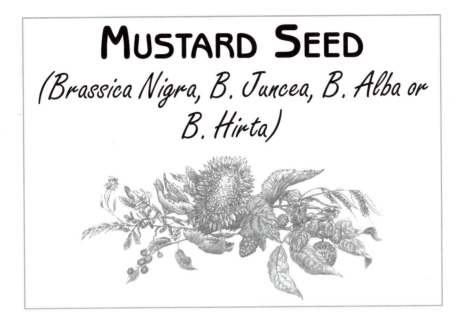

BRIEF DESCRIPTION

The mustard plant was known in ancient times and is highly valued for its oil content. It is mentioned five times in the New Testament. In Matthew 13:31–32 Christ compared "the Kingdom of Heaven…to a grain of mustard seed, which…when it is grown…is the greatest among herbs, and becometh a tree, so that the birds of the air come and lodge in the branches thereof." The term "tree," however, is to be taken only as an exaggerated contrast with the minute seed to infer that out of something every minute can come something very great. This philosophical point is best illustrated in the other reference to mustard in Matthew 17:20: "And Jesus said unto them…If ye have faith as a grain of mustard seed, ye shall say unto this mountain, remove hence to yonder place; and it shall remove; and nothing shall be impossible unto you."

The Gospel of Mark (4:31–32) furnishes us with an eloquent comparison of mustard in relation to other seeds: "…A grain of mustard seed…when…sown in the earth, is less than all the seeds that be in the earth: but when it is sown, it groweth up, and becometh greater than all herbs, and shooteth out great branches…." Palestinian mustard trees have been known to reach a height of almost twenty feet and are often a favorite place for birds to roost temporarily. Luke 13:19 confirms this by telling of a man planting a single grain of mustard in his garden: "…it grew, and waxed a great tree; and the fowls of the air lodged in the branches of it."

The final reference to mustard in the Four Gospels is found in Luke 17:6 and is a repeat of the seed-faith connection mentioned earlier in the book of Matthew. But in this instance, the writer has Jesus saying that if we have the faith of a tiny mustard seed, we "might say unto this sycamine tree, Be thou plucked up by the root, and be thou planted in the sea; and it should obey you." Probably for those with little or no faith at all, developing enough confidence within and in God to handle the replanting of a tree doesn't seem so impossible and is less discouraging than removing an entire mountain.

Looked at another way, some of the ancient rabbinical writings suggest that great dividends may be expected from a single effort. In Cunningham Geikie's classic treatise on *The Life and Words of Christ* (London: Strahan and Co. Ltd., 1879; 2:627 fn. c) may be found several quotes to this effect. "There was a stalk of mustard in Sichin from which sprang out three boughs, of which one broke off, and covered the tent of a potter, and produced three cabs of mustard (nearly six quarts)." Another "instance is given by the Rabbis, of the fertility of Palestine, to the effect that one man got three hundred-fold increase on the grain [of mustard seed] he sowed."

Of the three major types of mustard there are (black, brown, and white), the black mustard seeds are the most pungent and yield a yellowish, biting oil. Only a little bit of this mustard oil is necessary to bring about tremendous medical benefits for sufferers. This is undoubtedly due to the high concentration of sulfur in a very compact and tiny form, which helps to explain the previously cited Christian-Judaic references to the potent power locked up in a single grain of mustard seed. For further information on this spice, consult my other reference work, *Heinerman's Encyclopedia of Herbs and Spices*.

Grandma's Old-Fashioned Mustard Plaster

A number of decades ago, mustard plasters were in vogue; in fact, whenever I happen to mention this in an audience of appreciable size, invariably I will get at least two dozen or so hands raised out of a crowd of several hundred. These individuals can readily identify with it from their own childhoods.

My own grandmother Barbara Liebhardt Heinerman, who came from the "Old Country" of what was then Temesvár, Hungary (now part of Romania), employed her own kind of mustard plaster for a variety of ailments. She relied on them occasionally whenever her older children, George and Elsie (both deceased), became sick. My father, Jacob Heinerman, who was born in 1914, thinks she might even have used one on him at a very early age, to help clear up some congestion in his lungs.

My grandmother made her plaster by mixing powdered mustard with cold water until a thick paste was formed. The amounts used depended on how large an area was to be covered. She spread the paste on a muslin cloth. Another thin cotton cloth was then placed on the skin and the mustard cloth put over it. Her plaster remained in place until the surface of the skin began to redden and a burning sensation was felt. She then removed the plaster and washed away the remaining mustard with cold water and a wet sponge.

Grandmother Barbara never applied her plaster to tender or sensitive areas of the body. And if it seemed a bit too strong she would dilute its strength by adding a little bit of whole wheat flour. In order to prevent a rash from developing, she would sometimes smear the surface of the skin with a little virgin olive oil or the unbeaten white of an egg; both are wonderful protectants for hypersensitive skin. After removing the plaster and cleansing the area, she would usually sprinkle talcum powder or white flour on the skin and wrap it with dry cotton.

My father, who was 81 as of January 5, 1995, remembers his mother using such old-fashioned mustard plasters for the following difficulties: allergy, backache, bronchitis, colic, coughing, croup, hoarseness/laryngitis, muscle pain/"Charley horse," neuralgia, rheumatism, sciatica, and toothache. For some of these problems, a tiny amount of camphor spirits, eucalyptus oil, peppermint oil, or tea tree oil mixed in with the powdered mustard and water will hasten the "warming" of the skin and relieve pain more rapidly.

Removing the Onion Smell

A nifty little trick for removing the unpleasant smell from the hands after peeling onions was mentioned by British herbalist Mary Thorne Quelch in her *Herbs for Daily Use in Home Medicine and Cookery* (London: Faber & Faber Ltd., 1941, p. 255). She said that if the hands are rubbed with a little dry mustard powder *before* they are washed, all traces of onion odor will disappear.

NUTMEG SEED
(Myristica Fragrans)

BRIEF DESCRIPTION

Nutmeg and mace are the only spices in commercial trade that are produced by separate parts of the same fruit. Nutmeg is made from the dried seed, while mace is the dried seed cover known botanically as the *aril*.

The fruit of the nutmeg tree is fleshy in appearance, like an apricot, but can get as big as a peach. Upon ripening, it splits open, exposing the bright-red netlike aril wrapped around a dark reddish-brown and brittle shell within which lies a single seed. This dried brown seed, after its shell has been broken and discarded, is nutmeg.

For further information on nutmeg, please refer to my other book, *Heinerman's Encyclopedia of Herbs and Spices*.

Handy Paste for Insect Bites and Stings

In July 1994 I went to the Philippines and spent the better part of the month touring the different islands and visiting a number of local folk healers to learn some of their medical secrets. On the north end of the big island of Mindanao in the city of Cagayan, I met Ludivina de Padilla. She was a third-generation herbalist, and at age 31 a pretty one, too.

She took the time to explain to my interpreter and me how she made a simple paste to reduce the inflammation and itching and draw out the poison from insect bites and stings. The equivalent of one teaspoon of finely grated ginger root, mashed with a rock or hammer, is mixed with half that amount of powdered nutmeg and just enough Japanese saki or rice wine (any liquor can be used) to make a smooth paste. This is then applied directly to the afflicted site and left there for an hour or more. The addition of a little cooking oil, Ludivina said, would keep the paste from drying out.

Diaper Rash Cleared Up

I accompanied Ludivina to a nearby home in her slum neighborhood. A short, thin woman showed us the buttocks and genitalia of her 10-month-old son, which were fire-engine red. Ludivina explained that the baby suffered from an excruciating form of diaper rash, which she attributed to the mother leaving her son's soiled diapers on longer than she should. She took some powdered nutmeg from a little round metal can she had brought with her and showed the young mother how to lightly dust it over the sore and tender skin. She told her to make sure clean diapers were put on her child at least 3 times a day instead of the usual 1 diaper every 24 or 36 hours.

On the way back to her house, my host stated that the condition would clear up within a few days. About two months after this, I mentioned this to some of my anthropology students. One of them named Rosalind decided to try it for herself on her own infant girl who apparently was experiencing a similar problem. She reports back a week later that the remedy really worked—her child's diaper rash had completely disappeared.

CAUTION: If nutmeg is to be used orally, it must be used sparingly. Moderate dosages can induce mental confusion, hallucinations, double vision, tachycardia, and considerable joint-muscle pain following withdrawal of the substance. Only in rare instances have convulsions been known to be caused by this spice.

PEANUT
(Arachis Hyogaea)

BRIEF DESCRIPTION

The cultivated peanut is the hard, ripe, nutlike seed or bean of an annual herbaceous vine of the pea family. It is indigenous to South America, having originated in Bolivia at the base of the eastern slopes of the Andes. Some scientists, however, have noted strong resemblances between ancient forms found at various Peruvian archaeological sites and the kind of peanut commonly grown in the Orient. Carl O. Sauer, a professor of geography and formerly with the University of California at Berkeley, mentioned in *Handbook of South American Indians* (Washington: U.S. Government Printing Office, 1950, 6:499) that the peanut may have originally come from somewhere in the Orient via a trans-Pacific oceanic crossing in ancient times.

The *Book of Mormon,* an inspired translation of the history of the inhabitants of ancient America, sheds further light on how the peanut may have come here. The "Bock of Ether," toward the end of this volume of sacred writings, gives a brief account of the Jaredites, a very ancient people who left the Tower of Babel in central Iraq under the leadership of a man named Jared (hence, their name) and his brother, Mahonri Moriancumer. They traveled northward over the Caucasus mountains, then turned eastward and crossed the length of Asia, finally stopping for several years in the present Chinese province of Shandong. They eventually constructed unique vessels that were capable of traveling *beneath* or upon the water for great lengths of time; this is presumed to be the world's first submarine prototypes.

Into these vessels they put the beehives (called "Deseret" in their ancient tongue), many crops seeds (including peanuts), tanks of fish, beasts of burden (such as the woolly mammoth), tools, and some household articles and clothing they had brought along with them. There were a total of eight barges to accommodate an unspecified number of immigrants, who were the only ones, by the way, whose language had *not* been altered at the Tower. They launched their vessels in the Yellow Sea and with a terrific wind behind them crossed the mighty and uncharted waters that lay before them. It took them almost a year of travel, but they eventually reached this continent, landing somewhere near present-day Acapulco, Mexico. This was somewhere around 2009 B.C. In the centuries to follow they eventually filled all of North and South America. The peanut, of course, was widely domesticated by them, but seems to have been grown more in Central and South America.

Before the time of Columbus, the peanut was unknown in the Old World. It is first mentioned in Spanish chronicles and natural histories of the sixteenth century. In 1535 Captain Gonzalo Fernandez de Oviedo y Valdès, appointed historiographer of the New World and governor of Haiti by King Charles V of Spain, wrote in his *Historia General y Natural de las Indias Occidentales:* "Another fruit which the Indians have on Hispaniola is called *mani.* They sow and harvest it. It is a very common crop...about the size of a pine nut in the shell. They consider it a healthy food." Through the Spaniards it was reintroduced to the Old World.

The Ultimate Aztec Toothache Remedy

Ethnobotanical remains of the cultivated peanut have been found in the Tehuacàn Valley, Pueblo state, Mexico, dating from approximately 100 B.C. The peanut played an important part in ancient Aztec folk medicine. Friar Bernardino de Sahagun made an illustrated, encyclopedic study of the Aztecs in 1566 in which he wrote about the peanut. In the Nahuatl language (which the Aztecs spoke), it was called *tlalcacauatl* (from *tlatle,* meaning earth; and *cacauatl,* meaning cacao seed) or "earth cocoa bean."

A peanut paste, not unlike peanut butter, was prepared by the Aztecs as a toothache remedy. Almost 15 years ago I had a chance to test this out for myself. I was in New Orleans for a National Health Federation convention. One of the fillings in my upper right molar fell out. Soon my tooth was throbbing and hurting very badly; the pain alone nearly drove me crazy. A Creole woman in a tiny herb shop on Bourbon Street told me that a crushed garlic clove would help to relieve my suffering. So I bought some from her, peeled and mashed it, and stuck it into the filling hole, but it kept falling out.

Then I remembered this ancient Aztec remedy mentioned by Father Sahagun in his writings. I bought a small jar of peanut butter and a loaf of white bread. I spread a thin layer of peanut butter on one-quarter slice of bread. I laid some more crushed garlic clove over it. I then cut out a piece the size of a silver dollar and inserted it with my thumb into the empty hole. It remained there for several hours. The combination of the garlic and peanut butter stopped the pain for as long as I kept it there. I had to charge the packing material every 4—5 hours, but it served the purpose until I was able to get back home and see my dentist to get another filling put in. I've recommended this remedy many times since then and always with good results.

Peanut Butter, an Ideal Food for Anorexia Sufferers

Anorexia nervosa is an intense fear of becoming fat and the consequent act of self-imposed starvation. It affects women more than men. Two of the most evident signs are significant weight loss and the absence of menstruation. The nervous, gastrointestinal, cardiovascular, and reproductive systems are all adversely affected by this dramatic syndrome. Emotional factors are also to blame: perfectionist personality; low self-esteem; high self-expectations; and an over-acceptance of the culturally condoned ideal of slimness. If continued long enough, death can result.

I've counseled about half a dozen anorectic young women in the last two decades. They had all participated in lengthy fasts and barely ate enough to keep a parakeet happy. I put each one of them on just one basic food—peanut butter sandwiches. That's all they ate and nothing else except for reasonable intakes of water. Since I couldn't change their perceptual distortions about themselves, I decided the next best thing was to give them a single food that would keep them tolerably nourished, while at the same time allowing them to indulge in their very determined pronounced weight losses. *None* of the six women whom I advised died as a result of their anxieties about being overweight. Though all of them eventually came very close to looking like many of the Holocaust survivors from the Nazi concentration camps of World War II, and did, in fact, suffer some health problems, their conditions, when compared with other anorectic patients, were mild.

I attributed this to my success with peanuts in helping underweight invalids successfully recuperate from lengthy illness and regain their fleshy weight. Peanuts contain about 26 percent protein—higher than dairy products, eggs, fish, and many cuts of meat. In fact, the National Peanut Council claims that a glass of milk and two peanut butter sandwiches provide 83 percent of a growing child's daily need for protein. The total food energy in one pound of peanut butter equals 2 pounds of steak, a gallon of milk, or 32 eggs. Peanuts contain many of the essential B-complex vitamins including thiamine, riboflavin, and niacin, as well as appreciable amounts of calcium, phosphorus, potassium, iron, and magnesium—including a balanced share of calories, but no cholesterol.

Four of the anorectic ladies whom I worked with decided also to snack on raw peanuts sometimes and occasionally to make themselves small bowls of cream of peanut butter soup. While I certainly don't condone a phobia like anorexia nervosa, if nothing else will deter a person's mind away from this, then at least I'm going to try and persuade the individual to stick with a diet of peanuts in different forms. It could certainly spell the difference between life and death; at least six young women, who eventually overcame their problem, are still alive today, thanks largely to peanuts and water.

Anti-Bleeding Factor Found in Peanuts

Over three decades ago, a hemostatic factor was isolated from peanuts and reported in the scientific literature. A purified form of the extract was prepared by doctors in Washington, D.C., and in Copenhagen, Denmark, and administered orally to hemophilic patients. Hemophilia is an inherited blood disorder marked by a permanent tendency to hemorrhages, spontaneous or traumatic, due to a defect in the blood coagulating mechanism.

Medical researchers who worked with this factor in peanuts believed it was a protease inhibitor that accounted for the clotting action. The frequent consumption of peanut *flour,* they think, is the best form in which to obtain this hemostatic factor. This data appeared in *Drug Trade News* (July 23, 1962) and *Nature* (194:980, 1962).

Peanut Leaves Good for Insomnia

Peanut leaves have been used in mainland China for about three centuries. Its uses include treatment for hemorrhages, hypertension, and elevated cholesterol levels. The journal *Chinese Traditional and Herbal Drugs* (18(2):22, 1987) that I routinely subscribe to reported a while brick that a water extract of peanut leaves cause mice (10 in the group and 10 controls) to sleep for half an hour (no control mice slept). The mice were then fed 125 times the sedative dose for 3 days with no observed toxic side effects (though the test animals were very, very mellow, to say the least).

The best way to overcome insomnia is to drink a cup of peanut leaf tea 30 minutes before bedtime. Boil 1 $\frac{1}{2}$ cups water and add 2 tablespoons coarsely cut peanut leaves. Remove from heat, cover, and steep 40 minutes. Strain and drink while sill warm on an empty stomach.

PECAN
(Carya Illinoinensis)

BRIEF DESCRIPTION

The pecan is probably the single most important nut tree native to North America. Although named for its northernmost natural habitat, it is actually indigenous to a wide geographical area, including Texas, Oklahoma, Louisiana, Mississippi, Arkansas, Missouri, Kansas, Kentucky, Tennessee, Illinois, Indiana, Nebraska, Iowa, and Mexico as far south as Oaxaca.

For Native Americans tribes in the south-central region of the United States, especially in the Mississippi Valley, the pecan served as a dietary staple long before the arrival of Europeans. Later the Indians traded pecans to the settlers for furs, trinkets, and tobacco. Before the early Sixteenth century, no European had ever seen a pecan nut.

Lope de Oviedo, a member of a Spanish expedition to the New World in 1533, described pecans growing near the Guadalupe River in Texas: "There were many nuts on the tanks of this river which the Indians ate in their season, coming from twenty to thirty leagues about. These nuts were much smaller than the Spanish…walnuts."

Alvar Nuñez Cabeza de Vaca, a Spanish colonial official and explorer, was treasurer of the ill-fated Nàrvaez expedition to the

214

Gulf Coast of North America in 1528. When all the Spanish ships were wrecked during a violent storm in the Gulf of Mexico, Cabeza de Vaca and three other survivors were captured by Indians on an island near the Texas coast and imprisoned for several years. During his miserable captivity, he noted that for two months of the year his Indian captors subsisted on nothing but pecans ("noagles") when they habitually visited the so-called "river of nuts," which was the Guadalupe. A little historic aside here: It is from this Indian word for pecan that the Texas city of Noagles eventually derived its name.

In 1729, Jean Penicaut, a carpenter on a French ship, reported that the Indians at the village of Natche on the Mississippi River had three different types of walnut trees, one of which produced excellent, edible nuts as small as a man's thumb. They were called "pacanes." The French in Louisiana adopted this name for the pecan.

Two U.S. Presidents, George Washington (the "Father of our country") and Thomas Jefferson, were fond of pecans and frequently carried them in their pockets to munch on. They also planted numerous trees on their respective estates, since they both regarded the pecan as a handsome ornamental tree for American gardens.

The top five pecan-producing states in the nation are Georgia, Alabama, New Mexico, Louisiana, and Texas. Outside of America, pecans have been planted in Mexico, Australia, Brazil, South Africa, Israel, and a few other countries.

The pecan resembles a walnut in some ways, but is more elongated, has a much smoother shell and a higher proportion of kernel in its shell. In the pecan, the partitions that separate the two halves of the kernel are thinner than in the walnut. When mature, the husk of the pecan, unlike that of the walnut, splits open into four segments.

Terrific Recipe for Lack of Appetite and Loss of Energy

Lack of appetite can be due to any number of considerations, some of them mental, emotional, physiological, or a combination of several of these. Loss of energy may be attributes to mononucleosis, chronic fatigue syndrome, herpes virus, yeast infection, and hypoglycemia.

One recipe that an old Creole lady, skilled in the healing arts, gave to me some years ago in New Orleans has proven to be very useful in treating those who have no real desire to eat anything and in giving energy and stamina to those who always seem to be fatigued for one reason or another.

Ordinarily I would include this with the rest of the recipes at the end of this section. But because it is more remedial in nature, I felt it more appropriate to put it here instead. Since Mama Cass (for that was her name) originated this meal remedy, it naturally bears her name.

Mama Cass's Apple-Pecan Stuffed Squash

2 medium acorn squash

1/2 cup butter

2 cups green apples, finely chopped

1 teaspoon cinnamon

1/2 teaspoon mace

1/2 teaspoon cardamom

2 teaspoons lime juice

1 cup pecans, chopped

generous dash nutmeg

Cut the squash in half crosswise and remove the seeds. Bake with the cut side down in a shallow pan at 350°F for 45 minutes. Remove the cooked squash from its shells and mix with butter, apple, cinnamon, mace, cardamom, lime juice, and pecans, reserving 1/4 cup pecans for topping later on. Spoon this mixture into shells and top with nutmeg and remaining pecans. Bake at 350°F for 10 minutes.

I've encouraged several care givers of older enfeebled patients who refused to eat what was served them to prepare this instead. The aroma was so alluring that the patients soon greedily devoured whatever amounts were served them. And those requiring more energy have reported that a meal of this simple dish did wonders for their stamina afterwards.

Secretary Loses Weight by Snacking on Pecans

Luella Ritter, a secretary for an insurance agent in Sioux Falls, South Dakota, had a weight problem. It was difficult for her to go on any meaningful weight-loss program as long as her constant inclination to keep snacking kept getting in the way. She wrote to me after hearing a national radio program I did on "The Caveman Diet Plan."

I suggested that she stop all other forms of snacking and instead just stick with munching on pecans. But the secret to it, I said in my letter, was to *slowly* chew just a few, making sure that plenty of saliva was mixed in, before she swallowed each mouthful.

She followed my directions and happily reported back several months later that she, at last, had begun to lose some weight, thanks to my pecan snack plan. While the number of pounds itself wasn't too significant, for her, who had tried everything before, it seemed a major accomplishment.

Pine Nut
(Pinaceae)

Brief Description

The pine family is one of the most familiar groups of evergreen trees in North America since it furnishes most of our traditional Christmas trees, provides a strong, excellent softwood timber, and is an important source of turpentine and rosin. Less well-known perhaps is the fact that some members of the genus Pinus also bear edible seeds, commonly referred to as nuts. Worldwide, approximately 100 different species of true pines are recognized; of these, about a dozen—all in the northern hemisphere—produce nuts of sufficiently high quality and desirable flavor to make them worth gathering.

"Pine nut" can denote any of these edible nuts. The most common designation for pine nuts in Europe is "pignolia," a term that refers to pine nuts of the Italian stone pine, grown for the most part in Spain, Portugal, Italy, and North Africa. Nuts of a different species called "piñon," a name for the Spanish word for the pine nut, are produced in the western United States. These piñon nuts come mainly from the Colorado piñon tree, a two-needled pine that grows wild in the states of Utah, Colorado, Arizona, and New Mexico.

Pine nuts of lesser importance are harvested from other nut pines including the single-leaf piñon, which occurs in mountainous regions of the West and Southwest, even down into some of the states of northwest Mexico.

Well before the domestication of other food plants, the pine nut was a valuable source of food for many Native American tribes occupying the present southwestern United States. In 1540, for example, the chronicler for Francisco Vasquez de Coronado, the man who discovered the Grand Canyon, described how the Zuni Indians gathered and stored large quantities of these nuts. The piñon pine, in fact, provided food and fuel for many Native Americans of the Southwest, including the Navajo, Pueblo, Zuni, Hopi, Shoshone, Goshiute, and Cahuilla.

Southwest Indian Remedy for Head Colds and Coughs

The Hopi Indian Reservation is located in the northeastern part of Arizona, about 185 miles north of Phoenix and about 230 miles west of Albuquerque. On a map one can see that the Hopi Reservation is a lozenge-shaped area smaller than the state of Rhode Island located amidst the far vaster, nearly New England-sized Navajo Reservation.

Through the years I've had several occasions to visit this reservation. Back in 1981, while I was visiting with some potential informants at the village of Kykotsmovi on Third Mesa, I had a chance to peruse an issue of *Qua Tokti* ("Cry of the Eagle"), the Hopi newspaper, with one of my English-speaking hosts, who graciously translated some of the articles for me.

In one of them an unidentified old woman named Nampeyo, from the First Mesa village of Hano, gave her remedy for treating the head colds and coughs of all members of her extended clan. (Hopi society is distinctly matriarchal). She would take one cup of piñon nuts, shell them between her teeth, and then spit them back into another empty tin cup. After this she spread them out on her table between two pieces of waxed paper and rolled over them vigorously with her rolling pin. Then she gathered up the flattened nut meal and poured it into about a quart-sized jar filled three fourths full with hot water. She screwed on a lid, shook the contents well, and let the mixture steep for an hour. Then she strained out one and a half cups of liquid at a time and reheated it a little over the fire before giving it to a family member or relative to drink. She had the sick person drink four cups of this brew daily in between meals. She claimed that it always helped to clean up head colds and coughs in one day.

Infant Colic and Diarrhea Cured with Havasupai Remedy

In the cold, dreary month of December 1992, a graduate student from Ohio by the name of Howard Lowe and I took a trip to the northwestern part of Arizona. We parked our vehicle on top and descended by horseback with several Indian guides down the winding and slippery trail, made doubly treacherous by a heavy packing of ice on top, which eventually led us to the bottom of the Grand Canyon and the Havasupai village below. We spent part of one week gathering pertinent medical data, which I would later use in books such as this.

One Indian woman, about 40 years of age, gave me a simple remedy that she had often used for treating colic and diarrhea in both Indian and white infants. She would first shell and then grind $1/4$ cup of raw piñon nuts before combining them with $1/4$ cup water in a small saucepan. This she covered with a lid and boiled for 7 minutes. One tablespoon of honey was added. This amount could be doubled, if necessary, she added.

When sufficiently cooled to lukewarm, it would be fed to the sick infant. Colic and diarrhea would completely disappear within less than an hour. And whatever quantity the baby didn't eat she would add to regular pancake batter and cook pancakes for the rest of her family.

PISTACHIO NUT
(Pistacia Vera)

BRIEF DESCRIPTION

The pistachio belongs to the family Anacardiaceae, which also lays claim to the cashew, mango, sumac, and poison oak. There are approximately twelve different species of *Pistacia,* nearly all of which exude turpentine or mastic, and just a few of which yield small edible nuts. Only *Pistacia vera,* though, produces the pistachio nut that is popular throughout the Mediterranean world.

The edible pistachio is a deciduous tree that grows slowly to a height and spread of 25–30 feet. It can survive under dry, adverse conditions in poor, stony terrain where for most of the year there may be no rainfall. It can grow quite well on steep, rocky slopes suitable only for sure-footed goats. It can endure droughts very nicely but succumbs to abundant rainfall, so well-drained, somewhat sandy soil is important. It thrives in places that have winters cool enough to break bud dormancy and hot, long summers—the latter being essential for proper ripening of the nuts. It may be found in numerous quantities in certain parts of Iran where temperatures can vary from as low as 15°F in the winter to a sizzling 110°F in the summer.

This nut differs from other popular dessert nuts in the characteristic green of its kernel. This is an important clue in determining the freshness and quality of pistachios. The coloration varies from yellowish through various shades of green and isn't confined just to the exterior but also extends to the interior portion of the kernel. In general, the deeper the shade of green, the more the pistachios are valued.

The fruits grow in clusters resembling grapes. Though it is commonly known as a nut, the fruit of the pistachio is technically classified by botanists everywhere as a drupe, the edible portion of which is the seed itself. This oblong kernel is close to an inch in length and half an inch in diameter. It is protected from dust, dirt, and man-made air pollution by a thin, ivory-colored, bony shell.

When conditions are favorable, the shells split longitudinally along their sutures prior to harvest and have the appearance of a laughing face. In Iran this is termed "pistehkhandan," which, loosely translated, signifies the "laughing pistachio." It is a desirable characteristic since the nuts are usually marketed in the shell, and when the shell is split, the kernel can be more readily extracted with the fingers.

In the event, however, that unfavorable weather conditions have prevailed during the nut's growth and development, the shells won't split open as they should. A sorrowful, time-honored expression of nut growers in parts of Turkey covers this misfortune rather nicely in this eloquent way: "Too bad, our pistachios aren't laughing this year." The unsplit nuts are considered inferior and fetch a low price in the marketplace.

An Egyptian Cure for Dysentery

Pistachio nuts figured prominently in the ancient cultures of the Old World. The aged patriarch Jacob instructed his sons to take with them on their next sojourn back to Egypt "...a present, a little balm, and a little honey, spices, and myrrh, nuts, and almonds" (Genesis 43:11). The nuts he referred to were pistachios.

The Egyptians were especially fond of them, using the nuts as one of the ingredients in making sweetmeats and confectionery. However, as is often the case, some of their foods also doubled as effective medicines. In this instance, the outer shells of the pistachios, when they were in a "laughing" state or were naturally split open, were brewed in boiling water to make a tea for treating a medical condition, the described symptoms of which bore a close resemblance to what we today call dysentery.

When I first discovered this reference in an English translation of a very brittle medical papyrus estimated to be several millenniums old, I didn't give it much medical relevancy beyond being simply "cute and quaint." It wasn't very long after this that I had occasion to try this remedy for myself with amazing results.

Amedic dysentery is common in many Third World countries where good sanitation and hygiene aren't always practiced with the greatest of care. Infection with Entamoeba histolytica through bad food or water can be either mild or severe and is usually marked by diarrhea resulting from an ulcerative inflammation of the colon.

Fortunately, mine was very mild, but I still suffered a little from the effects of frequent watery stools mixed with some blood and mucus, as well as minor abdominal cramps, a slight fever, and brief dehydration. Being near an open-air marketplace in one of the suburbs of Cairo where I was staying at the time, I went in search of some garlic, first of all. Finding none, I then opted for some "laughing" pistachios and returned to the residence of my host.

I easily separated the kernels from their outside split shells with my thumb and forefinger. I then scooped up 2 handfuls of the outer husks, put them in a pint of water, and brought them to a boil. I reduced the heat and simmered them, uncovered, for about 15 minutes. After permitting the liquid to cool awhile, I strained it out and slowly drank a full 8-ounce glass of the lukewarm tea. This was sometime in the afternoon. I drank another glass at about 9:30 P.M., before retiring to bed.

I'm happy to report after all these years that Egyptian doctors some three millenniums ago knew *exactly* what they were talking about. The ancient remedy worked, believe it or not! I had no further recurrence of diarrhea, my cramps disappeared, and my fever dissipated. What I had copied down as mere folklore turned out to be a genuine medical fact!

Say "Nuts!" to Your Hypertension

An added bonus with pistachios is that they are rich in potassium, phosphorus, and magnesium salts. These three elements combined are an effective treatment for controlling hypertension. Admittedly one can get sick of snacking on a cup of pistachios every single day. But certainly three or four times a week isn't going to hurt.

I'm speaking, of course, in regard to *fresh* pistachios and not to any canned or packaged nuts, which are generally deep-fried and salted and not good for you. The person who has high blood pressure and likes to snack can munch on something that will help to normalize the condition, besides satisfying the craving to eat.

A Control for Alcoholism

Nothing is an absolute, especially when it comes to dealing with a complex social problem such as alcoholism. Substance abuse of any kind always has to be dealt with from many different angles. Nutrition is just one of them.

Back in the 1960s, experiments were conducted with glutamic acid (GA) on alcoholics. One study with GA began by giving volunteers 2 grams 3 times a day for a total of 6 grams daily. In the second month it was increased to 12 grams, and in the third and fourth months, the dose was increased to 15 grams daily. When compared to a placebo, the number of patients reporting a definite control over their drinking habits was an incredible 75 percent!

As mentioned early in the nutritional information section, a cup of pistachios has about 6 grams of GA. Certainly, they should be included in the daily snack regimens of recovering alcoholics because of their nutritional benefits.

Increase Your Energy Production

All nuts and seeds are fantastic for energy needs due to their high lipid (fat) and protein contents. But pistachios give energy in an unusual way.

Glutamic acid forms an interesting partnership with gamma-aminobutyric acid (GABA) and glutamine (GAM) in making the reactions of the brain run more smoothly. GA is a stimulant neurotransmitter; GABA is calming to the brain; and GAM is difficult to classify simply because it performs many different functions related to brain metabolism.

But the nonessential amino acid GA has the highest concentration of all the amino acids in the brain. It helps in the production of *mental* energy more than anything else. So, if you're cramming for a test or involved in some other kind of situation where a sharp memory is absolutely essential, the ideal snack foods would be a ham sandwich and a cup of shelled pistachios. Between the two, you would be getting almost 20 grams of *pure* GA.

Not B-a-a-a-d for Flavoring Lamb

In the Middle East, roast lamb figures very prominently. Its flavor is greatly enhanced by the addition of pistachio nuts, which impart a very delicate, nutty flavor to the meat! Try it next time you serve lamb. It's pretty g-o-o-o-d!

POKEBERRY
(Phytolacca Americana)

BRIEF DESCRIPTION

Pokeberry or pokeroot is a very common, smooth perennial road-side weed in eastern and central North America. In the South it can be of large and considerable size sometimes, often reaching a height of 10 to 12 feet and a breadth nearly as great. The stems are thick and fleshy, often several inches in diameter, and acquire a reddish color as they get older. The bland, greenish-white flowers are arranged in drooping spikes which, in late summer, give way to drooping clusters of distinctive, rich, purple berries containing a beautiful magenta-colored juice.

The shoots and tender plant tops are a springtime favorite pot herb of the hillbilly folks in the Ozarks and the Appalachias. The plants are gathered fresh, coarsely cut up, and parboiled several times before being eaten. In mountain lingo they're referred to as "poke salet." When I first heard the term applied by one Zeke Jones in rural Kentucky, I just assumed we would be having a tossed poke salad with dressing for lunch. But imagine my surprise when the "salet" turned out to be cooked wild greens, overboiled with salt, pepper, and lots of hog fat! But it was d-e-l-i-c-i-o-u-s, nonetheless.

The root is very long, thick, and fleshy, considerably resembling horseradish root. I went with Zeke into an area of the Kentucky foothills where the soil was fine and sandy. With his spade he dug up a poke root that, when held alongside of my arm, was nearly as thick in circumference, believe it or not!

WARNING: The root and seeds of the fruit can be poisonous if consumed raw and in great quantities! Caution and wisdom should always be used when either part are to be used internally. But they both make wonderful medicines. Interestingly enough, the rich purple *juice* of the berries can be consumed without any problems, even in large amounts. Apparently the juice is *not* toxic, only the seeds in the berries are.

A Remarkable "Cure" for Cancer and Other Skin Diseases

I remember telling an oncologist once about a remarkable "cure" that Zeke and other mountain folks have been using for decades. This expert in cancer (properly called neoplasm in medical terminology, which signifies "new growth") laughed in my face after I informed him how the berries and large root of pokeweed were made into a type of black salve. "Dr. Heinerman," he said with the typical arrogance you naturally expect to find in some doctors these days, "you've spent too much time with the Hatfields and McCoys. I know they're good at feuding, but I seriously doubt if they know much about cancer." Pausing, he thought for a moment, then added: "Tell me, do some of them still sign their names with an 'X' or can most of them read and write by now?"

I fired right back with a couple of salvos of my own. "I can see why you've earned the title of M.D.—*M*ethodical *D*rivel. Or maybe it's '*M*annerless *D*octor,' perhaps? But I prefer to think it's probably the *M*ean *D*evil in your title coming out about now." And with those Don Rickles-type insults, I walked away in disgust.

Cancer, of course, should never be taken lightly. Any kind of cancer is to be considered serious. Several different diagnostic opinions from a medical doctor, a naturopath, a homeopath, an herbalist, and a nutritionist should be obtained before any type of treatment begins. It is also a good idea to go to a local library and look up the particular cancer in a reference book. The best one available that I recommend and use myself quite often in my own research center is a massive, two-volume, 1,918-page tome appropriately entitled, *Comprehensive Textbook of Oncology* (Baltimore: Williams & Wilkins, 1991). It is definitive in every sense of the word and will help someone with cancer understand more about the type and nature of the neoplasm involved.

Once an individual is armed with such scientific knowledge and understanding, then the next logical step is treatment itself. A wide range of options exist, some involving powerful drugs, surgery, and cobalt radiation, while others are along more natural lines and non-invasive but still requiring potent plants with toxic capabilities.

My publishers tend to get a little nervous whenever I freely discuss this topic in any of my books. It is a rather touchy subject for them, and their in-house "legal eagles" always scrutinize every single word I write about the matter, *especially* when it comes to the self-treatment parts. But their extra concern is both for the benefit of this author and his huge reading audience. They are trying to protect both of us, only in different ways.

For the record, though, cutaneous malignancies account for about 22 percent of all cancers; this includes basal and squamous cell carcinoma and the melanoma family. In plainer terms, such a collection of skin cancers occur mostly in older Caucasians between the ages of 50 and 70, with better than 80 percent of most lesions starting somewhere above the neck. Long-term exposure to the sun, careless eating and drinking habits, an indiscriminate lifestyle, and stress are the leading causes of most cutaneous malignancies.

The appearance of such lesions is extremely varied, and they progress through different stages of advancement. This is not the place to go into details; that's what doctors and medical textbooks specializing in cancer are for. My purpose here is to describe how one of the most effective herbal remedies known to man is made and used by a backward culture of limited education and technological skills. But among the primitive are often found some of the best "cures" for common diseases that the greatest minds in science and medicine still haven't been able to solve in spite of the billions of dollars appropriated by them for research.

My old grizzled and unshaven friend from the hills of Kentucky probably gave the best description for identifying cutaneous malignancies. "If it looks like a squashed raspberry, blackberry, or prune that's been stepped on and flattened out, then it's probably skin cancer for sure," Zeke said, turning his head sideways and spitting out a stream of tobacco juice.

He showed me how they make the famous "black salve" known in those parts to "cure" just about any kind of external cancer. "They come from all over to get it from us," he said. First, he mashed up two cups of ripe pokeberries. Next, he washed off part of a large piece of pokeroot about the size of a big carrot, then finely grated it. In an old saucepan he melted $1 \frac{1}{2}$ cups of vegetable shortening. "Hog lard is just as good," he offered. Then he turned into the pot his mixture of berries and grated root. "I sometimes will throw in a couple of tablespoons of powdered golden seal root," he added. "Seems to help the formula work better." He stirred the mixture thoroughly with an old tire iron (I recommend a clean wooden ladle). "I like putting a little of this in," he grinned, and added what I judged to be $\frac{1}{4}$ cup of moonshine; afterwards. he threw his head back and guzzled some himself. Offering the jug to me, I politely declined. "Keeps the stuff from turning bad on you," he explained. (In lieu of moonshine, I suggest some vodka or whiskey, which acts as a preservative.)

After everything was well mixed, my informant poured the contents into a small empty coffee can that had been washed out prior to this. "Just let it set up until the grease hardens, before you put the plastic lid on," he said. Mr. Jones kept his supply in a cool dry place.

This black salve can be rubbed onto the cancer lesion with the back of a metal spoon, a popsicle stick, butter knife, or two fingers held together. We went down the long, winding road where every half mile or so were some of his neighbors who have been using this salve for generations. Elderly men and women pointed to their foreheads or faces where they had routinely applied this medicine with apparently very good success. "Them sores come and go with the sun" one oldster told us, "but the salve always helps them go away after that."

What more can I say, except that the remedy *works!* In the hills of Kentucky, they call it a cancer *cure* for sure, but in this book it has to be qualified with quotation marks (as in "cure") and adequate explanation so that readers know it is a *folk* remedy and not an approved medical treatment by any means.

Nevertheless, the stuff works and is also used for treating syphilitic sores, herpes lesions, shingles, ringworm, scabies, diabetic leg ulcers, and gangrene.

POPPY SEED
(Papaver Somniferum)

BRIEF DESCRIPTION

The poppy seed sprinkled on bread and cakes or included in various sweet stuffings comes from an annual ornamental with large white, pink, or lilac flowers. When the green unripe seed pods of the plant are slit, a gummy latex oozes forth that contains two dozen different alkaloids that are of considerable interest to doctors but I hope not to cooks. This is the potent narcotic known as opium to which millions of people worldwide are addicted. But when poppy seeds become ripe they no longer contain these powerful alkaloids.

There are many varieties of opium poppy and two quite different types of poppy seed. The type commonly met with in Europe is like blue-gray shot, but the seed usually seen in India is much smaller and a creamy yellow. From the point of view of flavor, there is really very little difference between the two.

Tea Helps with Breathlessness

Stanley Eubank, a freshman at a Midwestern university, loves to play collegiate football. He was having trouble with his running speed on account of his shortness of breath. Someone recommended poppy seed tea, which he made by simmering one-half teaspoon of seeds in one cup of boiling water on low heat for five minutes. He strained it and drank a cup of the *warm* tea 5 times daily for several days prior to his next game. Imagine his surprise when he discovered that he wasn't so shortwinded anymore and could run greater distances without any problems!

Poppy Seed for Insomnia

Stanley also reported that the same tea, drunk *warm* every evening before retiring, enabled him to get a better night's sleep than he otherwise could. He made the tea the same way as he did for his problem of breathlessness. Only he took *two* cups an hour before going to bed. He said that in the first couple of days he didn't notice any difference to speak of. But within a week's time he was sleeping like a baby after taking this tea.

CAUTION: Poppy seed is widely used in the Ayuvedic medicine of India and Pakistan. It is also a common culinary item in many favorite dishes of Indian cuisine. However, because of its highly potent nature, it is generally employed with other herbs and then, only in very small amounts. The cooking or baking of the poppy seeds renders them safer for consumption, which explains why Mr. Eubank benefited from his remedy without unpleasant results.

PSYLLIUM SEED
(Plantago Psyllium, P. Ovata)

BRIEF DESCRIPTION

Plantago psyllium has erect and branched stems, while *P. ovata* is nearly stemless. Both are native to the Mediterranean region, however.

Parts used are the dried ripe seed and its husk, a thin membranous layer on the seed coat. When soaked in water, the seed increases in volume manyfold but contracts to its original volume when excess alcohol is added.

Metamucil Cuts Elevated Cholesterol

An over-the-counter bowel regulator may also help to regulate cholesterol levels in the people who take it. In a study by James W. Anderson, M.D., a professor at the University of Kentucky College of Medicine, 26 men with elevated cholesterol levels took either a standard dose of Metamucil or an inactive lookalike 3 times a day. After just two months of treatment, serum cholesterol dropped an average of 15–20 percent in the men who took Metamucil. A cholesterol reduction of that magnitude would be enough to bring many people's cholesterol levels into the safe range.

The active ingredient in Metamucil is the plant fiber derived from the husks and seeds of psyllium. According to an interview I had with Dr. Anderson in November 1987, it could lower cholesterol by several mechanisms. One way, he said, is by increasing bile-acid excretion. Bile acids are digestive substances that are made from cholesterol. Normally, they are reabsorbed from the intestine after they do their job. But when they're excreted instead, the body has to take cholesterol out of the blood to make more. Psyllium may also slow cholesterol production by the liver, to help the cells elim-inate bad (low density lipoprotein) cholesterol, the kind believed to be responsible for clogging arteries.

Dr. Anderson told me by phone that he saw Metamucil or other psyllium seed products as an auxiliary treatment when diet alone doesn't bring blood cholesterol levels down enough. He said they may have distinct advantages over potent cholesterol-lowering drugs, which often have undesirable side effects.

Texas Farmer Stays Healthy with Psyllium Seed Drink

I've known the Robert Tipton family in Plainview, Texas, since 1984. He is farmer by trade and raises corn, cotton, and soybeans. I've been a guest in his home many times and have worshipped at Calvary Temple, a local Pentecostal church, with his wife Dora and their two sons, John and Joe.

Some years ago Dora became involved with a multilevel herb company and then eventually quit that to run her own health-food store for awhile. That was probably about the time she persuaded her husband to use psyllium seed. Every time I've been a guest in their home I've never failed to see Robert drink his healthful con-coction sometime in the evening before going to bed.

Robert would mix about one heaping tablespoonful of the featherlike, tasteless seeds and seed hulls in an eight-ounce glass of fruit or vegetable juice and drink it down. He told me that it helped him from becoming obese, diabetic, or constipated. I've seen evi-dence in the published medical literature that bears out these claims.

PUMPKIN SEED
(Cucurbita Pepo)

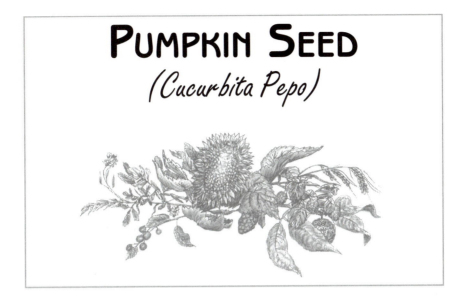

BRIEF DESCRIPTION

Pumpkins have been a dietary staple of Native American cultures since ancient times. Consider, for instance, the Moche civilization, which flourished on the north coast of Peru between the first and eighth centuries A.D. They were the first to implement a type of state government in the Andes, complete with municipalities, class divisions, politicians, and taxes. Their culture was centered in the Moche Valley.

Although they left no writing system, the Moche left a vivid artistic record of their activities, environment, and supernatural realm. Their extraordinary ceramics depict animals, plants, and anthropomorphic deities, and individuals engaged in hunting, fishing, combat, and elaborate ceremonies. Mocha metalworkers made remarkable jewelry and ornaments of gold, silver, and copper. Weavers created sumptuously decorated textiles of cotton and wool, and artisans carved and inlaid bone, wood, and stone, and painted colorful murals.

One particularly intriguing tapestry panel shows a couple of farmers holding what appears to be pumpkins. One kind of ceramic bottle depicting a human figure shows a seated man holding part

235

of a pumpkin in his hand. Moche burial sites have turned up skeletal remains covered with cloth and adorned with necklaces and bracelets. In the mouths of some were found small oval or circular sheets of gold. Beside these skeletons had been placed pottery or gourds that had been filled with funerary offerings, consisting of meat, pumpkin, pumpkin seeds, maize, mollusks, snails, birds, and so forth. It is clear from the archaeological evidence amassed that pumpkin and its seeds played a very important role in this ancient culture.

Marginal tribes of South American Indians residing in the Argentine pampa and the Uruguayan plains in modern times have depended upon the fruit and its flat, oblong, gently tapered seeds for food as well as for medicine. Consider the Chaco Indians and the various subtribes affiliated with them who inhabit this region. At harvest time, they make winter provisions out of pumpkins. The pumpkins are cut into halves, which are sun dried or smoked on a wooden platform. The seeds are roasted. Some Chaco subtribes boil the pumpkin seeds, pound them with a mortar, and then boil them again until they turn into a thick mush. Such preserved foods are later heaped into some corner of a hut or else stored in special granaries to keep rodents out.

The influence of shamans in Chaco communities was once considerable. Some shamans performed "miracles" to increase their prestige. An old anthropologist from Montevideo, Uruguay, informed me some years ago that he had witnessed one such shaman pounding a number of pumpkin seeds to a pulp in a stone mortar, after which he thoroughly rubbed the soles of both feet with them in private so no one else could see what he was doing. Then, much to the amazement of his tribal band, he proceeded to walk about on the hot ashes of a large fire that had just been used to roast a wild boar.

Pumpkins have always been a mainstay of different Indian tribes in the American Southwest. In the last century the Mescalero Apache would often construct a raft made of bulrush or cane, floated and supported on the water by some two or three dozen hollowed out pumpkin shells fastened together. The Apaches, Comanches, and Pueblos enjoyed frequent amusements in the forms of feasting, drinking, dancing, singing, and making music. There were cornstalk or cane flutes and wooden drums. Sometimes empty pumpkin shells were filled with pebbles and shaken to a constantly varying time, as singers would drone out impromptu songs in monotonous tones; this was a common form of entertainment with the Yuma Indians.

In Volume 1 of Hubert Howe Bancroft's *The Native Races* (San Francisco: A. L. Bancroft & Co., 1882; pp. 577; 625–626) there is given a very clever and rather novel way of duck hunting, using empty pumpkin shells. The Laguna Indians of southern California would cut the tops off pumpkins and carefully scoop out the interior contents. Then they would make holes in one side of the shells and invert them upside down over their heads. Through these slits they could both see and breathe. Very quietly then they would enter the water behind clumps of reeds or pussy willows and slowly float toward flocks of unsuspecting ducks. The only thing noticeable to the birds were different pumpkin shells gently bobbing up and down. By this artful deception Laguna braves were able to reach up with their bare hands and grab the ducks by both feet and pull them down under the water, where they quickly wrung their necks.

A Zuni Indian Cure for Tapeworm and Roundworm

Having been among the Zuñi Indians of Arizona in times past to do research, I discovered a very simple but highly effective way of getting rid of certain intestinal parasites. Zuñi women remove the seeds from pumpkins and place them on a tray to dry in the sun. After this the seeds are put into a bowl of some kind and just enough vegetable oil is poured over them to lightly coat them. The hands are used for mixing the oil with the seeds. Sometimes a little salt is added for flavor. Next the oiled seeds are spread on a metal tray and put into a 250° oven. The women stir the seeds occasionally with a long wooden spoon or metal spatula during the roasting process. The seeds are removed when they start turning brown.

Not only are these seeds consumed as a delicious and healthful snack treat, but they are also chewed by anyone, young or old alike, who may be bothered with tapeworm, roundworm, and other intestinal parasites. The equivalent of two cups of roasted pumpkin seeds is methodically chewed every day for a week on an empty stomach. Usually within that period of time, the worms will break loose from the intestinal tract and be discharged through the colon.

The same kind of remedy was recommended to my father many years ago by an old naturopathic doctor when it was discovered that I had a bad case of tapeworm around the age of nine or ten. Although I thoroughly detested every chewed mouthful, those seeds helped me to get rid of my long parasite. What this shows is not only that pumpkin seeds make a terrific vermifuge, but also that different cultures can come up with the same remedy completely independently of each other.

Great for Gout

A rancher just outside Santa Fe, New Mexico, told me a while back when I spoke at a chile festival in that city how he had utilized pumpkin seeds to help him get rid of his gout.

"It got really bad here and here," he explained, while at the same time pointing to his ankles and knees I was in so much pain, I couldn't stand on my feet for very long. And walking even a short distance would just about kill me. Got so I had to start using a wheelchair to cut down the hurt and still be able to move about. It was damn frustrating is all I can say."

Then someone told him about an old Pueblo medicine man, who had a reputation for curing people. "I went to him and told him what my problem was," the rancher continued. "I didn't have to do much explaining, because at the sight of me in my wheelchair, he knew I was in bad shape. He told my wife, who pushed me inside his house, to make a tea from pumpkin seeds and have me drink that 7 times a day instead of regular water. We thanked him for his advice and went back home. She made me a quart of tea at a time by boiling 5 cups of water and then adding $1\frac{1}{2}$ cups of pumpkin seeds. She left the pot uncovered and simmered the seeds on low heat for what I'd judge to be about 25 minutes. After her brew had sufficiently cooled, she strained the liquid into a big plastic pitcher and put it in the refrigerator. She made me drink one coffee cup of that funny tasting stuff every two hours or so.

"It may taste like crap, but I'll tell you this, doc," he finished with his story, "it sure as hell reduced my swollen knees and ankles and took away all the damned pain, so I could get out of that stupid wheelchair and walk again!"

RASPBERRY
(Rubus Idaeus)

BRIEF DESCRIPTION

Of all the raspberries, the red raspberry is the best known and most beloved. This cherished plant has arching canes that can extend as long as six feet, and sometimes they have a slight whitish tinge. An obliging shrub, the red raspberry doesn't even have as many prickles as other Rubus species, such as the blackberry. In the wild, it can be found growing on rocky hillsides and also in clearings. Even its leaves point to its sweet nature: they are heart-shaped at the base and have a whitened, downy underside. Raspberry leaves were brewed as tea by American colonists; the drink was known as Hyperion tea, named for the Grecian father of the sun god, for raspberries thrive on sunlight.

The red raspberry's flowers are a lovely white and blossom from May to July. The fruits, growing in fragrant bouquets, ripen from July through September. In North America, the hardy red raspberry may be found growing from Newfoundland to British Columbia, down through the Midwest, and south to North Carolina. It is especially prolific in California, where it boldly fruits into November, daunted only by the first frost. In the eastern states, 'Latham,' an early-to-midseason mainstay, is the grandfather of cul-

239

tivated red raspberries. In the West, berry connoisseurs are more likely to encounter the dependable, sturdy midseason 'Williamette' and the two-crop 'Heritage,' although the latter also grows well in the East. The red raspberry is equally hardy in northern Europe because it thrives in cool climates. Red raspberry varieties often seen in the British kitchen garden are 'Malling Jewel,' 'Glen Clova,' and 'Malling Admiral'—easily harvested and resistant to blight.

Most cultivated red raspberries are the result of crosses between the Eurasian species *R. idaeus* and the American native *R. strigosus* and are so finely melded that they are usually grouped under the European nomenclature. Even botanists are perplexed by the red raspberry's comings and goings. Cultivated European raspberries escaped from New England gardens centuries ago; they mingled with native red raspberries and produced their own transatlantic lineage.

Three other types of raspberries worthy of mentioning are the purple-flowering, the black, and the rare golden kinds. The first lacks the hooked prickles of red raspberry, and its fruits aren't as sweet as other raspberries. The second is often mistaken for a blackberry; when unripe, it can also masquerade as a red or even a yellow raspberry. Mountain folk of Appalachia harvest this ebony berry for preserves, wines, and liqueurs. The rare golden is, botanically speaking, really the same species as the red raspberry. A result of crosses between reds and native yellow Asian raspberries, it has merely lost its pigmentation. But it makes up for its lack of ruby color with a flavor that is infinitely sweeter than that of the red type.

Fight the Flu and Common Cold

Dr. Jaroslva Kresánek practiced medicine for many years in the former Czechoslovakia. While using some Western drugs and surgery for the more difficult cases he encountered, he was also very much a strong advocate of natural remedies. He believed that for common complaints, turning to herbs and foods was better for the body than simply writing a prescription.

For many years he has been using the fruit and leaves of red raspberry in decoction form to treat the common cold and flu in many of his patients. He discovered early on in his research that this combination worked best when it was sipped while still quite warm.

The addition of a small dose of rum helped to strip accumulated mucus from the bronchial tubes and sinus cavities, so it could be expectorated from the body.

Dr. Kresánek's recipe for making this incredible antibiotic tea is very simple. He shared it with me some years ago when we briefly met during a tour I made of the former Iron Curtain countries. Boil 1 quart of water. Remove from the heat. Add two tablespoons each fresh or dried berries and cut leaves. Mix well, cover, and let the brew steep for 25 minutes. Uncover, strain, and pour one 8-ounce glass. Add 1 teaspoon of brandy, stir, and slowly sip so as not to burn the mouth or tongue. Repeat every couple of hours until recovery is imminent.

By doing it this way. the loss of vitamin C is minimized. And by adding the alcohol just before drinking, it prevents its evaporation.

Childbirth Made Easy

The following anecdote in an abbreviated form appeared in *Heinerman's Encyclopedia of Fruits, Vegetables and Herbs* (West Nyack, NY: Parker Publishing Co., Inc., 1988, p 38). I believe it deserves to be repeated here in its original expanded form the way I received it.

A Mormon mother of nine children residing in West Jordan, Utah (who asked that I never divulge her name) had her virtually *pain-free* deliveries after her second child when she started drinking red raspberry leaf tea on a regular basis.

She made the tea by boiling a quart of water, turning off the heat, adding 6 tablespoons of dried raspberry leaves, covering the pot with a lid, and letting it steep for 40 minutes. She would drink a cup each day for the first eight months of her pregnancy. And when the nausea of morning sickness would set in, she would double her intake.

In the last month or a couple of weeks prior to the estimated delivery time, she would drink *four* cups of strong *hot* tea, always in between meals. Due to lack of space in my first *Encyclopedia*, I wasn't able to mention that her husband even brought her several thermos bottles full of the hot tea when she was admitted to the hospital a couple of days ahead of each delivery.

Other women with whom she shared rooms each time she was in to have another delivery always complained to her about how much suffering they endured during their labor periods. "But for me," she stated with a smile, "it was always a moment of joy, always a pleasant experience without hardship." That's what hot red raspberry leaf tea did for her multiple pregnancies.

ROSEHIPS
(Rosa Species)

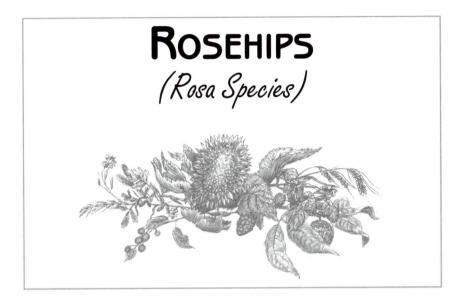

BRIEF DESCRIPTION

For many centuries, gardeners have adored the gorgeous aromatic flowers of the rose, but they have also prized the hips. These are the oval or rounded fruits of the rose that appear in late summer and fall. A rose hip is actually a receptacle that encloses the true fruits of the plant, called the *achenes,* or "seeds." Some linguists contend that the original English word for rose was *hip.*

Rosehips were once regarded as sacred. In fact, during the Middle Ages, the Catholic rosary was so named because rosehips were once used to count the prayers as they were being said. Come to think of it, the beads of the rosary do, indeed, resemble smooth, elongated rosehips, similar to the graceful fruits adorning many species of roses.

In general, species roses are easier to care for than hybrids, and they also tend to produce more succulent hips for eating. So if your intention is culinary as well as ornamental, you might wish to cultivate plants from this group. If you plant climbing roses and want them to fruit, remember to *not* prune them directly after their summer flowering.

Rosehips will usually remain on the plant throughout the early part of the winter or until birds, rabbits, and field mice have eaten or stored them. The hips have a zesty acidic but fruity taste, due to the rich amount of ascorbic acid present. Fresh rosehips contain 60 times as much vitamin C as oranges, and rugosa roses, with their large round fruits, are considered to have one of the highest contents. I've had the pleasure of eating some of them raw in the dead of winter in the high Uintah Mountains here in Utah. I ate only the walls of the hips and spit the seeds. I found them to have quite an exciting taste in the cold weather.

Preventing Infection

Treating infectious diseases when you have them is one thing, but trying to prevent them before they occur is even better. In parts of Europe rosehip syrup has long been a popular tradition for keeping the immune system strong enough so infections don't start. A French horticulturist, while admiring his lovely rose hedge, commented one time, "When I was very young my mother would give me a tablespoonful of rosehip syrup every day to keep me well. I never got sick that I can recall."

If you want to remain free from sickness, here is a time-honored recipe from a resident of Der Hague in the Netherlands. Translated from the Dutch, he writes, "Use about 1 $\frac{1}{2}$ pounds of rosehips for every 5 pints of distilled water. Mince the hips after removing the stalk and calyces. Cover with water and boil, then strain through a jelly bag. Reduce the liquid to approximately half of what it was before, add 2 cups of honey, and boil for 5 minutes to sterilize. Pour this mixture into sterilized bottles and seal up right away with sterilized screw top lids."

Rosehip tea is excellent for treating present infections. In a pint of hot water, steep 2 tablespoons of dried rosehips, covered, for 20 minutes. But DO NOT COOK or else the vitamin C, which is heat-sensitive, will be substantially reduced. Strain and drink 4 cups daily on an empty stomach.

ROWANBERRY
(Srobus Aucuparia)

BRIEF DESCRIPTION

The rowan, or European mountain ash, as it is sometimes known, was once considered one of the most magical plants in the wood, and it was planted liberally in northern countries. (Don't be misled by its common name, as it's not even related to the common ash, *Fraxinus excelsior*, but is actually in the same family as hawthorns and apples.) This striking tree, a native of Europe and western Asia, can grow to 50 feet or more and yields sour-tasting orange or scarlet berries in late summer.

More than 80 different species of deciduous trees and shrubs of the mountain ashes are distributed throughout the northern hemisphere. Their graceful foliage, showy flowers, and brightly colored fruits make them especially sought after for ornamental plantings. Birds and rodents thrive on the berries, while deer, moose, and elk enjoy browsing on the tender twigs. The strong, close-grained wood is sometimes used for specialty products.

Rowanberries have been held in deep esteem by northern peoples for many centuries. The Celts believed that the fruit could protect them against witches' spells. In the Scandinavian countries the berries were believed to hold magical charms. One such Finnish-

245

Russian belief suggested that if you were forced to spend the night
in the woods alone, sleeping beneath a rowan tree or on a pillow
of rowan boughs was the best protection against demonic influences.

Excruciating Sore Throat and Tonsillitis Cured

I met Mary Elizabeth Harker several years ago in London, England,
while attending an international health-food fair. Nearly all the
countries of the European Commonwealth were represented,
including some that aren't members. She had purchased one of my
New Age books, *Spiritual Wisdom of the Native American* (San
Rafael, CA: Cassandra Press, 1989) at a metaphysical book shop
somewhere in Liverpool and enjoyed it very much.

Because I had included several chapters on early Native
American remedies, she wondered if I was interested in hearing her
own recovery story with the use of plants. I indicated that I was
always on the prowl for new material to use in later writings. We
found a quiet place to talk, and I got out my little spiral notebook
I carried in my shirt pocket to jot in.

When she was 23 years old, Mary came down with a severe
cold. She took various herbal teas for it, including catnip and ver-
vain. These reduced her headache, runny nose, and slight fever, but
failed to improve her throat. "It was so tender and sore," she added,
"that even swallowing the teas proved difficult for me." Consulting
a medical herbalist (licensed practitioners permitted to diagnose and
prescribe by law), she was informed the infection had escalated into
tonsillitis.

This nature doctor prescribed ripe rowanberry juice as a gargle
every two hours during the day. The acidic and astringent properties of the berries soon reduced the swelling. Within three days the
inflammation totally disappeared and she was able to eat and drink
again as normal.

St. Johnswort Berry
(Hypericum Perforatum)

Brief Description

European lore has it that anyone who picks St. Johnswort on June 23, Saint John's Eve (also called Midsummer Eve), will have the power to see witches holding their traditional yearly festivities on Saint John's Day (Midsummer Day)—and consequently be able to avoid them. People commonly climbed to the roofs of their homes to get a bird's-eye view into the landscape to spot the hags. Perhaps this is what gave rise to the custom of placing wreaths fashioned from St. Johnswort on the rooftops of homes as a general projection against evil.

The purported powers of St. Johnswort are not limited to its namesake's day. In many European regions it was commonly planted by the door, hung up in the house, or burned in midsummer fires to ensure protection from the dark forces.

With so much intrigue surrounding St. Johnswort, it seems to deserve a place in the average home garden. Many a gardener has already been charmed by this herb, which is easily cultivated and can grow in partial shade. At home in the rock garden or the border, perhaps planted in the foreground of a stone wall, this unassuming undershrub is a joy to have in the garden. In midsummer its yellow flowers perk up the garden. Its natural habitat is woodlands and meadows.

Its foliage spreads thickly on the ground, prompting fussy gardeners to dub it a "weed"; however, if it's kept in check, it grows very nicely and agreeably. But it is the berries—known as *capsules* in botanical terms—that make St. Johnswort such a cherished plant. They can be a nice counterpoint to the tiny flowers and foliage of dwarf sedums and other low-growing rock garden plants. St. Johnswort berries turn from red to black as they mature and have been used to create a rustic effect when paired with flowers and greens in vases or wreaths for autumn decorations.

Cure for Bedwetting

Otto Günter plays the accordion in a *Hofbräuhaus* in Hamburg, Germany, where dark brew flows freely, the *Bier Steins* are never empty, and the packed crowd sings with a great deal of rousing merriment. He and his wife have two children, a boy of four and a girl of six. But for more than a year their son suffered from euresis, mostly due to nightmares.

Some psychological counseling helped curb this embarrassment to some extent, but there were still occasional recurrences, which were attributed to physiological causes. They conferred with a *natur Arzt* who prescribed for their young son a tea made from equal parts of St. Johnswort berry and sumac berry. This nature doctor instructed them to heat a pint of water to the boiling point, then to add two-thirds level teaspoons each of the dried berries of both herbs. Cover with a lid, reduce heat to a lower setting, and simmer for three minutes. Turn off the heat entirely and steep for an hour.

One-half cup of tea was strained and given, lukewarm, to the boy about two hours before bedtime. Within nine days his euresis problem stopped for good.

Depression and Anxiety Easily Treated

Many people are inclined toward melancholy moods that can leave them feeling depressed. Such negative "anxiety attacks" are more prone in women than in men. Some German doctors, who incorporate elements of natural healing in their individual practices, utilize a combination of St. Johnswort berries and valerian root to successfully treat those of their patients suffering from these psychological difficulties.

If the fluid extracts or tinctures are employed, then 15 drops of each herb are blended with 2 tablespoons of water and taken on an empty stomach. A quick and easy method of making a tincture is to combine $\frac{1}{2}$ teaspoon each of powdered St. Johnswort berries and valerian root in $\frac{1}{2}$ cup of brandy or vodka. Then dilute this solution with an equal amount of water. Put into a jar and let stand for 10 days, shaking twice a day; strain and pour the liquid into a bottle suitable for storage.

In some cases a decoction of both herbs is prescribed. Boil 1 quart of water. Reduce the heat and add 1 $\frac{1}{2}$ tablespoons each of dried St. Johnswort berries and cut, dried valerian root. Cover with a lid and simmer for 10 minutes. Remove from the heat and simmer for 30 minutes. Strain and drink one cup in between meals twice daily. Flavor with pure maple syrup or honey if necessary.

Wonderful Wound and Burn Dressing

A common German remedy for taking care of serious wounds is St. Johnswort oil. The oil is made by saturating crushed fresh flowers and pulverized berries of the plant with just enough sunflower seed, flaxseed, or olive oil to cover. This mixture should be made well in advance of anticipated emergencies and placed in a tightly sealed plastic bowl and stored at a moderate temperature for about six weeks. By then the oil will have acquired a dark red color.

Gauze compresses are soaked in this oil and applied like an ointment dressing, except that they need to be changed frequently. Good results have been obtained even with serious burns, following application of tampons soaked in this oil, to which has been added some onion juice. The oil-soaked dressings may remain *in situ* for up to a week and cause no pain upon removal.

CAUTION: St. Johnswort may cause photo-sensitivity in fair-skinned people.

SAW PALMETTO BERRY
(Serenoa Repens)

BRIEF DESCRIPTION

Saw palmetto usually appears as a stout, evergreen shrub with creeping horizontal stems. Occasionally, however, the species manages to attain the size of a small tree with an erect to oblique stem. The common name is derived from the ascending, palm-shaped leaves, which are rather stiff, with long petioles heavily armed with sharp, rigid, recurved teeth. Saw palmetto occurs from coastal South Carolina southward to Florida and westward to eastern Louisiana. It reaches its most extensive development in the pine flatwoods of the lower coastal plain of Georgia and Florida.

Saw palmetto provides wildlife habitat, and several species of wildlife consume the fruit. Large quantities of saw palmetto leaves are shipped north for Christmas decorations. The flowers are a significant source of honey, and the stems a source of tannic acid extract. The small white flowers are borne in panicles from April to early June, depending on the latitude. They appear on branches that are shorter than the leaves and that are usually numerous.

The fruit is a drupe, oval to oblong shaped, green or yellow before ripening, and bluish to black when fully matured. It contains a single globose seed. The odor of the berry is peculiar, somewhat cheesy, and not too agreeable. It has a sweet-sour flavor to it.

Popular Remedy for Benign Prostatic Hypertrophy

Saw palmetto berry is a very popular treatment for benign prostatic hypertrophy, a common problem in older men. Generally, it is taken in capsule form (3 daily), but also works equally well as a tea (1 cup daily) or tincture (15 drops twice daily beneath the tongue).

Antidote to Allergic Reactions

Richard Forman, an industrial engineer in Duluth, Minnesota, corresponded with me several years ago. He had been suffering from allergic rhinitis for quite some time. Repeated visits to different doctors in his city had not produced any real satisfying results. While the various antihistamines and decongestants that they had placed him on managed to reduce the severity of his symptoms, they failed to completely eradicate them.

The spring and summer months were the worst for him, he stated in his letter. His usual symptoms were as follows: a pattern of violent sneezing; watery nasal discharge; red, tearing, itchy eyes; nasal congestion; and an itchy sensation in the back of his throat and on the roof of his mouth.

I advised him to take three gelatin capsules of powdered saw palmetto berries twice daily with meals. I strongly encouraged him to avoid any foods high in sugar. Sugar, I said, was the main culprit of allergic reactions; remove it from the diet and 65 percent of the symptoms automatically disappear without the aid of herbs or vitamin-mineral supplements.

I wrote back that if the capsules didn't work, he had the option of making a tea. I told him to steep 1 tablespoon of dried saw palmetto berries in 1 $\frac{1}{2}$ cups of hot water, covered, for 20 minutes. He was to take 3 cups of this daily. Or if that didn't work, he had the additional option of making a tincture by combining one level tablespoon of the powdered berries in a 50 percent alcohol solution (1 cup each of vodka and distilled water) for 10 days, shaking twice daily. After straining, he was told to take between 30 and 60 drops a day beneath the tongue.

Some time went by before I heard anything more from him. Then, after getting home from my research center one night around 9:00 P.M., I received a long-distance telephone call from Duluth. It was Mr. Forman, calling to refresh my mind on who he was and then thanking me for helping him. He said he tried the different rec-ommended preparations for the berries without making a parallel change in his eating habits. He claimed that the saw palmetto helped him somewhat, but not as much as he expected.

He was getting rather discouraged while just on the herbal therapy and admitted to wanting to quit the program altogether. But his wife reminded him that I had *also* said to avoid sugar in *any* form. So with renewed determination, he accepted this dietary chal-lenge, though, "my craving for sweets darn near drove me insane," he wrote. But now that he was putting into practice *both* things, he discovered how quickly his allergic reactions diminished. "Within days I felt relief, could breathe better and see better," he explained. "And as long as I stay away from sweets and take the saw palmet-to capsules I manage just fine," he concluded.

His letter is not only a real testimony to the power of saw pal-metto berries to control allergies, but also evidence of the fact that there always *must be changes* in lifestyle habits such as food and drink preferences if recuperation from a particularly bad problem is to be total and not just partial.

SERVICEBERRY
(Amelanchier Species)

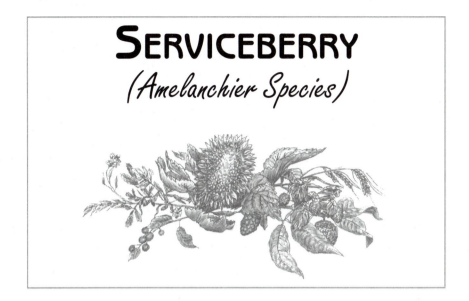

BRIEF DESCRIPTION

Serviceberries include about 25 species of small deciduous trees and shrubs native to North America, Europe, and Asia. Most species provide browse and edible fruits for domestic livestock such as cattle and sheep and wildlife such as deer and elk. Many species have attractive white flowers, which appear in terminal clusters early in the spring, before the leaves do (this is only in some species however).

The fruits are berrylike pomes that turn dark purple or black when they ripen. Each fruit contains from 4 to 10 small seeds, although some of these are usually abortive. The early Winnebago Indians prized the berries for food, calling them *Haz-shutsh* (*haz,* fruit; *shutsh,* red).

Saskatoon serviceberry (*A. alnifolia*) is one of the more common species. Its conspicuous white flowers, with their quintets of strap-shaped petals, decorate many of North America's shrubs and trees in the spring of each year. Having about twenty stamens, appearing in short duration in long, slender assemblies, the white flowers are often so thick and showy that their parent trees and shrubs many times seem rimed with frost and snow, silhouetting them against abrupt slopes and swarthy undergrowth. Saskatoon fruit is similar to blueberry in color, but with the rose family's distinctive five-pronged pucker at its summit. Saskatoon fruit is actually an applelike pome rather than a berry per se. Ten large seeds give an almondlike flavor when they are dried or cooked to the otherwise rather insipid berries.

The saskatoon differs markedly from other serviceberries in the fact that its fruit and ovary are separated into chambers, each of which holds a single seed. The filiform prolongation of the plant ovary bearing a stigma at its top, however, usually numbers five. The petals are much narrower than those in the other serviceberry species. Rather than being arranged in a cluster, the fruit ascends the small branches one by one.

Blurred Vision Improved

One of my Native American informants from the Crow Agency in eastern Montana, Joy Yellowtail Toineeta, told me this story some years ago during the time I spent with her. A grandson had been out canoeing in mid-July for a number of hours with friends on a river. The sun's rays high overhead constantly reflected off the top of the water into their faces. By the time their trip was finished, each man suffered from sore eyes. Joy's grandson's vision was especially blurry on account of the strong glare.

He came to his grandmother for help. Joy made an infusion of the berries and inner bark by simmering half handfuls of each in about 1 $^1/_2$ pints of water for approximately 20 minutes. When sufficiently cooled, some of this infusion was strained and used to wash the grandson's eyes every 30 minutes. Joy also laid a cool poultice of the tea over each closed eyelid. By the next day, the young man's vision was again 20/20.

I should add here that this same remedy also works well for snow blindness, which isn't blindness at all but rather inflammation caused from too long exposure to the continued shine and glint of ice and snow on insufficiently protected eyes. (Interestingly enough, snow blindness can be incurred on an overcast day and even through the canvas of a tent. Always be sure to wear tinted or dark glasses when spending any length of time in the outdoors.) Joy's infusion always gives relief from visual discomfort incurred from dust during farm work (such as plowing a field, for instance) or traveling in dry weather on landscape that has very little vegetation.

Diarrhea Stopped

Several of Joy's customers who came to her for medical services while I was a guest in her home happened to have been elderly Native Americans. Two men and a woman each suffered from prolonged watery stools. Joy picked enough serviceberries, while they were still *unripe,* to fill 2 measuring cups; these she added to 1 $\frac{1}{2}$ quarts of water and gently simmered for about half an hour. When cool, she gave a strained pint to each of them with instructions to drink half cupfuls every 4 to 6 hours. She told me that after the berries have fully matured, they lose their astringent quality and are no longer useful for treating diarrhea.

Loss of Appetite Improved

Among the early Cheyenne serviceberries were often employed to create a sensation of hunger in young children or the elderly who had experienced loss of appetite, usually due to sickness of some sort. Squaws would gather the ripe berries, mash them well, and then spoon-feed them to ailing kids or adults. In more recent times, serviceberries have been juiced and slowly sipped from a cup for the same purpose. Not only do the berries provide nourishment, but they also stimulate appetite as well.

Chippewa Gynecological Aid for Female Problems

In the first quarter of the present century, ethnologist Frances Densmore spent a great deal of time interviewing Chippewa Indian men and women on the White Earth, Red Lake, Cass Lake, Leech Lake, and Millie Lac reservations in Minnesota, on the Lac Court Oeilles Reservation in Wisconsin, and on the Manitou Rapids Reserve in Ontario, Canada. His field notes were eventually compiled into a lengthy scientific article, "Uses of Plants by the Chippewa Indians," which appeared in the *44th Annual Report (1926–1927) of the Bureau of American Ethnology* (Washington, DC: U.S. Government Printing Office, 1928, pp. 281–368).

Many of his principal informants were medicine *women* or *female* shamans, who practiced the combined arts of healing and magic simultaneously among their people. Most notable were three women, in particular: Mcmacka'wanamo'kwe (Woman with a powerful respiration) from White Earth, Minnesota, who was married to a Mr. Agness; Meya'wigobiwîk (Standing strongly) from Red Lake, Minnesota, who was married to a Mr. Defoe; and John Quaderer's wife, Ogima'bînêsi'kwe (Chief bird woman), who was from the Lac Court Oreilles reservation in Wisconsin.

Their favorite botanical medicine for treating an assortment of gynecological problems in young, pregnant women and older squaws past the age of menopause was a compound decoction made from the berries, bark, and root of guzigwa'komînaga'wûnj or "thorny wood"—their name for a Canadian species of serviceberry. Guzigwa'komînaga'wûnj was their "all-purpose" answer to preventing miscarriage after an injury, to stop excess bleeding during the monthly menstruation period, to alleviate abdominal cramping, to smooth the transition to menopause in older women, and, in general, for any other "female weakness" they didn't have any particular names for.

In those times Native American men and women didn't work with the standard units of measuring that their white neighbors did. Everything was done by partial or whole "handsful" of this or that, indiscriminately thrown into any receptacle of boiling water, to gently simmer (usually uncovered) over an open fire outdoors or on a stove top inside closed quarters. But for the benefit of my readers, I shall assign some details to the above generalities. Figure on using 1 tablespoon of serviceberries with 2 tablespoons each of root and bark in about 2 quarts of boiling water. Reduce heat to lowest setting possible, stir thoroughly, and simmer uncovered for about 30 minutes. Allow to cool before straining.

It is important to keep in mind, however, that the prescribed amounts depend a lot on the problems for which the tea is to be used; also, whether it is to be taken warm or cold. For use by expectant mothers in the first trimester of their pregnancies, the *warm* tea works best. One cup twice daily is suggested for this. To prevent hemorrhaging, one to two cups of *cool* tea daily are recommended on an empty stomach. For menopausal problems, these Indian medicine women had their patients consume three cups of *cool* tea a day. The same tea will also work for vaginal discharges due to yeast infection and endometriosis.

SESAME SEED
(Sesamum Indicum)

BRIEF DESCRIPTION

Sesame is one of the world's most economically important oil seeds. Since ancient times it has been extensively cultivated in Greece, Egypt, Iran (Persia), India, and China. The latter two countries still command the lion's share of harvested crop, however, but sesame is also the chief vegetable oil in Mexico.

The plant is an annual, reaching almost six feet in height and can be either bushy or without branches. The flowers are white or pink, and the seeds may be red, brown, or black, but more often than not are a creamy white, depending, of course, on the variety.

Sesame seed is extremely oily; some modern strains contain nearly 60 percent oil. The pure oil is almost without taste or smell and doesn't easily go rancid in hot countries, which is one reason for its huge popularity. European countries import a lot of it to use in making margarine.

Sesame seeds make an excellent cooking oil. In the Near East the seeds yield a delicious nutty taste after slight roasting. The seeds are scattered on bread and cakes in much the same way as poppy seed, and with a somewhat similar result. In Syria and neighboring countries the sweetmeat known as *halva* (of which there are many varieties) is best known when made of ground sesame. It has a very characteristic rich nutty taste.

In Greece, Cyprus, Lebanon, Jordan, and Syria, a creamy or creamy-gray-colored paste called *tahini,* which is similar to peanut butter in texture, is made from finely ground sesame seeds. In this region *tahini* is used as a basis for various salad dressings and to flavor a puree of chick peas (*hummus*), which is one of the staple Arab dishes. Mixed with water and flavored with garlic and lemon juice, *tahini* is a very frequent part of the *meze* (appetizers with drinks), a saucer of this delicious garlicky substance being served with chunks of bread for dunking. As Mostafa Ghandehari, a Persian scholar once told me: "A *meze* in good company is like a beautiful sunset: It lasts for hours and then ultimately becomes the dawn."

Fattening Food for Underweight

Doctors in various Arab countries routinely prescribe sesame seed for malnourished or underweight patients. The form that works best is to mix some finely ground sesame seed powder (about two tablespoons) with one and a half ripe, peeled, and mashed bananas. This is usually fed to such patients in the morning for breakfast and again sometime in the evening as a bedtime snack.

The same mixture can be combined in a food blender or Vita-Mix with a little milk (1 1/2 cups) to make a tasty shake. Variations of this basic recipe, which can include different fruits (figs or dates) or nuts (cashews or pecans), are often made by body builders seeking to add more bulk to their physical frames.

Parents concerned with nutritious snack foods for their children should give this sesame seed-banana mixture some serious consideration as a foundation for delicious after-school treats. They are a nourishing combination when used in conjunction with other natural foods.

Excellent Burn Medicine

Medical doctors have made immense progress in treating severe burns over the past few decades. Thanks in large part to skin grafting and other innovations, patients with burns covering 80 percent of their bodies now stand better than a 50–50 chance of survival.

Just 30 years ago, however, the same odds applied to people with burns only half that extensive.

Burn patients often spend weeks in sterile isolation, at a cost of more than $2,000 a day. They shriek in pain as their wounds are scrubbed and bandaged. And thousands still die from infections each year. Grotesque scars darken the lives of many survivors.

But a revolutionary treatment from mainland China has, since 1988, rendered much of this modern burn therapy nearly obsolete. Dr. Xu Rongxiang developed a remarkably simple herbal salve of finely ground sesame seeds, honey, and other organic substances that has become a near "miracle medicine" in the treatment of burns. Beginning back in 1979, this unassuming physician began applying his Moist Emergency Burn Ointment with wooden ice-cream-style sticks on severe burn patients. The new remedy not only eased their pains, but actually sped up healing, significantly reduced scaring, and drastically cut the cost of saving lives.

By late 1988 the Chinese government had seen the value of his amazing work and set him up with his own institute besides appointing him head of the national burn treatment center in Beijing. Over 65,000 people have been successfully treated with his singular therapy, and Xu has trained more than 4,000 fellow physicians to use it. He also set up a partnership with George Liu, an entrepreneur who works out of Hong Kong and New York, to market the expensive ointment worldwide.

In 1989 business Liu approached Harry Gaynor, president of the National Burn Victim foundation in Orange, New Jersey, with a briefcase full of photographs. At first the American suspected a terrible scam. "The pictures just looked too damn good," he recalled later on. But when Gaynor and Dr. Anthony Barbara of the Hackensack Medical Center Burn Unit in New Jersey traveled to mainland China, they managed to interview many of the pictured patients whom Dr. Xu had previously treated. Some had received just standard therapies on one part of their bodies and the doctor's special moisturizing paste on another. "The differences were nothing short of incredible," Barbara recalled. "The conventionally treated skin was rough, scarred, and marked by patches of excessive or reduced pigmentation." But the herbally treated flesh (which had appeared just as charred in earlier photos was now "unbelievably supple and unblemished."

Gaynor and Barbara also witnessed Dr. Xu treating five patients who had developed serious infections during the course of conventional burn therapy. In any American burn center, the infected tissue would have been surgically removed, and such patients might not have survived. But Xu kept his patients in rooms of half a dozen people, and their attendants wore no caps, gowns, or masks. Yet after one week all five were totally free from infection.

While a home preparation of this special anti-scarring medication can be made, I recommend that the manufactured ointment be purchased and used instead. Pure sesame seed oil and unpasteurized or raw honey can be mixed together until a thick syrup consistency has been achieved that isn't too runny; if necessary, a little powdered wormwood herb can be added to increase thickness. A little powdered golden seal root and Kyolic aged garlic extract powder (emptied from some gelatin capsules) should also be added for antibiotic effect. The mixture can then be applied with a clean, wooden ice-cream stick or similar device.

But the manufactured product, known as Moist Emergency Burn Ointment or MEBO, is guaranteed to work better, even though it is very expensive. MEBO stops dehydration, chemical ulcers, and lacerations in all burn wounds. It has the capacity to reduce pains and infections. It stops the progressive necrosis of the burn tissue and heals deep wounds without scarring. Besides the principal ingredients of sesame seed and honey, MEBO also contains yam root, bee propolis (bee glue), and amurente. A 40-gram tube costs $29.95 and may be ordered from: Chi's Enterprise, Inc., 5140 East La Palma Avenue, Suite 103, Anaheim, CA 92807. Or call: (714)-777-1542 (day); (714)-921-1957 (evening); or fax: (714)-998-6090.

This same salve preparation is equally useful in treating hemorrhoids, scalds, diabetic leg ulcers, insect bites and stings, severe skin rashes, and leprosy.

Relief for Colitis, Gastritis, Heartburn, and Indigestion

A very delicious sesame seed milk can be made for various gastrointestinal disorders. Place in a Vita-Mix blender $1/4$ cup sesame seeds and 2 cups of water or goat's milk. Secure the lid and blend for $1\,1/2$ minutes. Then strain through a fine wire strainer or double layers of cheesecloth in order to remove the hulls. Add 1 tablespoon of carob powder and 6 dates. Return to the blender and mix again for another minute. A banana, stewed raisins (soaked in boiling water for 30 minutes), frozen apple concentrate (thawed), or seedless grapes can also be substituted.

Drink one cup of this delicious milk about 30 minutes following a meal for relief of colitis. gastritis, heartburn, or acid indigestion. This is a wonderful drink for gaining weight and can be used as an effective base for healthful salad dressings.

Clinical Use of Sesame for Fracture Wounds

In 1980 I had an opportunity to go to mainland China with the American Medical Students Association. The group of nearly three dozen medical students and several faculty advisers (including myself) went there to learn more about the empirical folk medicine, which had been elevated to clinic and hospital status by the Communist Chinese government.

I met with Doctors Wang Baoquan and Yao Shuyuan of the Orthopedics Department at Tianjin Hospital in the city of Tianjin. Through an interpreter provided for the occasion, I learned that since 1970 they had been using an ointment called *Shengji* ("tissue-growing") in 127 cases of infected open fractures of long bones with good results. Of those treated, 103 were males and 24 were females, ranging in age from 6 to 68 years (average age was 33 years). Injuries were mainly caused by crushing in 93 cases, collision in 20 cases, falling in 8, and gunshot wound in 6 cases. The bones injured included tibia and fibula in 82 cases, radius and ulna in 24 cases, femur in 13 cases, and humerus in 8. Nine cases were complicated with neurovascular injury and 18 with closed fracture of other bones. Size of lesions ranged from 4 centimeters squared to 600 centimeters squared. Five of these 127 patients required amputation of limbs due to the severity of their infected open fractures. Bacterial cultures taken from the wound surfaces in 109 cases revealed Gram-negative bacilli in 74 cases and Gram-positive bacteria in 35 others (the majority of these being staphylococcus aureus).

Both doctors demonstrated for me on several patients how they applied this special Shengji ointment, the principal ingredient of which was sesame seed oil. They first cut away all infected, dead tissue in the injured area, then wiped it clean with absorbent cotton. It struck me odd, though, that they didn't follow the routine pattern American doctors do in using alcohol and tincture of iodine. I inquired about this and received the reply that with Shengji it wasn't necessary to do the other.

After reduction of the fracture, the wound was covered with this special ointment spread evenly about 0.15 centimeters thick on an absorbent cotton pad that extended 1 centimeter beyond the edge of the wound surface. The dressing was changed every day or every other day according to the amount of discharge. Skin grafting was performed when there was fresh granulation, and more Shengji ointment was then applied to the grafted wound surface.

Then I boldly ventured where no Western observer had ever gone before—I asked them for the ingredient list and preparation instructions for their famous Shengji ointment. It took a few hours of discussion between them and their hospital superiors before permission was finally granted. Dr. Xu Erzhen was called in from the biology department at the local Nankai University to assist in the explanation.

Now what I am about to give in the way of ingredients may seem rather strange by American standards. But keep in mind that Chinese medicine for many centuries has included things other than herbs, which are believed to be equally efficacious. Therefore, don't condemn what your ignorance may want to outright reject. Here are the ingredients in metric measure as exactly given to me:

Crinis carbonisatus (charred human hair)	15 grams
Plastrum testudinis (inside tissue of turtle shell)	25 grams
Rehmannia glutinosa (Chinese foxglove root)	25 grams
Angelica sinensis (tangkuei or dongquai root)	15 grams
Gypsum fibrosum (calcium sulfate, selenite, or alabaster)	30 grams
Calamina (calamine or zinc oxide with 0.5% ferric oxide)	50 grams
Cera flava (beeswax)	90 grams
Corium elephatis (thickened wing or skin of certain insects–chaetopod worms)	20 grams
Oleum sesami (sesame seed oil)	500 grams

Methods of preparation for the Shengji ointment went something like this. After human hair was burned and cleaned with lye, it was dried in the sun. The soft underside tissue of turtle shell was scraped away with a sharp knife, and the thick part of certain insect wings or worm skins were cut into fine pieces. These three materials were then heated with talcum powder or sand until they became yellow in color and somewhat brittle in consistency; afterwards they were finely ground in a mortar with a stone pestle and then sieved through very fine gauze mesh.

Next, Chinese foxglove and tangkuei roots were finely cut with a sharp knife. The zinc oxide and calcium sulfate were finely ground and sieved as with the former first three items. Sesame seed oil was heated in an iron pot to 250° C. or until the dripping oil looked like pearls, after which the hair was added and scooped out 15 minutes later. Following this the turtle shell tissue was fried to the color of chestnut shell (approximately 15 minutes), and then the roots of foxglove and tangkuei were added. They were all scooped out 5 minutes later. After this, the sesame seed oil itself was filtered, any unwanted debris was discarded and then returned to the same iron pan to be reheated again to 200°C.

Following this procedure, the calcium sulfate and zinc oxide powders were slowly added to the oil and the mixture gradually cooked for 3 $1/2$ hours or until it turned dark brown in color. Then the beeswax was melted, filtered, and added to the hot oil. Ten minutes later the pot was removed from the stove. The final ingredient to be added was the dried bug wing or worm-skin powder; the mixture was stirred constantly until it became pasty thick like cooked cereal. This, they proudly declared, was how the famous Shengji Ointment was made.

Both doctors informed me that they followed up 97 of their original 127 cases for 6 months to 3 $1/2$ years. In 76 cases the fracture wounds remained totally healed; in 21 cases there were small areas of superficial ulcerations. Eighty seven of the 98 fracture wounds were healed. These 87 fractures involved: humerus 1, radius and ulna 14, femur 6, and tibia and fibula 66. The average turnaround time for recovery was 4 months for humerus, radius, and ulna, 5 months for femus, and 5 months for tibia and fibula.

Furthermore, they said through our interpreter that among two dozen serious cases that would usually have required amputation, 19 patients were spared surgery by receiving this Shengji treatment.

Based on the medical data provided by them, results in 60 (65.2 per-cent) of the 92 patients followed up (5 amputated cases excluded), could be classified as "excellent"; in 28 (30.4 percent) as "relatively good"; and in 4 cases (4.3 percent) as "rather poor." They figured that there was an overall effectiveness rate of 95.7 percent.

Admittedly, this is a rather lengthy rehearsal of case studies in a clinical setting. Obviously not all of the ingredients or preparation time will be readily available for most consumers. But, at least, it shows the medical relevancy of sesame seed oil in the treatment of complicated fracture wounds.

STRAWBERRY
(Fragaria Ananassa)

BRIEF DESCRIPTION

Strawberries have had a curious dichotomy about them throughout history. On the one hand, they have been portrayed as a spiritual, noble fruit. Fifteenth-century religious miniature paintings often depicted garden scenes to represent abstract spiritual values. Different plants signified specific virtues. Strawberries, in particular, represented the fruits of righteous living, and their leaves symbolized the Holy Trinity.

On the other hand, around the sixteenth century they were cast in a completely different light, or maybe I should say "shadow." Hieronymous van Aeken (better known as Hieronymus Bosch) was a famous Dutch painter of religious pictures, caricatures, and fantastic representations of devils, monstrosities, and other gruesome subjects. In his famous triptych *Garden of Earthly Delights*, strawberries are synonymous with carnal lust and pleasure: Evil creatures are shown gorging themselves on the carmine fruits; some members of this wicked horde from Hell were even drawn with strawberries for private body parts.

And King Henry VIII only helped to further the association of strawberries with debauchery by his inordinate fondness for this then very expensive fruit. Historical records depict the bloated British monarch reclining in his elaborate padded-sleeved costumes, draped in a fur-lined robe, devouring bowls full of the dainty berries. As strawberries were an old standby for gout, from which he suffered a great deal, this was undoubtedly the motivation for his huge berry consumption. It is said on some good authority that one of his several wives lost her head, quite literally, because she failed to have ready for him his evening bowl of strawberries and cream.

In the sixteenth century strawberries were still being eaten surreptitiously for pleasure by an enlightened few. This fruit was one of the first packaged foods in recorded history, being sold in pottles or cone-shaped straw baskets. Because they had to be harvested, packaged, and brought to market as quickly as possible to prevent spoilage, they were rather expensive and could be afforded only by nobility and the wealthier class. This contributed to their reputation of being a snobbish food consumed by the upper crust of British society, much in the same way caviar is regarded today.

If you're amused by now with this much of strawberry's checkered past, then you'll be further delighted to know about some of its promiscuous botanical history. It seems that in the early 1700s, while on a spying mission of unknown purpose in South America, a Frenchman named Amédée François Frézier became intrigued by the deep-red, large-fruited strawberries of Chile. He smuggled the species (*F. chiloensis*) to France, where it was introduced to the king's gardens in Paris. Eventually, this smuggled species met up with its British cousin somewhere in a very indiscreet way and they cross-pollinated with each other: today's garden variety of strawberry is a result of premarital plant "sex" between two different "unwed" species.

Strawberries are so common that they need no description here. Unfortunately, though, most of the strawberries sold today are picked while still unripe and rushed to supermarket produce sections where they remain for a week or ten days before starting to turn old and moldy. Strawberries harvested in this hurried manner are without flavor and taste dull and woody.

But if you really want to find out what *true* strawberries *really* taste like, then check out wild strawberries. These tiny, intensely sweet strawberries that have been with us all along are unsullied by human intervention, growing naturally all over Europe. Their heady aroma and flavor have lured berry pickers into woodlands for centuries. In fact, one of the first records of them in cultivation is under England's Edward I (reigned 1272–1307), who had the little strawberries transplanted from the wild forest to his castle garden.

If you're into gardening at all (or know of someone who is), then you might want to consider adding the strawberry not just for its fruity flavor, but also for its delightful *scent*. Here's what I consider to be the "ideal" fragrance garden: lemon verbena, bergamot, mints, savories, roses, snapdragons, pinks, and lobelia, all interspersed, of course, with plenty of strawberry plants. A walk through such a charming mix is the next best thing to Heaven itself—a real *nirvana* for the nose.

Strawberries for Dental and Cosmetic Needs

It's hard to imagine that a single, plump, red, delicious strawberry could be a useful dentifrice and cosmetic agent. But some medical herbalists in Great Britain, who by law can diagnose and prescribe, find this fruit to be quite beneficial for teeth stained by tobacco juice from chewing or smoking this filthy weed.

They instruct their patients to cut up one ripe strawberry and then mash it to a pulp with the back of a large metal spoon or the bottom of a coffee mug or drinking glass. The pulp is then put into a small dish. A wet toothbrush is repeatedly dipped into it and some of the pulp is brushed directly onto the teeth and left there for about six minutes, after which the teeth are rinsed with warm water to which has been added a pinch of baking soda.

Mary Donovan, M.H. (Medical Herbalist) of Chatburn, England, prescribes this beauty tip for women concerned about their complexion. After washing the skin, cut a large strawberry in half. Holding one piece in each hand, lightly rub in a circular motion over the skin, starting with the forehead and working down on each side of the cheeks over the nose, above and below the lips, and finally up and down on the throat.

This procedure should be done once a day to help whiten the skin and remove slight sunburn or a badly sunburnt face, she suggests massaging the juice from the strawberries directly into the skin, leaving it on for 45 minutes, and then washing it off with warm water to which have been added a few drops of simple tincture of benzoin. If the latter isn't available, pulverize one aspirin and add the powder to the warm water before washing the face with this solution. Above all, *don't* use any soap when doing this as that will only irritate the sunburn more.

The Perfect Foods for Obesity

Maurice Mességué was once one of the world's most famous natural healers. His inspired use of ordinary plants and herbs had helped thousands of men and women in Europe and Asia. Among those whom he treated were Ali Khan, King Farouk of Egypt, Pope John XXIII, Cocteau, and Charles De Gaulle.

He used only fruits, vegetables, and herbs to cure crippling diseases, make complexions smooth and fresh, eyesight brilliant, smiles radiant, and hair clean, healthy, and with a soft, silky feel to it. One of his several books on the way to natural health and beauty became an overnight best-seller in France.

Under the entries of "Strawberry and Raspberry" in his book, *C'est la nature gui à raison* (Paris: Opera Mundi, 1972), Monsieur Mességué had some interesting things to say about these fruits in regard to obesity. First, he noted that both berries were ideal snack foods for overweight people who constantly crave sweets because they satisfy such desires without doing injury to the body. Second, he noted that they detoxify the system of accumulated poisons that obese bodies have a difficult time throwing off. Third, strawberry and raspberry are recommended for obesity-related diseases such as gout, arthritis, diabetes, constipation, hypertension, and kidney stones.

Monsieur Mességué put it this way: "If you want to feel wonderful in the morning, do without your regular supper and eat a quart of strawberries instead." He meant without cream or sugar added. "Go to bed early and in the morning you will empty your bladder and bowel with a rare feeling of well-being, for your entire system will have been cleansed. In addition, you will have passed a remarkably restful night, for strawberries contain a bromide that promotes sleep."

This great French herbalist put many of his heavier subjects on a nut (for the protein) and berry (for the carbohydrates) diet with outstanding results. Not only did they experience more energy, but they lost on an average between 7 and 11 pounds within a 3-month period. This inspired me to include berries as part of my "Caveman Diet Program" featured in the recent audio album, *Dr. Heinerman's Healthy Prescriptions*. (This album consists of 6 tapes and a 100-page remedy book, costs $75, and may be ordered from Dr. John Heinerman, POB 11471, Salt Lake City, UT 84147.)

SUMAC BERRY
(Rhus Typhina)

BRIEF DESCRIPTION

The sumacs include about 150 species of shrubs and trees of the temperate and subtropical regions. Their handsome foliage often assumes brilliant colors in the fall, and the showy red fruits provide additional ornamental value. Because of their suckering habit, edible fruit, and browse value, many sumac species are valuable for erosion control and wildlife habitat.

One of the most recognizable of the sumacs, which thrives throughout southern Canada and the United States in meadows, pastures, and around bodies of water, is staghorn sumac. Its large, stout, and velvety twigs look so much like the branched and fuzzy antlers of a buck deer when in velvet that the quickly growing tree is easy to spot, even for a novice. As if that weren't enough, you've only to cut one of these twigs open and a white, sticky, gelatinous sap will ooze onto your knife blade and at once change to black. Furthermore, all these shrubs and small trees with the red berries on them are edible and harmless. It is the sumacs with white or somewhat yellowish, and incidentally sagging, berries that are poisonous—poison ivy, poison oak, poison sumac.

270

All sumacs belong to the cashew family, which has in it those trees that produce the edible cashew nuts. The bark of most members of this family are smooth, often striped orange to greenish in color, and rather picturesque. In fact, the wood is so distinctive looking that it is frequently used commercially in the manufacture of picture frames and the napkin-ring holders used in some fancy restaurants.

Even the fruits are rapidly recognizable. They start with small, tawny, and somewhat greenish flowers, the males and females growing on separate medicinals. The male clusters are many times about a foot in length and are spreading. The smaller, denser, feminine panicles are tinier, forming compact fruit bunches that are made up of small, single-seeded, berrylike drupes that mature early in the fall and, startlingly crimson, stay on the shrubs or trees throughout the winter months. They are covered with bright scarlet hairs, pleasantly sharp to the taste with malic acid, the same substance that flavors grapes, by the way.

Marvelous Drink for Dehydration and Excessive Thirst

Joy Yellowtail Toineeta, my Native American contact from the Crow Reservation in eastern Montana, told me about an "Indian lemonade" that her people used to make in the summertime. She described it as being "a very agreeable beverage to help keep you from 'drying out' in hot sun." Apparently the properties of the red sumac berries are such that they prevent dehydration.

She remembered as a little girl, her grandmother making this favorite drink of many Indian people. The berries always had to be picked in the late summer or early fall *before* the first full rainstorm; otherwise, they wouldn't be as good. (Recent evidence shows that the malic acid content in the berries drops substantially following the first rains. Malic acid is very soluble in water.) Her grandmother pressed juice from the berries, mixed it with an equal amount of water, stirred in a little white sugar (honey may be substituted) and then set the pitcher in a pan of cold water to keep cool. Joy said that one glass of this crimson-colored drink cured the worst case of thirst.

Indian Dental Plan for Pain

One of the most unusual uses I believe I've ever seen for the gelatinous substance oozing from the cut twigs of sumac came about quite by accident. I was in the home of an old Cheyenne medicine man years ago, conducting one of my typical interviews for the usual field research into folk remedies. Our conversation was interrupted by one of his grandchildren opening the front screen door and entering the room holding his jaw with one hand. He was a boy of about eleven, I'd judge, and was moaning and groaning. His grandfather kindly asked what was the matter, and the kid informed him his tooth started hurting like crazy.

Upon examining the inside of the boy's mouth, the grandfather discovered a deeply recessed cavity that had probably been there for quite some time but had now apparently struck a nerve, which was the source of all his pain. I accompanied the elderly gentleman outside to a sumac tree nearby. He retrieved a jackknife from his back pocket and with the blade opened, cut off two twigs. He returned to the house and had his grandson sit in a chair with his head tilted back and his mouth opened wide. He then squeezed the sticky sap into the cavity where it soon hardened up. *Within 15 minutes the pain ceased!* This is only a temporary measure, however—please see a dentist for proper medical treatment.

Nifty Ointment for Scratches, Cuts, Wounds, Sores, Moles, and Warts

When we returned to our interview a little later on in the morning, I asked the medicine man more about the use of sumac sap. He said he had used it for many years among his people in healing scratches and cuts encountered by thorny bushes and other sharp objects, wounds suffered from knife fights, bed sores and leg ulcers from being bedridden or having diabetes and moles and warts that frequently show up on the skin. He sometimes added the sumac berries to the sap, believing it promoted faster healing.

Dan Whistle-in-the-Wind, for that was his name, claimed there were two ways of making the ointment: the old way of his ancestors or the new way of the modern generation. With the exception of just one thing, directions for making both types of salve pretty much remained the same. In the old way, bear fat or beaver grease was used, but nowadays such animals weren't as plentiful. So, the only other option left for younger medicine men was to use lard or vegetable shortening.

After the lard has melted, he said, the sumac berry juice and some white twig sap should be added, along with some melted beeswax. The adding of these ingredients should be alternated back and forth: melt all the lard, add *some* berries and sap, and then a portion of the beeswax; then add some more berries and sap and a little more beeswax; continue this procedure until everything is added. Cover the pot with a lid and allow the mixture to get hot enough to the point where it begins to bubble. Remove from the fire, pour into individual jars, let harden, seal with lids, and store in a cool, dry place until needed.

Big Help with Burns, Scalds, Blisters, Eczema, Ringworm, Shingles, and Gangrene

My aged Cheyenne informant told me that the juice of the red sumac berries was an excellent wash for the skin in cases of minor burns and scalds from accidents with fire or overexposure to the sun. The twig sap was very nice for applying on water blisters suffered from walking in ill-fitting shoes or working too hard with the hands. Both the berry juice and the twig sap alone or in an ointment worked miracles for eczema, ringworm, and shingles. They stopped the redness and itching very quickly. And in his time, Dan Whistle-in-the-Wind saved the legs of several people who had contracted gangrene and were scheduled for amputation by rubbing into their terrible infections a combination of the sticky sap mixed with a tiny amount of crimson juice.

SUNFLOWER SEED
(Helianthus Annuus)

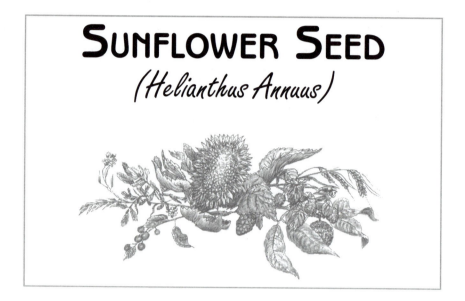

BRIEF DESCRIPTION

Scientists think that sunflowers may have come from Peru, but they've been cultivated for so long that their true origin is still something of a botanical mystery. They are cultivated as an important cash crop in Russia, Bulgarian Hungary, Romania, Argentina, and parts of Africa. Sunflower seeds contain about 40 percent oil, which has become recognized of late because it is very unsaturated and affords considerable protection against arterial disease. The oil is fine, almost tasteless, and of a light yellow color. It is excellent for cooking and in making salads. The buds of the sunflower are often used in Europe in salads. When the seeds are roasted in their husks and lightly seasoned with an herb salt, sea salt, or granulated kelp (a seaweed from health-food stores), they can be eaten by the handful, just like peanuts.

Mucus Accumulation Removed

Charlie Raymond of Manly, New South Wales, Australia, wrote me a long letter in August 1993 in which he praised my book, *Heinerman's Encyclopedia of Fruits and Vegetables* as being "one of the best books I've ever read on home remedies." Then he proceeded to share with me some of his own experiences with natural means and encouraged me to use any of it in one of my next books.

He described a very bad mucus problem that developed in his lungs. No matter what he tried—"strong whiskey, day old coffee boiled with the grounds, or hot tea"—nothing seemed to work to his satisfaction. "I was always spitting up phlegm, mate," he wrote, "and me wife was getting purty disgusted with all my hacking."

Then someone (he never said who) suggested that he make a strong tea from sunflower seeds and drink that for awhile. The method he employed for this was a little unusual for the way most teas are made. To 1 $1/2$ pints of boiling water, he added $2/3$ cup of slightly crushed sunflower seeds. (He crushed them by spreading the seeds inside a pillow slip and running his wife's rolling pin back and forth over the top for a couple of minutes.) Charlie "boiled down the water by leaving my container uncovered" for 30 minutes. The liquid was strained, "strengthened with wild honey," and 1 cup of the *very warm* tea slowly sipped every 4 hours.

"It only took me about five days to get rid of all that green junk inside my lungs," he boasted.

Cured of Prostate Problems

Charlie wrote in his lengthy correspondence about a sheepherder friend of his named Zeke Davison. "Old Zeke can plumb shear a ewe in 'two shakes of a lamb's tail,'" he wrote, with some obvious exaggeration. Anyhow, his friend suffered from an inflamed prostate; urination was painful, not to mention other activities that place stress upon this particular gland.

"I told him about my own recovery, and he decided to try some of my tea for himself," Charlie wrote. "Old Zeke claimed he got back to his 'natural self' in nothing flat!" As I read this last line in Charlie's letter, I wondered to myself if Zeke's turnaround had been in "two shakes of a lamb's tale," or maybe longer.

The same tea, by the way, drunk regularly every day while somewhat hot, will promote urination and perspiration very nicely.

SWEET CHERRY
(Prunus Avium)

WILD BLACK CHERRY
(Prunus Serotina)

BRIEF DESCRIPTIONS

The genus *Prunus* is one of the most important genera of woody plants. Its five well-marked subgenera include the plums and apricots, the almonds and peaches, the umbellate cherries, the deciduous racemose cherries, and the evergreen, racemose, or laurel cherries. Nearly 200 species, ranging from prostrate shrubs to trees over 100 feet tall, are found in the north temperate zone with a few species in Central and South America. By far the greatest number of species occurs in eastern Asia, but most of the long-established food-producing species originated in Europe and western Asia. Over 100 species have been brought into cultivation.

Many of the stone fruits have been cultivated since ancient times for their edible fruits and a few for their edible seeds. Wild species of cherries were a source of food for early Native Americans and early settlers of the western frontier; they are still collected for their food value. Several species of *Prunus*, including those of different cherries, are valuable ornamentals because of their attractive flowers and relatively rapid growth in a variety of soils.

Chinese Cure for Constipation, Edema, Gout, and Inadequate Urination

Years ago the late Mao Tse-tung, former leader of mainland China, inaugurated a unique health-care system throughout his country that brought the most basic of medical services to its one billion inhabitants. Several million men and women with the equivalent of a Western high school education were taught the fundamental principles in the prevention and treatment of disease. They were schooled both in Chinese traditional medicine, which included Oriental diagnosis, acupuncture, and herbs, as well as in orthodox techniques, such as simple surgery, immunization, and the dispensing of some common Western drugs.

They were then sent out into all the rural areas of China to serve the vast population that had never had access to basic medical care. They were nicknamed the "barefoot doctors" because they often worked in the rice paddy fields like any other faithful commune member, barefooted and with trouser legs rolled up. But through them the health standards for one third of earth's people were raised considerably higher than they had been before.

Shortly after the late U.S. President Richard M. Nixon paved the way for normalizing relations with Red China, the country slowly began opening up to Westerners. I was fortunate to be with one of the first medical groups ever invited into the country by the Communist government in Beijing. I and four other faculty advisers, all of whom were medical doctors, by the way, accompanied about 27 third- and fourth-year medical students on this historic trip. I got to see firsthand many of China's hospitals and clinics, which *no* foreigners had ever been allowed to see heretofore.

I made extensive notes of this historic trip, which now. some 15 years later, I still keep referring to every so often. In the course of our visit, we had many opportunities to meet a number of these "barefoot doctors," many of whom I interviewed through different interpreters provided for our group by the Chinese government. I was asked to come along because of my extensive knowledge of medicinal plants and Oriental culture. During the trip, I had the opportunity to give several lectures to our small group.

Cherries played a prominent role in the remedial therapy advocated by these "barefoot doctors." The name they used to identify them was *yu-li jen*. There was no finer "food medicine" (as they termed yu-li jen) for stimulating sluggish colons and evacuating the worst case of stool blockage than this. They had their patients eat several small bowlsful of sweet cherries a day, which never failed to produce the desired results within about six to eight hours.

Most of the Chinese we met were slender, as a rule. Very few of them suffered from the disease of obesity. However, in some of the more prosperous village farming communes we visited there were an alarming number of cases of edema and gout, usually in the older residents, on account of the huge amount of pork and duck they consumed. Here again, cherries were brought into play, both as a fresh fruit to be eaten regularly and as a tea made from *yu-li jen*, which had been sun-dried. Anyone who has ever experienced the marvelous diuretic effects of cherries will know that they automatically increase urination. For more information on this fruit, see CHOKE CHERRY.

WALNUT
(BLACK AND ENGLISH/PERSIAN)
(Juglans Nigra, J. Regia)

BRIEF DESCRIPTIONS

There are about fifteen different species of walnuts growing throughout the world. They are indigenous to eastern Asia, southeastern Europe, and North and South America. All walnuts are edible. However, the Persian or English walnut is probably the most delicious and certainly the most important. It is believed to be native to a vast region including Turkey, Iran, Iraq, Afghanistan, southern Russia, and northern India.

In ancient times *Juglans regia* was known as "the nut of the Gods." In the first century A.D., the Roman scholar Pliny stated that the walnut had been sent to Greece from Persia "by the kings"; the best quality walnut was, therefore, known as "Persian and royal." At that time the walnut was considered to be superior to other common nuts such as acorns, beech nuts, and chestnuts.

Those unacquainted with walnuts may not be aware of the fact that they can be tapped in the spring for their rising sweet sap; the liquid is then boiled down into sugar. This procedure is widespread in eastern Russia, Mongolia, and northern China.

A distinction should be made between commercial walnut growing for nut production on the one hand, and the cultivation of the tree as an ornamental or for timber on the other. Nut-producing trees should have large crowns and considerable branching to develop abundant fruiting wood, while timber trees should have narrow crowns and long, straight trunks. Dispersed as it was across Europe and eastward toward Asia, the walnut tree was found to be tolerant of a wide range of temperatures when planted for ornamental or timber purposes, in cooler climates, though, nut production was minimal or virtually nil. In northern Europe, for instance, the Persian walnut will grow to a fair size, but it ripens nuts only when above average winter temperatures are experienced.

The eastern black walnut is native to the deciduous forests of the eastern United States and Canada. It is the largest of the native species of North America, reaching a height of up to 150 feet. It bears dark-colored, edible nuts within a thick, hard, black shell, smaller in size, more circular in outer shape, and with a somewhat stronger flavor than that of the Persian walnut. Its high-quality wood has long been prized for furniture, cabinet making, and gunstocks. Black walnut is, in fact, the most valuable hardwood in America. Fantastic prices have been paid for black walnut trees, up to $30,000 for a single tree with an especially long, clear bole.

There is a brisk demand for black walnuts—especially during the Thanksgiving and Christmas holidays—for use in candies, cakes, and ice cream. The nuts are scarce and expensive—the average retail price in late 1994 was roughly $5.49 per pound.

Walnuts are oval-shaped, green, leathery, aromatic, and occur in groups of one to three. The hull encloses the familiar tan-colored fruit; the smooth, large nuts of the Persian walnut separate easily from the hulls at maturity. In the cultivated varieties, the shells are thin and easily broken. The kernel consists of two identical lobes, united at the apex; the ivory-colored nut meat is protected by a thin, light-brown testa. The hulls fall away from the shells more readily in the Persian or English walnut than in the black walnut. The kernel of the former is likewise easier to withdraw from the shell intact than that of the black walnut, which has a somewhat denser endocarp. The inner shell of the black walnut is more difficult to crack without damaging the kernels, so they are usually sold already shelled.

Walnuts for Physical Weakness

I discovered one of the most amazing uses for walnuts some years ago when I was in mainland China again for more research. It was in the summertime while I was attending the annual Nadam Festival, staged in a large arena called the Race Ground in Inner Mongolia's capitol of Hohhot (pronounced Hu-He-Hot). (Since 1993, however, this event has been held in a huge, new structure built on the vast open spaces of Gengentala Grasslands some 85 miles away.)

I saw many different wrestlers munching on quantities of walnuts prior to their respective turns inside the ring. They were stocky, muscular men, built like squat fireplugs. They were clad in loose trousers embroidered with animals, flowers, or decorative patterns. Their bare upper bodies were partially covered by leather harnesslike vests that were studded with copper or silver rivets and encircled the waist and shoulders, leaving the arms free. Colorful sashes in red, yellow, or blue adorned their solid waists.

I stood with other spectators in a wide circle on the barren earth. At a signal from one of the referees, two wrestlers would prance into the ring, bow to each other and the audience, and then at the referee's signal begin to encircle each other like two aggressive bulls.

The leather harness, like the wide belts worn by Japanese sumo wrestlers, provided a facility for competitors to grab and lift their opponents. The objective was for one to throw, push, or trip the other to the ground. The first to do so won.

At first, the wrestlers seemed to me to spar with each other, each seeking a handhold on his opponent's leather harness or arms. With a loud grunt, one of the larger guys grabbed the harness of the other, a medium-sized fellow of very stocky build. In a quick move, the larger man swung his adversary about. But the grip slid, and the other wrestler stumbled and tottered, but somehow managed to stay on his feet as he broke free.

Suddenly, the medium-sized one with the heftier build wrapped his arms around the torso of the other and lifted him bodily off his feet; then, with a quick jerk, he turned his hip out and swung his foe to the ground. The referee raised his hands over his head and then grasped and raised the arm of the standing wrestler who was by now dancing in joy over his victory. With a sheepish grin, the fallen warrior arose and moved back to join his other defeated companions, while the winner walked over to a table and scooped up a fistful of shelled walnuts out of a large wooden bowl and methodically began munching on them again. Through my interpreter, I was told by some of those present that walnuts are considered the prime food source for becoming strong in this autonomous region of mainland China.

Effective Treatment for Diarrhea, Sore Throat, and Ringworm

During my short stay in Hohhot, I learned from several local doctors a few other medical applications for this particular nut, which requires neither roasting nor salting to enhance its flavor.

Green walnut husks were routinely gathered and then boiled in enough water to cover them to a depth of about 2 inches for 1 $\frac{1}{4}$ hours or until half the liquid remained (no lid was put on the pot in which they were cooked). This bitter-tasting brew was strained and stored in corked jugs until ready to be used.

Some of the liquid would be heated to lukewarm and given to a patient in one-cup amounts twice daily on an empty stomach to stop diarrhea. One-half cup of the same lukewarm liquid was prescribed as an effective gargle for sore throats and tonsillitis with very good success. And poultices steeped in some of the cold juice and put on areas of the skin afflicted with ringworm would soon clear up that problem; powdered walnut bark was also liberally sprinkled over the area for the same purpose.

Runny Nose and Head Cold Cleared Up

A popular remedy in parts of Germany for many decades has been a tea made from walnut leaves to help dry up continual sinus discharges in young chidden and adults. Two tablespoons of walnut leaves are added to boiling water, stirred, covered, and removed from the heat and allowed to steep for 30 minutes. One-half cup of the lukewarm tea, strained, is given to young children every 4 hours to help stop a runny nose. One cup of the warm leaf tea every 3 hours is suitable for adults with head colds.

Acne, Eczema, and Psoriasis Benefitted

The same tea makes an excellent wash for a variety of skin afflictions. Some German teenagers suffering from bad cases of acne vulgaris who have been treated by their grandmothers or mothers with this remedy on a regular basis in time have regained clear complexions. They also drank the tea internally.

Older people who have been troubled with eczema and psoriasis reported considerable relief after washing their afflicted body parts with this same tea several times a day. The tea not only relieves the itching and inflammation, but actually helps to heal the skin, too. Sometimes, burdock root is added for greater effect; in such cases, one tablespoonful of coarsely chopped, dried root is simmered for 10 minutes before the walnut leaves are added and the mixture steeped for 40 minutes. The tea can also be taken internally.

Walnuts Head Off Heart Disease by Reducing Serum Cholesterol

In the summer of 1992 researchers at Loma Linda (California) University Medical School reported epidemiological data suggesting that Seventh Day Adventists who rarely eat nuts suffer heart attacks and coronary deaths at roughly twice the rate of those who typically eat nuts five times a week. Then, in the spring of the following year, these same researchers came up with the reason for this. By comparing the results of two four-week-long dietary intervention trials in 18 men, they found that eating moderate amounts of walnuts, without increasing total dietary fat and calories, "decreases serum-cholesterol levels and favorably modifies the lipoprotein profile in healthy men."

Both experimental diets derived 30 percent of their calories from fat—a level recommended by the American Heart Association and 14 percent lower than the typical American diet, which contains a whopping 35 percent fat. Writing in the March 4, 1993, *New England Journal of Medicine,* Joan Sabaté and her coworkers reported that substituting walnuts for two thirds of the fat in such a relatively low-fat diet further lowers cholesterol concentrations in the blood by more than 10 percent.

Since the walnut diet contained roughly three times the ratio of polyunsaturated to saturated fat found in the other low-fat diet, some drop in cholesterol was expected anyway, said David Kritchevsky of the Wistar Institute in Philadelphia. But what no one anticipated, he noted, was the magnitude of the walnut's cholesterol-lowering and heart-saving effect.

Why Walnuts Are a Natural Sedative

In Appendix III of the second section devoted to berries, there is considerable information on a natural substance called ellagic acid. It occurs in fruits such as strawberries and in certain nuts, like those from Brazil. It has cancer-prevention properties about it. This is probably why grapes have been routinely recommended for many decades by folk healers and naturopathic physicians for getting rid of tumors (because of their high ellagic acid contents).

Walnut meat and the husk contains a fair amount of this substance, which also has sedating activity. Native Americans and some blacks and whites have previously employed walnuts to stupefy fish; as the fish floated to the surface, they were easily scooped up with large nets in great numbers; which prompted at least one southern state, Mississippi, to pass a law barring the use of walnuts, dynamite, or gunpowder to land the catch of the day.

But just how effective is this ellagic acid in walnuts? Can it really induce sleepiness? Consider this, told to me by a worker, who wished to remain anonymous, who is employed by the Walnut Lumber Co. in Kansas City. "After those computerized saws have done their work," he confided to me awhile back, "then our job is to sweep up the sawdust. But we deliberately delay making a fast job of it, because the sawdust has such a sweet smell that we can't seem to get enough of sniffing it. The other guys and myself find that its aroma has a very soothing effect on our minds and nerves. The pleasant smell helps us to relax. It's similar, in some ways," he finished, "to smoking a joint [marijuana cigarette], but perfectly legal!"

WATER CHESTNUT
(Trapa Natans)

BRIEF DESCRIPTION

There is a pair of similar but unrelated plant products known as water chestnuts. *T. natans* is an aquatic plant found throughout Europe and belongs to the family *Trapaceae*. But if the proper name "Chinese" is substituted for "European," then it has reference to *Eleacharis dulcis,* an Asiatic sedge of the family *Cyperaceae*.

The European water chestnut is a dark-brown, hard-shelled, woody fruit with four hard, spinelike projections protruding from its surface. The fruits are two to three inches wide from tip to tip of their woody horns and about one inch deep. Inside each fruit is enclosed one large, white, starchy kernel, which is the edible nut of the water chestnut. This floating annual aquatic plant, with beautifully mottled foliage, grows luxuriantly in standing water; it strikes root in muddy bottoms and floats on the surface of ponds, pools, lakes, and irrigation tanks.

The flowers are small, white, and inconspicuous; the fruits are hidden beneath the aquatic foliage until they ripen, drop off, and sink to the bottom. During the harvest, the nuts are scooped up from the depths in small nets.

The Chinese water chestnut, commonly called *matai* in Cantonese, is familiar to devotees of Chinese foods. A grasslike, annual plant common to marshy environments, it is a paddy crop that reaches three to five feet in height and spreads by means of horizontal rhizomes along the edges of shallow marshes and lakes. It is not a true nut as the name might imply, but is the edible, dark-brown corm or tuber of an Asiatic sedge. The Chinese characters for matai mean "horse's hoof," referring to the shape of the tubers. The Chinese water chestnut has a delicious flavor, reminiscent of sugar cane, sweet corn, and coconut; it is starchy, similar to white potatoes in composition, and possesses a unique crisp texture, which it retains even after cooking. Sliced, peeled water chestnuts provide crispness to chop suey in America, while shredded matai is an ingredient in a variety of Oriental soups, salads, and meat and fish dishes. The raw corms are eaten out of hand in mainland China as a substitute for fresh fruits, or are frequently cooked alone as a winter vegetable.

Heartburn and Acid Indigestion Greatly Alleviated

Many people suffer from intestinal discomforts due to inadequate chewing of each mouthful consumed, eating in a hurry, bad food combinations, or several of these together. This results in an excess production of hydrochloric acid and an abnormal concentration of gas within the gut.

Chinese water chestnut is especially good for this. When I made my first trip to China in 1980 with the American Medical Students' Association, we learned from a number of barefoot doctors the value of this. These barefoot doctors—the medical equivalent of our own physicians' assistants here—made a tea from water chestnuts for their sick patients to drink. Three coarsely cut water chestnuts were simmered in boiling water for ten minutes; both the liquid and nuts were consumed, either together or separately, when sufficiently cooled.

At one commune hospital, I had a chance to sample some of this remedy in the form of a clear broth soup, topped with several of these water chestnuts chopped into tiny slivers. Not only was it quite flavorful, but it also helped to settle my stomach after I overdid it on a sumptuous duck dinner the previous evening. I was mildly surprised and quite pleased to see just how quickly my intestinal discomforts disappeared because of this Chinese water chestnut remedy.

Conjunctivitis Successfully Treated

When our medical group visited what was then called the People's Republic of China in the summer of 1980, we discovered that conjunctivitis was widespread in some provinces. A few of those barefoot doctors with whom some of us were privileged to work as they made their village rounds used an eyewash made from this water chestnut to clear up this eye infection and inflammation in their patients. The tea was made similar to that used for stomach distress.

WATERMELON SEED
(Citrullus Lanatus)

BRIEF DESCRIPTION

The garden variety of watermelon hails from ancient Persia (now Iran), but is now extensively cultivated in the warmer climates of earth's seven continents. It can, however, be grown in the temperate regions of the world where 130–140 days of growing weather prevail. There are several small-fruited varieties developed especially for the northern states and provinces of North America.

The plant is a trailing vine with deeply lobed, medium-sized leaves and yellow flowers that are borne in the axils of the leaves. The fruit ranges in size from a large grapefruit to a large field pumpkin, while the shape is anything from oval to cylindrical. The color is light or dark green, with gray-green stripes running lengthwise in some varieties.

"Sure Cure" from Finland for Kidney Failure

Kai Laakso, aged 42, suffered from kidney failure. Various urologists whom he consulted in Helsinki, Finland, failed to offer him any lasting help for his increasing inability to urinate. He started getting sick, and very soon his situation looked pretty grave.

But family members who waited on him called in a homeopathic doctor who prescribed capsules (6 a day) and tea (3 cups daily) of watermelon seeds. Two level tablespoons of watermelon seeds were simmered, uncovered, in 2 $^1/_2$ cups boiling water for 15 minutes. The tea was strained and drunk in between meals. Within a month, by using this tea and faithfully taking the capsules, Kai fully regained his health.

Istanbul Doctors Baffled by Remedy

Mostaupha Ghandehare is a successful merchant in the huge and bustling capitol of Istanbul, Turkey. But his one passion was a craving for sweets; he just couldn't seem to get enough of things that were loaded with sugar. In time, this man developed a serious case of diabetes, for which large injections of insulin on a daily basis were an essential requirement for his survival.

One day, while finishing prayers in a local mosque, an *imman* with whom Mostaupha was well acquainted took him aside and discussed his health problem with him. The holy leader informed Mostaupha that a sister of his in the Turkish city of Ankara had completely healed herself of the same problem by routinely drinking watermelon seed tea. He said she took that in place of water and consumes about six to eight glasses every day.

Mostaupha thanked him for the information and went home and shared it with his wife. She started making large batches of the tea for him. He later informed me through a mutual friend of ours who was in the United States on a temporary visa that he began noticing improvements in his health within the first couple of weeks of drinking the tea. He mentioned that his wife added a couple of handfuls of watermelon seeds to a coffeepot full of boiling water and cooked them that way for close to 45 minutes; every so often she would add a little more water as she deemed necessary.

Mostaupha averaged seven glasses every day for a period of five solid months. At the end of that time, he no longer needed the insulin injections. Several doctors familiar with his case were utterly baffled by the astonishing effectiveness of this simple remedy.

WILD GRAPE
(Vitix Labrusca)

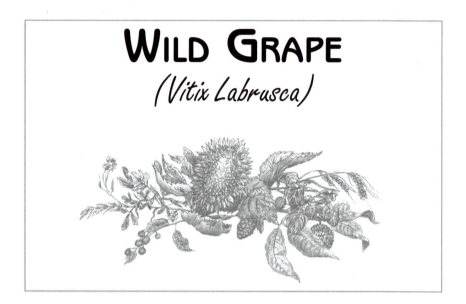

BRIEF DESCRIPTION

In the second of my food remedy series, *Heinerman's Encyclopedia of Healing Juices,* I presented a strong case under GRAPE JUICE for this particular item being the "forbidden fruit" that Adam and Eve deliberately partook of in the Garden of Eden, contrary to the wishes of God. I backed up my argument with historical evidence from ancient writings found in the Apocrypha, the Pseudepigrapha, literature of the early Jews and Gnostics, as well as the histories of Philo and Josephus compiled two millenniums ago.

Grapes have been with us ever since. It has been estimated by some viticulturists (those who grow grapes for a living) that at least *half* of this world's innumerable grapes are native to North America. And most of the species of this trailing, climbing, tendril-clasping, wide-leaved, and quickly picked fruit can trace their origins back to a common ancestor—the fox grape. This deciduous, woody vine ranges from New England to Illinois and south to Georgia and Arkansas. It sustained the frequently famished members of the Lewis and Clark Expedition on more than a few occasions. The leaves are mainly heart-shaped and unlike most vines often have no tendril or fruit cluster opposite every third one.

Fox or wild grape is the ancestor of the world-renowned Concord grape (developed in Concord, Massachusetts). It is a loftily climbing vine that thrives in rich forests, by streams, and in thickets. An individual fox grape can have three to six seeds, is somewhat sweetish and musky in flavor, and is usually on the purple side.

An Alternative Cancer Remedy

Earlier in the text, I discussed at some length the subject of cancer under the entry for POKEBERRY. There I used the word "cure," which was deliberately set off in quotation marks to imply more of a folk remedy than a medical fact. I cautioned readers *always to consult* knowledgeable medical practitioners who have had extensive training in health-care procedures and understand the problems of cancer in particular. Then, after receiving several different learned opinions, one could at least make more of an intelligent choice as to which types of treatment were preferred.

Certainly there are some other sensible selections available in what is called *alternative* health care, meaning therapies that are practiced *outside* the purview of accepted medical science. The many modalities offered by the different cancer clinics located in Tijuana, Mexico, would fall into this realm. Most, if not all of them, are considered quite controversial, and because of this have to be used *outside* the United States, in countries where laws prohibiting them do not exist.

I cannot say to my readers directly, "Grapes will cure you of cancer!" Not only would that give my editors at Prentice Hall renewed cases of heartburn, but it would probably give their legal department major anxiety attacks. However, I *can* tell you that grapes have been very prominent in the alternative movement for many decades as one of the *more* efficient and reliable therapies that has an impressive track record for tumor reduction.

Cancer is a very sad disease, not so much for the pain and suffering it brings to its victims, but more for the sense of hopelessness that it engenders for the patient and his or her family and friends. A mood of desperation sets in, which compels the sufferer and the loved ones tending that individual to reach out to anyone and everyone who may have a possible answer or new solution to the problem. Unfortunately, those who act in desperation often become the unwitting pawns of unscrupulous people who are interested only in making a fast buck and really don't give a damn about the suffering families who seek them out as a last resort.

Over a decade ago, I wrote a book entitled *The Treatment of Cancer with Herbs* (Orem, UT: Bi-World Publishers, 1980). It was definitely *not* a "do-it-yourself" cancer cure guide; instead it was simply a compilation of natural substances and alternative programs that have been used around the world in the treatment of this hideous disease. The book had modest sales and soon went out of print. But renewed interest has revived in it recently with the publication of Richard Walter's book entitled *Options*, in which he praised my volume as being one of the most "definitive works" on alternative cancer therapies.

Lo and behold, I started getting calls and letters from all over the country from people with cancer or in behalf of those who had it. Most of them had been through the usual programs of chemotherapy, radiation, and surgery with less than happy results and were now in despair. They looked to me for things I could not entirely supply them with, because (as I explained to them) I'm not a medical doctor nor am I licensed to practice. I am only a research scientist who has specialized in the study of alternative medicine or folk remedies on a worldwide scale. I could give them sound information based on reliable evidence I had meticulously gathered from trustworthy folk healers and alternative practitioners in many different countries. That is the best they could hope for, but, I'm happy to report, in many instances their expectations did *not* end in disappointment.

Thus it is against this background setting that I now come around to the subject of wild grapes once again. Because *all* commercial grapes today (unless they're organically grown) are *heavily* sprayed with pesticides, I cannot in good conscience recommend them to be eaten or their juices drunk, which is why I'm so much in favor of the wild varieties such as fox grape or the trailing or climbing muscadine, to name just two. They are devoid of chemical poisons and can offer diseased bodies hope for recuperation where everything else has pretty much failed.

Small clusters of blackish-purple wild grapes such as these are generally tough-skinned with a musky, sweet flavor. But they are incredibly rich in vitamins A, C, and P (bioflavonoids) and trace elements such as germanium and selenium—nutrients that have been favorably evaluated in the regression of cancer.

Their royal-appearing juice will purify the blood, invigorate the immune system, and put flesh and weight back onto bodies that have become severely wasted and weakened by the ravages of cancer. That has been my experience with wild grapes in this disease treatment. And see one of my other books, *Heinerman's Encyclopedia of Healing Juices* (pp. 140–141) for an incredible true story of a photographer friend of mine by the name of Ogden Kraut, who completely cured himself of a tumor that doctors had declared to be malignant, by fasting and drinking nothing but Concord grape juice!

WINTERGREEN BERRY
(Gaultheria Procumbens)

BRIEF DESCRIPTION

The genus *Gaultheria* consists of about 100 species mostly native to Asia, Australia, and South America, with 6 species found in North America. Salal has a distinctly woody stem, while creeping snowberry and wintergreen berry (also called checkerberry) are semi-shrubs. All three attain their best development in moist, acid soils. They provide cover and food for wildlife. The leaves of wintergreen contain an important oil (oil of wintergreen), which is extracted for pharmaceutical use. When the shiny, waxy evergreen leaves are crushed and the winter-clinging little red berries are tasted, they give off a familiar wintergreen aroma.

The small trailing perennial creeps through and under the woodland humus, moss, and ground, thrusting up separate blooming and leafing clusters. The frosty flowers appear like chaste white miniature bells, with their unions of five petals, growing between stems and leaves about summertime, maturing into solid red fruits in fall and winter, each with a distinctive pucker on top. The leaves, which become leathery and ruddy with age, have tiny teeth, each with bristlelike tips.

Aspirin Alternative for Fever, Sore Throat, and Headache

Aspirin has been described as an "all purpose" medicine, because tens of millions of people take it for a variety of general physical complaints. But aspirin is synthetic and not always good for the body, although its primary ingredient, acetylsalicylic acid, was originally synthesized from the true salicylic acid found in wintergreen leaves and berries. In fact, it was the Bayer Company in 1899 that first coined the term "aspirin" from the combination of "a" for "acetyl" and the original generic name *Spiraea* = spirin, from which salicylic acid was first isolated. (Salicylic acid was first observed in the flowerbuds of *Filipendula* (Spirae) *ulmaria* or Eurasian queen-of-the-meadow in 1839.)

A more preferred alternative to this much overused medication would be wintergreen berries and leaves. Tea is the recommended form in which they are to be applied. A conservative way of making this tea is to immerse a tablespoonful of the chopped berries and a teaspoonful of the dried, cut leaves in one pint of boiling water. Stir, remove from heat, cover, and let steep for an hour.

Depending on what you're taking it for determines the temperature of the tea. For fevers, drink the tea *warm* on an empty stomach, in half-cup amounts every few hours. For a sore throat, gargle with some of the *cool* tea before swallowing every few hours. For any kind of headache, drink a cup twice daily when the tea is *cold*. But to apply compresses of the tea across the forehead to relieve throbbing pain and pressure, the tea should be somewhat *hot*.

APPENDIX I

THE FOOD VALUE OF NUTS AND SEEDS

The Role of Nuts and Seeds in Prehistoric Diets

Nuts and seeds constituted two of the most important sources of nutrition for paleolithic man. Scientists, such as archaeologists, paleobotanists, and palynologists, who excavate ancient ruins and examine plant fragments and fecal remains (called coprolites) for clues as to what people ate long ago have discovered at a number of important archaeological sites around the country that nuts and seeds predominated in the diets of prehistoric societies.

Janet Ann Stock, a graduate in anthropology from Texas A & M University in College Station, Texas, participated in several explorations of the Hinds Cave in Val Verde County, in the southwest part of Texas, back in the late 1970s and early '80s. She compiled her field work into a published report entitled *The Prehistoric Diet of Hinds Cave, Val Verde, Co., Texas* (College Station: Dept. of Anthropology, Texas A & M University, August 1983).

People inhabiting the Hinds Cave tens of thousands of years ago subsisted on vegetative foods of high-protein yield. These included sunflower seeds and walnuts, both rich in amino acids and strength-giving once ingested and fully absorbed into the body. The seeds in many different wild fruits, such as Texas persimmons, fox grapes, currants, hackberries, and crab apples, were also eaten along with their fruits, instead of being spit out as we're in the habit of doing today.

Ms. Stock was of the opinion that men and women in those times were in much better health than many of us are at present, even if the lifespans then were considerably shorter than they are now.

One of my scientific colleagues, fellow anthropologist Vaughn M. Bryant, Jr., is a member of the distinguished faculty at Texas A & M University, where he has taught both anthropology and biology at various times. He has been the editor of the scientific journal *Palynology* for some years now and is considered by many to be one of the most renewed palynologists in the world; these are scientists who conduct microscopic research on the invisible grains of different plant pollens left behind in coprolites and other garbage residues of ancient caves.

Every year since 1968, Texas A & M holds a premier lecture program for faculty and students entitled the University Lecture Series. It is set apart from other campus speaker programs by the general interest of each lecture topic and the recognized eminence of the speaker involved. And lectures that are deemed to be of exceptionally scholarly merit are published by the University. On November 28, 1979, my friend Vaughn gave the twelfth speech in this much-honored lecture series; it was subsequently published a short time later under the appropriate title *Prehistoric Diets*. It is from this publication that I briefly quote.

In speaking about our very ancient ancestors, who lived "millions of years ago," Dr. Bryant noted that "their meals were not like ours" at all. "Today our lifestyle dictates that we eat most of our food at three specific times of the day, yet this is contrary to the true needs of our bodies. We are designed to be snackers who never eat much at any one time but instead nibble on food throughout the day."

Two of the central ingredients in prehistoric snacking were nuts and seeds, he stated. "...In the dimming light of early evening they...huddled together...and munched on whatever leftover seeds, nuts, and dried pieces of meat they had carried back to camp at the end of each day." "But this was nothing like our modern concept of an evening meal," he continued, "with its variety of main courses and desserts. Food was the main focal point of their lives...." They cared very much about what they ate and through "a system of trial and error...learned which plant foods were good to eat and which were poisonous." In other words, they were more careful in choosing good foods than we are in our time.

"Most of their foods came from plants," he added. "Meat was a luxury since most of it came from small animals they could easily catch or from carrion left behind by large carnivores. Their food was nutritious, high in tough fiber and provided *all* of their dietary needs. Since they lacked an understanding of how to use fire, their food was eaten raw and thus lost none of its vitamins. With a wholesome diet [of nuts, seeds, berries, tubers, leaves, and small game] accompanied by lots of daily walking, these people were lean and fit. Obesity was probably unknown, and the remains of their skeletons suggest malnutrition was not a problem."

Vaughn observed that as long as our early ancestors clung to this simplified eating program, they enjoyed remarkably good health. But once they added more meat and additional fats to their diet, in the forms of milk, pork, cheese, and eggs, and began domesticating crops and refining and cooking foods then they soon became subject to obesity and a whole host of other diseases.

Energy Utilization from Nuts and Seeds

The amount of carbohydrates, fat, and protein in a food determines its energy value. Man and beast alike are dependent on food as a source of energy to do body work and maintain body temperature. After a particular food is ingested, digested, absorbed, and metabolized, the food energy from it is transferred to form the important compound adenosine triphosphate (ATP). (ATP has been called an "energy currency" because it can be created and expended by the cells themselves.) The energy from ATP is used by the cells as energy for the synthesis of body nutrients, proteins, nucleic acid, and other materials; for the contraction of muscles; for the conduction of nerve impulses; for glandular secretion; for the transport of substances through membranes (for example, sodium and potassium exchange in cells); and for other functions.

The protein and fat contained in many nuts and a few seeds provide some of the greatest physiological fuel value to the body. When many foods are consumed and go through the usual assimilation process, there are generally varying losses of energy due to waste production of feces and urine and further losses due to defects inherent in the digestive system. But the actual amount of energy lost from consumed nuts and seeds through these various factors is considerably *less* than for most other foods eaten.

The following table shows the caloric, protein, and fat contents of eleven different nuts and seeds. But although obviously high in fat and calories—most have over 160 calories per ounce—strangely enough, they do not necessarily contribute to obesity.

COMPARISON OF SOME NUTS AND SEEDS
(1 ounce, dried or roasted)

Type	Calories	Protein (grams)	Fat (grams)
Almonds	167	5	15
Brazil Nuts	186	4	19
Cashews	163	4	13
Chestnuts	70	1	1
Hazelnuts (filberts)	188	3	19
Macadamia Nuts	199	2	21
Peanuts	164	7	14
Pecans	187	2	18
Pine Nuts	146	7	14
Pistachios	162	6	14
Walnuts, English/Persian	182	4	18

Medicinal Benefits of Some Amino Acids

In 1958 scientists in the former Soviet Union discovered that walnuts, pine nuts, pistachios, almonds, and peanuts were extremely rich in arginine, according to *Chemical Abstracts* (55:6723, 1961). Experiments conducted in animals have shown, that diets enriched with just 18 percent arginine produced significant reductions in serum cholesterol. Arginine inhibits fat absorption; hence, the higher the arginine in the diet, the lower the cholesterol level. Now meats contain more of another amino acid, lysine, which can be harmful to the heart because it promotes atherosclerosis. However, the inclusion of arginine-rich nuts and seeds in the diet frequently helps to prevent coronary heart disease.

Two other amino acids are especially useful to the brain; these are tryptophan and tyrosine. They affect neurotransmitters or chemicals within the brain, which, in turn, produce mood changes. Tryptophan stimulates serotonin, the neurotransmitter that causes a sense of relaxation. Conversely, for sharpening brain concentration, tyrosine is needed; it triggers the neurotransmitters norepinephrine and dopamine, which may be described as "alertness chemicals," in that they assist the brain to think and react more quickly.

Almonds, chestnuts, peanuts, pecans, and walnuts have more tryptophan for relaxing the body. So if you want to unwind after the end of a hard day at work or play, then snack on any of these. On the other hand, if you're driving long distances at night or taking a test, both of which require enhanced mental alertness, then you'll went to munch on either Brazil nuts, cashews, hazelnuts, macadamias, pine nuts, and pistachios.

Nuts Enhance Brain Power

I know what I'm talking about because of a personal experience I had with pine nuts a couple of years ago. Our family has a large ranch of about 400 acres in the beautiful Painted Desert wilderness of southern Utah. Pink and red sandstone formations and copper-colored soil make the scenery very pretty and unusual.

The distance from our ranch to our temporary residence in Salt Lake City is approximately 300 miles. I usually make this ten-hour round-trip drive every six weeks or so to see how our hired ranch hands are doing with their labors. During one of my return trips home in the late afternoon, I began feeling little tired. Knowing that wasn't good, I stopped for gas at a service station in the little town of Tropic, about 17 miles from our spread. I walked around and inhaled the crisp, cold autumn air to revive my brain. This made me fully alert for a short time.

While paying for my fuel inside, I happened to notice some small plastic bags of fresh pine nuts that were on sale at the counter. I bought two bags, figuring they would make a useful snack treat on the way back. Going through a long, winding canyon for some miles until I finally reached a highway took all my mental energy and concentration. By then I was beginning to feel drowsy again. I also happened to be a little hungry, so I opened one of the bags and commenced chewing on small handfuls of pine nuts.

I unconsciously kept this routine up for the next few hours until all of the nuts in both bags were gone. It was only then that I realized for the first time that I was no longer tired. In fact, during the entire episode of snacking on those pine nuts I had become mentally alert again without even noticing it. Something in them had given my exhausted brain a badly needed boost and pickup. It was only later on, while researching through some of the scientific literature on nuts that I learned about their rich tyrosine content.

Trace Elements for the Body

It is known that the human body currently requires 18 different minerals for good health and growth. Certain ones—calcium, phosphorus, sodium, chlorine, potassium, magnesium, and sulfur—are found in the system in appreciable amounts (0.05 percent or more) and are, therefore, called macrominerals. But others—iron, iodine, manganese, copper, zinc, cobalt, and fluorine—appear in very small amounts or traces and are thus called trace elements or microminerals.

There are indications that several other trace elements, particularly selenium, strontium, boron, molybdenum and chromium, may also be vital in the nutrition of the average human being. Nuts contain appreciable or even significant amounts of the first four; only in chromium do they seem to be rather deficient.

Selenium is a potent antioxidant. It helps protect the immune system from damage caused by scavenger molecules called free radicals. Selenium is also vital for proper function of the pancreas and keeping muscle tissue elastic. Where selenium reserves are low, there you will find cancer and heart disease. According to the *British Journal of Nutrition* (39:394–95, 1978) seven types of nuts contain varying amounts of selenium. Brazil nuts lead the pack; in fact, they are far higher in selenium content than previously thought, averaging 22 micrograms per kilogram of nut meat. Next in line for fairly high amounts were peanuts, cashews, and walnuts; those with minimal amounts included hazelnuts, sweet chestnuts, and almonds.

The next trace element in nuts that is only now beginning to be seriously looked at by scientists for its role in body health is strontium. The following table shows its distribution in different types of food (measured in parts per million).

Element	Grains and Cereals	Vegetables	Meats	Nuts
Strontium	3.00	1.90	2.00	60.00

(From *The Analysis of Prehistoric Diets* by Robert I. Gilbert and James H. Mielke (eds.) (Orlando, FL: Academic Press, 1985, p. 374.)

Because it's too soon to tell all the ways in which strontium might be potentially useful in the body only a few functions can be stated based on current scientific evidence. For one thing, strontium is vital to the production of immune system macrophages, which move about the body like garbage collectors, consuming foreign debris and harmful bacteria that could injure the system in various ways. This trace element is also closely allied to certain brain activity, but more investigation needs to be done in this area to determine specifically what role it plays there. Strontium is also a key component in intracellular functions; it's presence in the body keeps cells from mutating due to environmental (chemical) or social (stress) considerations. Strontium is also involved in the bonding of calcium with magnesium, phosphorus, potassium, and sodium to form strong bones. Without adequate amounts of it, bones become weaker over the course of time. The same thing applies to tooth formation as well.

Boron is essential for calcium uptake and healthy bones and teeth, just as strontium is. A recent study conducted by the U.S. Department of Agriculture showed that within a week's time of boron supplementation (3 milligrams daily), a test group of post menopausal women lost 40 percent less calcium, 33 $1/3$ percent less magnesium, and about 29 percent less phosphorus through their urine.

Molybdenum is needed in extremely small amounts for nitrogen metabolism. This assists the body in better utilizing nitrogen. This trace element helps in the last stages of conversion of purines to uric acid following meat consumption.

It stimulates normal cell activity and is part of the enzyme system of xanthine oxidase. Molybdenum concentrates primarily in the liver, bones, and kidneys. Low intakes have been frequently associated with male sexual impotence, higher incidents of cancer, and frequent mouth and gum diseases in both sexes.

Seeds Are Sensational for Healthy Teeth

Many things might be said in favor of seeds for snack foods. They help develop good complexion and strong bones on account of several wonderful minerals in which they are rich. They also help to prevent sagging jowls and fatty accumulation around the throat, resulting in the "double-chin" effect seen on many obese people. When the jaws are constantly exercised by frequent seed or nut chewing, excess deposits of fat stored in the muscle tissue of the face, neck, and throat is gradually "burned up" through increased chemical combustion.

But there is another benefit to seed consumption that not too many people are aware of. They help keep the teeth free of cavities and plaque and the gums free of inflammatory infections like periodonitis and gingivitis. When sunflower seeds, for instance, are routinely chewed, they help to remove other food particles that may have become stuck in between the teeth from previous meals. They also reduce the acidity level of saliva in the mouth due to sugar consumption. Both measures help to prevent cavities. Gingivitis is a progressive, painful infection marked by craterlike lesions covered with slough; foul breath, increased salivation, and frequent bleeding from the gums are additional features. Chewing seeds often helps to "massage" these tender gum areas so lesions can heal, and it removes the dirty film covering them. Believe it or not, seeds and also nuts to some extent are nature's forms of inexpensive and nutritious dental care.

Nuts and Seeds Promote Longevity

Flavius Josephus (A.D. 37–A.D. 100) was a prominent Jewish historian and soldier, born in Jerusalem. Josephus' historical works are among the most valuable sources for the study of early Judaism and early Christianity. Having studied the tenets of the three main sects of Judaism—Essenes, Sadducees, and Pharisees—he became a Pharisee himself. At the beginning of the war between the Romans and the Jews, Josephus was made commander of Galilee, despite the fact that he had opposed the uprising. He surrendered to the Romans instead of committing suicide when the stronghold was taken. He won the favor of the Roman general Vespasian (Titus Flavius Vespasianus was his full name) and took his name, Flavius. He lived in Rome under imperial patronage, where he wrote the Greek-language historical works for which he is so renowned. His most famous work, of course, is the *Antiquities of The Jews,* which has appeared in different English editions. I use the William Whiston translation from the original Greek and published by David McKay of Philadelphia, sometime in the nineteenth century.

In Book 1, Chapter 3 (p. 45) of this particular edition may be found a comment about a somewhat lengthy commentary as to the reasons why people *before* the Flood (known as Antediluvians) lived centuries longer than people did afterwards.

Josephus attributed it to three basic factors. The first was that "those ancients were beloved of God." The second reason was "because their food was *then* fitter for the prolongation of life." And finally, "God afforded them a longer time of life on account of their virtue."

Philo Judaeus of Alexandria, Egypt, was a contemporary of Josephus, though it is doubtful either of them ever met. Philo's writings, like those of Josephus, were composed at a time when both men had unrestricted access to many ancient documents found in the library archives at Alexandria and Rome, which since then have become lost or destroyed through the ravages of time and war. The edition of *The Works of Philo* I rely on is that which has been translated by C. D. Yonge (Peabody, MA: Hendrickson Publishers, 1993). Philo recorded in his *Legum Allegoriae,* III, that when Adam and Eve were cast out of the Garden by God for disobedience to divine Law, they were commanded to eat different things of the field. Among these specifically were a variety of nuts and seeds, which were intended to *minimize* but not totally do away with their intake of animal flesh.

Both ancient historians were of the opinion that the Antediluvians were able in live to such incredible ages because of their almost dally subsistence on things such as nuts and seeds. Various analyses of their nutrient contents show that they are rich in certain trace elements, which are, in fact, the very *key* to keeping the body alive and in a reasonably good state of health for a very long time. My own studies with centenarians in different cultures over the last several decades has proven to me that their longevities can be attributed, in part, to the nuts and seeds they love to snack on.

APPENDIX II

A COLLECTION OF TASTY NUT RECIPES

Delicious Almond or Cashew Milk

1 cup raw almonds or cashews

3 cups water

$1/_4$ tsp. pure maple syrup or blackstrap molasses

Place ingredients in a Vita-Mix Total Nutrition Center or equivalent food machine container. Secure complete 2-part lid by locking under tabs. Move black speed control lever to HIGH. Lift black lever to ON position and allow the machine to run for two minutes.

If you wish to strain away the pulp, simply place a fine mesh sieve over a large bowl. Pour the almond or cashew milk slowly into the sieve and allow it to filter through. Or stir the milk in the sieve with a spatula to encourage it to pass through more rapidly. Makes 2 $1/_2$ cups (strained).

(NOTE: Consult the end of this appendix for information on how to obtain a Vita-Mix Whole Food Machine.)

Wonderful Almondaise

1 cup blanched raw almonds

1 cup distilled water

1 teaspoonful Kyolic liquid aged garlic extract

1 teaspoon sea salt or 1 teaspoon Mrs. Dash

2 tablespoons fresh or reconstituted lemon juice or an equivalent
  amount of apple cider vinegar
1/4 teaspoon paprika
1/8 teaspoon granulated kelp (a seaweed)
2 cups canola oil

Place blanched almonds and water in the Vita-Mix unit. Secure complete 2-part lid by locking under tabs. Move black speed control to HIGH. Lift black lever to ON position and allow machine to run two minutes or until creamy. Stop machine and run a spatula inside container to integrate ingredients, add Kyolic liquid garlic extract, sea salt or Mrs. Dash, and kelp. Blend briefly. While the machine runs on LOW, slowly drizzle oil into the nut mixture until thickened, (Approximately one minute or less.) Continue adding more oil if desired. Any oil sitting on top can be mixed in with a fork. Pour into a jar, cover, and refrigerate. Keeps one week. Makes 3 1/2–4 cups.

(NOTE: Kyolic garlic and kelp may be obtained from any health-food store or nutrition center. In the event you cannot find Kyolic, call 1-800-421-2998 or write to Wakunaga of America Co., Ltd., 23501 Madero, Mission Viejo, CA 92691 to obtain it.)

Vitality Powerhouse

1 cup canned pineapple, with juice, chilled
1/4 medium apple
1/2 small banana
1 tablespoon English/Persian walnuts
1 tablespoon black walnuts
1/2 cup carrots
1/3 cup celery
1 large Romaine lettuce leaf
1 large spinach leaf
1 tablespoon raisins

1 small parsley sprig
1 cup ice cubes

Place all ingredients in the Vita-Mix machine in the order listed. Secure complete 2-part lid by locking under tabs. Move black speed control lever to HIGH. Lift black lever to ON position and allow machine to run for 1–1 $1/_2$ minutes until smooth. Serve immediately. Makes 1 $3/_4$ cups.

(NOTE: Fresh pineapple can be substituted for canned pineapple, but it will create a much thicker drink. If desired, thin with a little canned pineapple juice.)

Pine Nut Delight

$1/_2$ cup cold apple juice or cider
$1/_2$ cup cucumber slices, peeled
$1/_2$ apple, cut in half
$1/_4$ cup pine nuts
1 tablespoon frozen apple juice concentrate
$1/_2$ cup ice cubes

Place all ingredients in the Vita-Mix Total Nutrition Center or equivalent food machine container in the order listed. Secure complete 2-part lid by locking under tabs. Move black speed control lever to HIGH. Lift black lever to ON position and allow machine to run for 1–1 $1/_2$ minutes until smooth. Serve immediately. Makes 1 $1/_3$ cups.

Pineapple Coconut and Yogurt

$1/_2$ cup fresh or canned pineapple with juice
$1/_4$ cup low-fat pineapple yogurt
3 tablespoons shredded coconut
$1/_2$ cup regular milk
$1/_4$ cup ice cubes

Place all ingredients in the Vita-Mix unit in the order given. Secure complete 2-part lid by locking under tabs. Move black speed control lever to HIGH. Lift black lever to ON position and allow machine to run for 10–15 seconds. Makes 2 $\frac{1}{4}$ cups.

Polenta with Hazelnuts

This unique blend of ingredients was inspired by the farcement, a potato pudding with many possible garnishes, including a variety of dried fruits, from the Savoie area of France. Be sure to make the tomato sauce and roast the hazelnuts ahead of time to cut down preparation time.

2 cups tomato sauce

$\frac{1}{2}$ teaspoon ground cinnamon

$\frac{1}{2}$ teaspoon ground cardamom

1 cup pitted prunes, packed, coarsely chopped

1 clove garlic, minced

2 tablespoons Kyolic liquid aged garlic extract
  (available from health-food stores or nutrition centers)

2 tablespoons fresh parsley, chopped

$\frac{1}{2}$ cup hazelnuts

1 cup cornmeal

1$\frac{1}{2}$ cups cold water

1$\frac{3}{4}$ cups boiling water

$\frac{1}{2}$ teaspoon granulated kelp
  (a seaweed available from health-food stores)

$\frac{1}{4}$ teaspoon grated nutmeg

$\frac{1}{4}$ teaspoon ground cloves

2 tablespoons unsalted butter

2 large fresh eggs, cracked and beaten

1 tablespoon extra virgin olive oil

Preheat the oven to 350°F. Place the tomato sauce in a pan and add the cinnamon, cardamom, prunes, both kinds of garlic, and parsley. Simmer on medium-low heat for 10 minutes and set aside.

Next, spread the hazelnuts in a square cake pan and roast in the oven for 20 minutes or until aromatic and lightly golden. Watch them carefully so as not to overcook. Pour them into a clean cotton-cloth hand towel and wrap up. Rub the nuts together through this towel to remove their skins for disposal. Then chop the nuts and set them aside. Increase oven temperature to 400°F.

Place the cornmeal in a large bowl, add the cold water, and mix well. Pour the boiling water over the mixture, whisking until it is smooth. (By doing it this way, lumps won't form as readily.) Transfer this mixture to a heavy stainless steel pot. Add the kelp, nutmeg, and cloves. Slowly bring the polenta to a rolling boil over medium heat, whisking constantly. After boiling for $1-1\frac{1}{2}$ minutes, lower the heat and cook the mixture, stirring frequently with a spoon, until it is thick enough so that the spoon will stand up in the mixture without falling over. (In order to make the polenta deep enough to conduct this test, simply tilt the pan and scrape all the polenta into one corner. Then stand the spoon up in the middle of the mixture.) When it is thickened, remove the pan from the stove. Add the butter and mix until it melts. Let the polenta cool slightly.

Lightly oil a 9" × 13" baking dish. Add the beaten eggs to the polenta, mixing constantly until they are incorporated. Add seasoning to taste and pour half of the polenta into the baking dish. Spread half the tomato-prune sauce over the polenta in an even layer. Pour and spread remaining polenta over the sauce and sprinkle with the hazelnuts. Bake the polenta until it is bubbly, about 30 minutes. When cooked, remove it from the oven and let it settled for about 10 minutes before serving. Serves 6.

Hearty Vegetarian-Nut Soup Stock

Basic soup stock generally consists of about 50 percent allium vegetables (onions, leaks, shallots, garlic) and 25 percent each of celery and carrots, plus herbs, spices, and water. Some chefs will add dried or fresh mushrooms or dried beans, but try to avoid vegetables that have a strong dominating flavor, such as broccoli, cauliflower, cabbage, and peppers.

During my earlier years when I worked in several different restaurants (including a fancy country club) in Utah and Idaho, I often experimented with basic soup stocks in hopes of discovering exciting new flavors along the way. After some trial and error, I came up with this one-of-a-kind recipe, which includes several different kinds of nuts. I found, to my great delight, that they added a rich, mellow flavor to an otherwise straight vegetarian soup. This strained stock works incredible flavor miracles when added to stews, sauces, grain and bean dishes, salad dressings, poached fish, and braised tempeh and tofu.

The standard method for making stock is to place the vegetables and nuts in a large pot, add 3 $1/2$ times as much water as ingredients, and then bring to a boil. Salt can be added, if desired, but I would do so *very sparingly*. Simmer the contents, uncovered, for 2 $1/4$ hours. (The vegetables and nuts will become bitter if cooked any longer than this.) Discard them and strain the stock.

An old Japanese chef once shared a secret with me that I've never divulged until now. He said that if I wanted to add some real body to my basic stock, I should add a small amount of miso paste or nutritional yeast; better still, "add both after you've strained the broth," he concluded with a wink.

The stock is now ready. It can be eaten plain just as a simple broth or it can be added to any recipe that calls for water. Stock can be stored in the refrigerator for up to 1 $1/2$ weeks or in the freezer for 3–4 months. To make frozen stock easier to use in small amounts, freeze it in an ice cube tray. When frozen, place the stock cubes in a plastic bag; then use as needed.

5 cups unpeeled Bermuda onions, sliced in half-moons
$1/4$ cup shallots, cut in half
2 cloves garlic
2 large carrots, unpeeled and sliced
4 stalks celery, sliced
1 medium parsnip, sliced
$1/2$ cup parsnip root, diced

2 medium unpeeled potatoes, sliced

1/4 cup canola oil

1/4 cup sweet rice wine (mirin)

1 gallon water

1/4 cup navy beans, soaked overnight and drained

1/4 cup green lentils

1/8 cup chopped walnuts

1/8 cup pistachios

1/8 cup pine nuts

1/8 cup hickory nuts

1 1/2 cups tomatoes, diced

2 tablespoons tamari

6 parsley sprigs

2 bay leaves

1/4 teaspoon dried thyme

1/4 teaspoon dried rosemary

2 cloves (spice)

8 whole peppercorns

Preheat the oven to 450°F. Place the onions, shallots, garlic, carrots, celery, parsnips, and the potatoes on a large, flat baking sheet and brush with oil. Leave them uncovered while roasting in the oven for approximately 1 hour and 10 minutes or until nicely brown; be sure to turn them every so often with a metal spatula.

On a separate oiled baking sheet, spread out the different nuts. Put them on a lower rack inside the oven, but roast for only half the allotted time. Be sure and use *raw* nuts for this, not any that have been previously roasted and salted in oil. Remove the nuts and set aside until the vegetables are finished.

Place the roasted vegetables and nuts in a stock pot with the sweet rice wine and 1 cup of water. Cook over medium heat until some of the liquid evaporates. Then add the remaining ingredients. Cock uncovered for 1 1/2 hours and strain.

Almond-Cranberry-Pumpkin Bread

Heather O'Leary of Portland, Maine, created this recipe from two different ones that her mother made. "At our annual Thanksgiving Day feast, Mom's delicious pumpkin bread and cranberry nut bread were always on the help-yourself table. I decided to combine both flavors into my own special Christmas bread," she told me in September 1993, following an 8-hour alternative-health workshop I had finished giving to almost 3 dozen people. I am indebted to her for this recipe.

4 cups all-purpose flour

2 tablespoons baking powder

2 teaspoons ground cinnamon

1/2 teaspoon baking soda

1/2 teaspoon ground nutmeg

1/4 teaspoon ground ginger

1 cup brown sugar

1 cup molasses

2 cups canned pumpkin

4 large eggs

1/2 cup canola oil

2 cups coarsely chopped cranberries

*   (or the equivalent in frozen cranberries, thawed)*

1 cup chopped roasted almonds

Grease two 9" × 5" × 3" loaf pans; set aside. In a medium bowl stir together flour, baking powder, cinnamon, baking soda, nutmeg, and ginger; set aside. In a large bowl combine sugar, molasses, pumpkin, eggs, and oil. Add flour mixture to pumpkin mixture; stir just till moistened. Fold in berries and almonds.

Pour batter into the prepared pans. Bake in a 350°F, oven for 1 hour and 10 minutes. Cool for 15 minutes on wire rack. Remove from pans; cool. Wrap and store overnight. Makes 2 loaves or a total of 36 servings.

Chicken Pecan Salad Sandwich

1 cup cooked chicken, diced

1/4 cup chopped celery

1/4 cup, fresh or canned, sliced mushrooms

1/4 cup chopped pecans

1 two-ounce jar chopped pimento

1/4 cup low-fat mayonnaise

Combine all ingredients and mix well. Spread four slices of pumpernickel or rye bread or English muffins with butter. Place Romaine lettuce and tomato slices on bread and top with filling. Serve open-face style, hot or cold. Serves 4.

Amazonian Potato Salad

6 boiled potatoes, unpeeled and cubed

1 cooked beet, unpeeled and cubed

3 small pickles, cut fine

1 stalk celery, chopped fine

pinches of salt and pepper to taste

1/2 tablespoon grated Bermuda onion

1/2 can mushroom soup, undiluted

1 cup sliced Brazil nuts

1 hard-boiled egg, shelled and sliced

Mix potatoes, beet, pickles, and celery together. Then season this mixture with salt, pepper, and grated onion. Moisten with just enough undiluted mushroom soup to give thick consistency. Add half the sliced Brazil nuts. Chill. Serve on a Romaine lettuce leaf, garnished with the remaining nuts and hard-boiled egg. Serves 6.

Peanut Chicken Dijon

1 medium red or green pepper, cut into strips

5 teaspoons peanut oil

1 pound boneless chicken breasts, cut into thin strips

1/4 cup dijon mustard

2 tablespoons dry white wine

1/4 teaspoon cornstarch

3 tablespoons dry-roasted, unsalted peanuts, chopped

2 cups hot cooked rice

In a large skillet over high heat, cook peppers in oil until tender-crisp. Remove from pan; keep warm.

Blend mustard, wine, and cornstarch; add to skillet mixture. Cook over medium-high heat, stirring constantly until mixture thickens. Return chicken and peppers to pan; cook with sauce for 3–4 minutes or until heated through. Stir in peanuts. Serve over rice. Serves 4.

An Amish Salad with Black Walnut

Some years ago, while lecturing among some Amish folks in the rural area just outside Smicksburg, Pennsylvania, I was treated to a very special lunch in the home of Amos Yoder and family. His wife, Anna, served me some delicious cream of stinging nettle soup. But it was the salad I remember most. It contained not only the standard bibb lettuce from her garden, but fresh violets (flowers and all), some slices of Jerusalem artichoke, and sliced daylily shoots (which she also fixed like asparagus), the whole of which was sprinkled with crumbled black walnut meats. That was the most elegant and sumptuous repast, I believe I had in years. And instead of eating it in a fancy four-star Manhattan restaurant, I partook of it in a humble abode with simple but genuine friendly folks, who often used the Bible and prayers as their guides for daily living.

Cream of Black Walnut Soup

The evening of the same day that I ate lunch at the Yoder residence, I was invited to stay over for supper. Anna prepared an unusual but delightful soup, which still lingers fondly in the memory after all these years.

2 cups black walnuts, chopped
3 tablespoons chopped celery
1 tablespoon chopped chives
5 cups chicken stock
2 tablespoons cream sherry
2 teaspoons butter
1 cup heavy cream
pinch salt to taste
grated nutmeg for topping

I watched as Anna combined the black walnuts, celery, and chives with some chicken stock in a saucepan. She brought it to a rolling boil, then moved the pan to medium heat at another spot on top of her coal-and-wood range and left it for 20 minutes.

After this, she stirred in the sherry, butter, cream, and salt with a wire whisk. She then reheated the soup before serving it in individual wooden bowls. She ladled some chopped black walnut meats into each bowl and topped it off with a sprinkle of nutmeg. As I remember, her soup served 8 of us.

Brown Rice with Chestnuts

1 cup rice
8–10 dried chestnuts
1 1/2 cups water
pinch of sea salt to taste

Wash rice. It's easy to remove the dark skin of the chestnuts if they're first soaked or roasted in a dry skillet on a low flame for 7 minutes. Add to rice and pressure cook for an hour. Serves 2.

Amish Chestnut Stuffing

While staying with the Yoders near Smicksburg, Pennsylvania, for a couple of days, I got a chance to taste some of Anna's incredible chestnut stuffing, which she used to stuff an 8-pound goose for a wedding coming up.

1/2 pound chestnuts
1/4 cup melted butter
2 cups soft bread crumbs
1 teaspoon salt
2 teaspoons poultry seasoning
1 well-beaten farm-fresh egg
1/4 cup chopped celery

Wash the chestnuts and make two slits in each shell before baking at 475°F for 15 minutes. Then shell each one and boil them in enough water to cover for 20 minutes. Chop them fine. Mix in with the melted butter, bread crumbs, salt, poultry seasoning, egg, and celery. Stir thoroughly with a wooden spoon.

Hazelnut-Vegetable Pie

1 cup fresh broccoli, chopped
1 cup cauliflower, sliced
2 cups fresh spinach, chopped
1 small onion, diced
1/2 green pepper, diced
1 cup cheddar cheese, grated
1 cup coarsely chopped hazelnuts
1 1/2 cups milk

1 cup biscuit mix

4 eggs

2 tablespoons Kyolic liquid garlic extract
(found in most health-food stores or nutrition centers)

1/2 teaspoon pepper

Precook broccoli and cauliflower until almost tender (about 5 minutes). Drain well. Mix broccoli, cauliflower, spinach, onion, green pepper, and cheese and put into a well-greased 10-inch pie tin. Top with hazelnuts. Beat together the milk, biscuit mix, eggs, Kyolic liquid garlic, and pepper; pour over hazelnuts and vegetables. Bake at 400°F, for 40 minutes. Let pie stand 5 minutes before cutting. Serves 6.

Macadamia Nut Fettucine

7 quarts water

1 pound egg noodles

1/2 cup butter

1/2 cup heavy cream

1/2 cup grated Parmesan cheese

One 3 1/2-ounce jar macadamia nut bits

Bring water to a boil and cook the noodles. Drain. In a medium saucepan, melt butter, stir in cream. Remove from the heat and stir in the Parmesan cheese, reserving a little of it for the top. Fold in hot cooked noodles and macadamia nuts. Sprinkle with reserved cheese. Serves 4.

Arizona Indian Acorn Stew

1 pound stewing meat

1/2 cup finely ground acorn meal

pinches salt and pepper to taste

Place beef in heavy pan and add water to cover. Put lid on pan and simmer beef until it is very tender and almost ready to fall to pieces. Remove the beef from the liquid and chop the meat very fine. Return it to the liquid in the pot. Stir in the acorn meal. Add salt and pepper to taste. Heat the mixture and serve. Serves 3–4.

Sichuan Chicken with Gingko Nuts

During the summer of 1980 I was privileged to visit what was then called the People's Republic of China. I was one of several different faculty advisers accompanying about 29 third- and fourth-year med students with the American Medical Students' Association to this part of the world to learn more about traditional Oriental medicine. We were served this dish, and it tasted so good that I asked one of our interpreters to get the recipe for me from the chef, which she gladly did.

12 oz. fresh or canned gingko nuts

1 2 1/2 pound chicken

3 green onions

6 slices fresh ginger

2 tablespoons rice wine or dry sherry

pinches of salt and white pepper to taste

Soak the fresh ginkgo nuts in boiling water, then drain and scrape off the skin. Pick off the two ends, push the bitter core through with a toothpick, then soak again.

Blanch the chicken in boiling water, then hold beneath cold running water to rinse. Drain and place the breast facing upward in a casserole dish.

Add the remaining ingredients, except for the gingko nuts. Cover with water, bring to boil, reduce the heat and simmer for 15 minutes. Turn the chicken over, add the gingko nuts and continue to simmer until the chicken is completely tender.

Remove the chicken and cut in half lengthwise, then cut the meat diagonally from the center into slices. Arrange in its original shape on a serving plate. Lift the gingko nuts from the stock with a slotted spoon, arrange around the chicken and serve at once. Serves 4.

Vita-Mix Peanut or Cashew Butter

Place 4 cups roasted peanuts or cashews in the Vita-Mix Total Nutrition Center or equivalent food machine container. Secure the complete 2-part lid by locking it under the tabs. Move speed control lever to HIGH. Lift the black lever to the ON position and allow the machine to run for *no more* than 1 minute; any processing longer than this could result in serious overheating of the unit.

As the machine is running, the tamper that comes with each unit can be slid through the lid to compress the nuts into the blades, as they're apt to bounce around a little while the blades are running. Almond butter can be made by substituting an equal amount of almonds in place of the other two nuts. Add $1/_2$ cup pure virgin olive oil if necessary, refrigerate, and pour off excess oil the next day. Makes $1 1/_2$ cups of delicious peanut, cashew, or almond butter.

Raw peanut butter can also be made in the Vita-Mix blender. For this you will need $4 1/_2$ cups raw peanuts and 3 tablespoons pure virgin olive oil. After putting both ingredients into the container, proceed as described above; process *no more* than one minute. Remove the peanut butter with a rubber spatula. Makes $4 1/_2$ cups peanut butter.

I highly recommend the Vita-Mix Total Nutrition Center since it is the only unit on the market that is versatile enough to make nut butters, grind whole wheat into flour, and make hot soup. To purchase a unit for yourself, write or call:

Vita-Mix Corporation
8615 Usher Road
Cleveland, OH 44138
1-800-VITAMIX (800-848-2649)
Fax: (216)-235-3726

Appendix III

Sources for Nuts

In many large metropolitan areas, a person is apt to find one or several different companies specializing in different kinds of nuts. They usually offer them in raw or roasted forms. Some nuts, such as black walnuts, for instance, are seasonal and carried only during the traditional period spanning Thanksgiving to New Year's. By consulting the yellow pages in your local telephone directory under NUTS and calling or visiting several of the places listed there, you should be able to find many of the more common nuts.

There is however, a Florida business that specializes exclusively in nuts, seeds, dried fruits, exotic coffee blends, and assorted herbs. I've personally known the people who run this business for almost 20 years and can vouch for the integrity, wholesomeness, and freshness of their products. Because they are Jehovah's Witnesses, they feel duty-bound to their strange religion to act in an ethical way in how they choose to conduct their business affairs.

Because of the worldwide contacts they've developed over the years, they are able to procure for their mail-order customers just about any kind of nut, seed, fruit, coffee, or medicinal herb requested of them. Their prices are fair, their service excellent, and their products fully guaranteed. You may write or call Ron or Louise Hamilton for more information on what you need.

Great American Natural Products, Inc.
4121 - 16th Street North
St. Petersburg, FL 33703
(813) 521-4372
Fax: 1-800-522-6457

If you want more information on nuts than what has been given in this section, I recommend a book by a colleague of mine. His name is Dr. James A. Duke, recently retired from the United States Department of Agriculture's Germplasm Research Laboratory in Bethesda, Maryland. Jim has written one of the most comprehensive books ever assembled on the subject of nuts. Appropriately entitled, *CRC Handbook of Nuts,* it covers 109 different nut species.

Each write-up includes detailed discussions of uses (all uses of the plant), folk medicine, chemistry, toxicity, description, germ plasm, distribution, ecology, cultivation, harvesting, yields and economics, energy and biotic factors. This highly detailed compilation is of greater interest, I think, to farmers, producers, food technologists, chemists, pharmacognosists, and those in research and development of food and medicinal plants than it would be for the average consumer.

Still, there is a great deal of data you simply won't find in any other single work, even including this section of my book. The bibliography alone contains almost 450 references. However, before I give you the cost of it, I advise you to sit down first. The truth of the matter is, you have to be (quite literally) "nuts about nuts" (encompassing all definitions of the word nut) to want to pay a heart-stopping $175.00 price tag for this most useful reference work. If you've got the dough, here's where to go:

CRC Press
2000 Corporate Blvd., N.W.
Boca Raton, FL 33431

Appendix IV

Berry Cultivation and Harvesting

Mulching

Mulches are any material that are spread on the ground to protect the soil and the roots of trees, berry bushes, and garden plants from the effects of soil crusting, erosion, or freezing; they are also employed to retard the growth of weeds. For larger areas under cultivation, a tilled layer of soil serves the purpose of mulches.

Mulches are especially important in berry cultivation. Besides the aforementioned advantages, they also encourage earthworms, and as the mulches rot, they contribute humus and fertilizers to the soil. Soil to which some type of mulch has been added is enriched with the minerals and trace elements left behind during the decaying process.

Mulch materials fall into two basic categories: the decomposing and nondecomposing kinds. Mulches that decay very nicely are citrus pulp, coarse shavings, cocoa shells, composted bark, evergreen needles (pine are best for blueberries), farm wastes (spoiled ensilage, straw, hay), lawn clippings (dry slightly before using to keep from heating), tree leaves (oak is best for blueberries), old magazines, discarded newspapers, peanut shells, peat moss, shredded bark, and wood chips. Mulches that do not decompose are black plastic, commercial landscaping fabrics, crushed rock or gravel, flat rocks or slate, marble or granite rock chips, and paving blocks.

Avoid using shavings, wood chips, or other slow-to-rot mulches on strawberry beds. The best material to use is straw—in fact, this is where the berry originally got its name from. It was customary in the Middle Ages to cover them with straw, hence *strawberries*. Besides the previously mentioned benefits of mulches, in the case of strawberries and other low-growing berries, such materials keep rain from splattering dirt on the ripening fruits.

Professional and serious berry growers unanimously support mulching for the home gardener, preferably with an organic mulch. A professional berry gardener in upper New York State explained it this way: "Berries respond to mulch better than any other plant simply because they are plants of northern climates, are shallow-rooted, and like moisture in the soil." A very cost-effective method for mulching is to prune your berry bushes, then chop up the trimmings and work them back into the ground. This works well with all bramble fruits, including raspberries, blackberries, and roses (for the rose hips).

Nonorganic mulches can be used if your berry bushes or plants are part of your home landscape. Professional landscape experts usually choose the clean appearance of crushed rock, flagstones, marble chips, or slate around their plantings, and blueberry and strawberry growers often spread black plastic between the rows. Such nonorganic mulches last for years and offer many of the advantages of organic materials except for the all-important one of contributing humus and nutrients to the soil.

Watering

Commercial berry growers use self-running irrigation systems that ensure measured dosages of water to berries; the slow-drip method is one of the more popular of these. A sprinkling system is adequate for the purposes of the home gardener. It is especially important to water during the hot summer months. It isn't too difficult to tell when berries require a lot of water: they wilt, and some of the fruits may have a sunburn, which gives them a wilted appearance. High bush blueberries and cranberries, in particular, require generous amounts of water.

It is best to water berry bushes and plants every five days, preferably in the morning or midafternoon. This allows the berries a chance to dry before nightfall so that they don't become susceptible to rot. Once the fruits are harvested, the plants or shrubs need a thorough soaking.

Planting

The first rule of thumb to remember in growing *healthy* berry shrubs and plants is *never* to accept gift plants from a generous neighbor or relative, no matter how well intentioned that individual might be. You might think you're saving money, but in the long run such gift plants will usually end up costing you more than they're worth, simply because the majority of them are likely to come with hidden diseases and insects; these will spread through the rest of your garden like wildfire and be hard as hell to get rid of.

Always purchase *all* your berry bushes or plants from reliable nurseries. Such establishments go to great lengths to ensure that the plants they offer for sale to the public are disease-free and reasonably *healthy*. This way you have *total* control over what you're working with and can start out properly with a bug-free, disease-free berry patch. You'll have less to worry about in the long run.

Planting instructions vary with the type of berries involved. Because of the limitations of space, only the bramble fruits, strawberries, bush fruits, blueberries, and one vine fruit (grapes) will be briefly dealt with here.

When buying berry plants make sure that they are suited for the climate in which you reside. Berries that have been developed especially for one region are often unsuitable in another, even if climatic differences seem slight. Experimenting is fun, but if you are relying on a crop, plant the cultivars you are absolutely sure will yield in your part of the world. Add a lot of compost or manure (15 pounds dried or 10 bushels fresh per 100 square feet of garden space) to your soil, work it in well, and get rid of all grass and weeds. The soil should be rich, loose, and crumbly, so the roots will be able to start growing as soon as you set the plants in.

When planting brambles, make sure you don't crowd them. In other words, allot plenty of space between such items as raspberries, blackberries, dewberries, and elderberries, since they all sucker badly. And don't plant them near a vegetable garden, strawberry patch, or ornamental flower bed. Plant them some distance apart from shade trees with large roots, too, and away from large fruit trees that may require spraying during the summer when the berries are ripening.

Berry plants received through the mail are generally shipped bare-rooted and are often dry upon arrival. After unwrapping them, soak their roots for six hours in a bucket of water. However, potted plants from a local nursery will take off faster because their root systems are already somewhat established.

Brambles need to be well mulched with thick layers of shredded bark, leaves, shavings, or wood chips to prevent grass and weeds from growing around them. Don't use sawdust, however, because it packs too tightly and steals nitrogen from the soil. Don't rototill or hoe around brambles as such actions can damage the root systems.

Brambles need to be planted at least three feet apart. Set each plant to the same depth as it originally grew in the ground or pot. Saturate the soil heavily with water to which has been added a weak solution of liquid fertilizer. Make sure that each plant sits in a muddy mixture and is free of any air pockets around the roots. Continue to water the newly set plants thoroughly every three days for three weeks unless it rains heavily. Once a week use the liquid fertilizer solution. Remember that water is cheap fruit insurance.

If you use potted plants, no pruning is necessary at planting time. With bare-rooted plants, however, it's important that the canes be cut back to two inches above the ground after they're set in. If not, the tops will grow faster than the roots, resulting in a weaker plant. Plants that have been cut back will not produce any berries the first year, but the idea is to develop a lot of canes that will produce heavily in the third year.

Remember that bramble roots are perennial, but their canes are biennial. This means the roots live for years, but each cane sprouts and grows its full height in only one year, bears fruit the next, and then promptly dies after that. So to keep your berry patch productive, cut each dead cane to ground level after it has finished bearing.

I asked two professional berry growers which ones were the easiest to start with and invariably, both pointed to the blackberry. Nita Gizdich of the Gizdich Ranch in Watsonville, California, remarked that "of all the berries we've ever grown, the blackberry seems the easiest for people to get into. There always seems to be a home for them. no matter where the customer may live." And Perry Kozlowski of the Kozlowski Berry Farm in Sebastopol, California, concurred: "The easiest berries I know of are blackberries; they seem to thrive even under the most adverse conditions."

So, how many plants should you grow? This depends on the size of your family and their preferences, whether you intend to preserve the fruit or not, and how much room you have available for planting. Here is a suggested berry garden I've laid out for two people: 4 blackberry plants (yield 8 pints fruit); 2 blueberry (yield 25 pints fruit); 2 currant (yield 5 pints fruit); 2 elderberry (yield 5 pints fruit); 2 gooseberry (yield 6 pints fruits); 5 black raspberry (yield 25 pints); 20 red raspberry (yield about 35 pints); and 13 strawberry (yield 13 quarts).

Strawberries do well in soils that will also grow vegetables. Never plant them in soil that you know is infested with nematodes, tiny root eaters that can destroy young plants in no time at all. Plant them very early in the spring. There are two planting methods to choose from: the matted row or the lesser-used hill system. Either way, they should be planted with their crowns at ground level. Removing the blossoms by hand in the first year will allow for large fruits on stronger plants in the second year.

Like the brambles just mentioned, the bush fruits come in a variety of rich colors. There are the red, white, and black currants; the green, amber, pink, and red gooseberries, the blueberries; and the wine-dark jesters, elderberries, and saskatoons. They all furnish a tremendous amount of good eating in return for the small amount of time and money you need to spend on them. They begin to bear at an early age, bear big crops each year, and add exciting variety to any home grower's fruit collection.

The culture of all bush berries is pretty much the same. Plant them six feet apart in well-drained soil, except for elderberry, which enjoys moist ground. All do well in humus-rich soils.

Growth habits of bush fruits vary considerably. Gooseberries and red and white currants are well behaved and stay within bounds, but black currants and elderberries sucker so much that they can overwhelm an entire parcel of ground.

Because such bush berries are, in reality, small trees, they don't require planting in soil that is as carefully prepared as that needed for strawberries and brambles. Just dig a big hole, mix an equal amount of well-rotted manure or compost with the soil you remove, and fill the hole with water. Set them as you would fruit trees, at the same depth they grew originally in the pot or before they were dug if bare-rooted.

Birds seem to be one of the biggest threats to bush fruits. This is especially true with regard to currants and elderberries. Keeping a cat outside near them, setting up a human-looking scarecrow and moving it about from time to time, and tying strips of foil on the branches of such bushes will keep these pesky and hungry critters away.

Blueberry plants are slow growers and take at least eight years before reaching their full production potential. The soil must be rather acidic, well mulched and comported, and fairly loose in consistency in order for blueberries to do well in it. They also require cross pollination, so plant at least three different cultivars just for good measure. Mix up the plantings and keep the different cultivars near each other, in order to attract bees more easily. High bush and rabbit-eye blueberries need to be set five feet apart, while low bush plants require only one foot spacings. Of all the berries, these seem to need more nitrogen than any others so be sure to fertilize and mulch them thoroughly and frequently. Because blueberry plants are much harder to start than other kinds of berries, they generally cost more as a rule.

Finally, a few words about grapes. They happen to be the world's oldest cultivated fruits. Apocryphal, pseudepigrapha, and early rabbinical writings suggest that red grapes were the original "forbidden fruit" in the Garden of Eden, of which Adam and Eve partook in order to acquire the necessary mortality to sire and give birth to mortal children.

Grapes are one of the easiest fruits to propagate. Hardwood cuttings taken in the early spring root easily and become husky, well-developed plants by late fall. The following spring the cuttings can be transplanted to more permanent homes where they will start yielding fruit after a couple of years. Grapes can also be started by layering and by softwood cuttings. On the other hand, grape seeds are likely to produce mostly wild-type plants with little food value to them.

An early spring planting is best for grapes because they require an abundance of heat and sunlight to get established before winter.

Pruning is essential to grape growing and must never be neglected. Because of the grape's tendency to grow vigorously, after it reaches maturity a lot of wood must be cut away every year.

Unpruned grapevines become so overgrown and dense that the sun is unable to reach into the areas where fruit should form, and the further the grapes are produced from the main stem, the smaller the crop is likely to be.

Spring planting in slightly sandy soil is advisable. Plant the vines nine feet apart, with a post midway between each plant and one on each end of the row. String two strands of smooth nine-gauge wire on the posts; the first one should be two feet above the ground, and the second, about two feet higher.

If you bought your vines bare-rooted, cut them back directly after planting so each is only half a foot long and has just two or three fat buds. This pruning will encourage the roots to start growing rapidly and help them to keep up with the top growth. On the other hand, if potted vines are being planted, then this cutting back can be eliminated. Be sure to water the vines frequently and allow them to grow freely, without further pruning the first year. In the second and third year, more vigorous cutting is needed to encourage faster growth.

Obviously in the space allotted, only basic essentials have been covered with regard to the planting of berries. The reader will need to consult other books that specifically deal with these issues in greater detail. I recommend these three, in particular:

D. E. Bilderback and D. Hinshaw, *Backyard Fruits and Berries* (Emmaus, PA: Rodale Press 1984).

L. Hill, *Secrets of Plant Propagation* (Pownal, VT: Garden Way Publishing, 1985).

L. Hill, *Pruning Simplified* (Pownal, VT: Garden Way Publishing, 1985).

Harvesting

In the short time I spent among various Native American tribes of the West, Northwest, and Southwest, I discovered an easy way to remove most berries when fully matured. A large canvas or black plastic tarp is placed under and around the shrub or small trees. If they are prickly and have stickers or thorns in them, the hands should be protected at all times with leather work gloves. With a long stick, cane, or even an old crutch the branches are gently tapped to knock the ripe berries off and onto the covering below. After this, the berries are removed to a large pot or tub of water, poured in, and washed. Any leaves, stickers, or other debris will float to the top where they can be skimmed off. This is basically the method employed by Crow, Sioux, Cherokee, and Mescalero Apache Indians with whom I've associated in times past.

Another method—again wearing thick leather gloves—is to raise a branch with one hand and strip the pendant berries off with the other. They can be collected in a plastic bucket or handcrafted basket of some kind, held in midair beneath the branch being stripped. Or else a covering can be laid out on the ground and the berries can be permitted to fall down on it.

For lower-growing berries, a stool or folding chair may be necessary to avoid back and leg strain from excessive bending or squatting. Some berries, such as currants, need to be gathered by pinching off each cluster with the thumb and forefinger. This can be rather tiresome and boring, to say the least.

When picking blueberries, remember to taste them first. Just because they're blue doesn't necessarily mean they're ripe yet. You'll know a blueberry bush is ripe for harvesting when the berries easily separate from the stems. To collect them, simply rake your fingers lightly across the blueberries. The ones that are ready to be eaten right away will fall into your bucket or container. If you watch your blueberries carefully, you'll know exactly when they're ripe.

Raspberries separate from their cores when picked; but other brambles such as blackberries take the core with them. Raspberries are very tender and must be handled gently. Don't pack too many in a container. You'll know raspberries are ripe when they turn deep red, purple, glossy black, or golden-yellow tinged with pink, depending on the variety. Picking thornless brambles is a much more pleasant task than struggling through brambles. Blackberries are soft, but not as fragile as raspberries and will easily separate from the plant when fully ripened.

When picking strawberries, always be sure to break the stem by pinching it with your thumb and forefinger. Never just pull the berry from the plant, as this can damage the fruit or separate it from its cap—which will cause it to wither.

Most berries can be harvested in late summer or early-to-late fall. It's best to collect them on a sunny, dry day, because high humidity or wet conditions will cause picked fruit to spoil very quickly. Many berries can be kept in a refrigerator for a week to ten days provided they are dry and the temperature is set at just above freezing.

Berries are delicious as well as nutritious and provide their consumer with quick energy and a deep sense of eating satisfaction and pleasure on account of their unique and wonderful flavors.

APPENDIX V

BERRY PROCESSING: PRESERVING, DRYING, AND STORAGE

Preserves

Two excellent methods of preserving berries are to bottle or freeze them. Preserved berries packed in attractive glass jars make stunning gifts. Not only that, but fresh berries can be made into luscious jams and jellies without much difficulty. Berries can also be packaged in tight zippered plastic bags, which keep air and moisture out to retain freshness, and stored in the freezer until needed. Frozen berries retain more of their original color, taste, and nutrients than those that have been cooked for use as preserves.

Cook your berry jam or jelly to the thickness desired (substituting honey or pure maple syrup instead of white sugar) using your favorite recipe, and use a wide-mouthed funnel to ladle or pour the cooked preserves into jars. Fill the jars to within one-quarter inch of the top. Then seal with a sterilized lid. Use paraffin or flat lids to seal jars. Afterwards, use a jar lifter to transfer the jars to a rack. Let them cool for several hours.

I highly recommend the book *Putting Food By,* by Janet Greene and others. This tome should be read by every prospective home berry preserver because of the valuable "how-to-do-it" information offered inside. The book may be ordered from The Stephen Greene Press (an imprint of Penguin USA), 375 Hudson Street, New York, NY 10014.

Aside from turning them into jams and jellies, you can make fresh berries into other marvelous concoctions. Add Madeira wine to a jar filled with blackberries or raspberries and let the mixture stand for a minimum of two weeks. This luscious sauce can then be poured over pound cake or short cake for a truly pleasing dessert.

It also goes very well with wild game such as venison, pheasant, or duck, as well as other types of cooked meat.

Sun-Dried Patties

Sun drying fresh berries for the wintertime when plant foods are scarce was a common practice of many Native American tribes in the last century and before then. With just a few exceptions among some elderly Indians, it has just about died out for the most part. I was fortunate enough to have learned it firsthand from Joy Yellowtail Toineeta on the Crow Reservation in eastern Montana several decades ago.

Firm berries such as blueberry, choke cherry, cranberry, currant, gooseberry, huckleberry, and wild plum dry the best. They need to be washed free of debris, thoroughly drained of water, and then dried between two towels by gently rolling them around with the palms of the hands lightly placed on the top covering. After this they are run through a food or nut grinder. (Choke cherries and plums need to have their internal seeds removed by hand. Cook 1 cup of whole chokecherries in 2 cups of boiling water for 20 minutes; drain liquid and give each cherry a little squeeze with the thumb and forefinger and the pit will pop right out. Plums, on the other hand, can be slit in half with a sharp paring knife and the point of it used to lift out the stone. When chokecherries are cooked this way, they need to be *very well drained* before proceeding to the next step.)

After running berries through a grinder *twice*, their pulp is ready to be converted into patties. Joy had a couple of ways of doing this. To each gallon of mashed berries, she added 1 cup of vegetable shortening and $2\frac{1}{2}$ cups of brown sugar. This she mixed well with both hands and shaped patties $\frac{1}{4}$ to $\frac{1}{2}$ an inch thick and about $2\frac{1}{2}$ inches in diameter. In the other method, she just mixed some brown flour with the berry pulp to form patties that way. After this the patties were placed on clean muslin or an old bed sheet on top of a table or drying rack outside the house where they could be well exposed to the sun. She turned these berry patties over every day with a spatula so they would dry thoroughly. They were covered with a thin layer of cheesecloth during this several-day drying process to keep flies and other insects away.

After this Joy gathered them up and carefully put them in an empty flour sack, which she tied at the top with some twine and hung on a nail in a well-ventilated room for a few more days. Following this the patties were then permanently stored in dry #10 coffee cans with plastic lids or in wide-mouthed glass gallon jars with tight-fitting screw-on metal caps. I recall her telling me that it wasn't necessary to always make patties; the berry pulp could be spread out on a sheet and dried that way. But it had to be stirred often for several days to make sure no moisture remained in it. The dried berry patties or pulp was then used throughout the long cold winter by crumbling some of them into stews and soups for added flavor and nutrition.

Joy made some elk stew to which was added three or four crumbled gooseberry patties. I was amazed at just how delicious this dish was because of them. If hot, sunny days aren't always available, berries like this can be dried in your oven or in an indoor dryer. The book mentioned earlier or any other authoritative work on food preservation will give specific instructions for drying procedures.

Berry Breads

Berry cornbread is another innovative way of preserving your favorite bush fruits. Cornbread, even when hard as brick, keeps for quite awhile if always stored in a cool, dry place with *no* humidity and in a tightly sealed container. I learned this method from a Zuñi Indian woman in Arizona some years ago. Her standard recipe for *any* type of berry cornbread is as follows:

1 cup cornmeal (yellow or white)
1 cup stone ground whole wheat flour
2 teaspoons baking powder
1 teaspoon salt
1 egg
1 tablespoon honey
2 tablespoons vegetable shortening or butter
1 cup milk or cooked berry juice
2/3 cup berries of your choice

Heat oven to 425°F. Grease a 9-inch cast-iron frying pan and put it into the oven to heat. Combine all of the dry ingredients. Then add the egg, honey, and shortening or butter. Measure berry liquid or milk and add liquid to make $3/4$ cup. Add to the other ingredients. Stir the berries in next. Pour the batter into the hot pan and bake at 425°F for 30 minutes. Muffins and cookies that keep awhile can also be made from berries.

Teas and Wines

Berries make delicious beverages. They can be sun-dried (but without rolling them in fat or flour) by washing, draining, and then spreading them out on a clean sheet or screen dryer where the sun can get to them. They are then stored in tightly closed containers until needed. About a half cup of dried berries is added to one quart of boiling water and simmered for 5 minutes on low heat. After this the brew is removed from the stove, covered with a lid, and steeped for 45 minutes. A little honey, cinnamon, or mint leaves may be added for extra flavor. The strained liquid makes a variety of delicious teas with very exciting berry flavors to them.

Home brewing of berry wines is another possibility for the adventurous berry preserver. Gooseberry wine is a surprising sparkling beverage; it goes especially well with fish. Currants make excellent dessert wines. A real berry connoisseur friend of mine residing on Vancouver Island in the Pacific Northwest brews this delightful beverage for his clientele in the gourmet restaurant he owns and operates. He reported to me that he couldn't keep enough of this in stock to satisfy his customers. The blackberry has a mellow flavor that is very pleasant as a table wine. There are different books on wine making; one of the best is *Guidelines to Practical Winemaking* by Julius H. Kessler (This can be ordered for $45 from Anthropological Research Center, POB 11471, Salt Lake City, UT 84147.)

All the blackberries and especially the loganberry and boysenberry varieties, raspberries, and strawberries produce very good quality wines. Currants, gooseberries, and elderberries have somewhat similar characteristics but less distinctive flavor. They are made into wines by identical procedures.

Ripe fruit in sound condition produces the best wine. Fresh or unsweetened frozen berries are equally satisfactory as starting material. Frozen berries, *without* added sugar and at reasonable prices, make the wine-making procedures easier to control. Freezing destroys the cellular structure and permits high yields of juice with moderate pressures. The home freezing of berries *first* BEFORE making wine is definitely encouraged wherever possible.

Crush the berries, by hand if the amount is small, or with a wooden paddle or roller crusher as the amount becomes greater in size.

Each ten pounds of blackberries, raspberries, or strawberries should receive three pints of water after crushing. Mix well and transfer to the container intended for fermentation purposes. Each ten pounds of currants, gooseberries, and elderberries should receive six pints of water after crushing.

Weigh out almost two pounds of white sugar for each gallon of mixture in the fermentation vessel. Add one quarter of the total weight to the mixture. Stir well to dissolve the added sugar. Set the remainder of the sugar aside. When a vigorous fermentation is in progress, remove a small portion of the liquid, dissolve another one quarter of the required amount of sugar in this portion, and then add the mixture to the fermentation container. Repeat this procedure at daily intervals until all of the sugar has been used up in this manner.

Some judgment of fermentation characteristics is necessary at this stage as the sugar must be added only while the mass is in active fermentation. Conditions such as temperature, variety of fruit, kind of sugar, kind of yeast, and the like may require adding sugar at a faster or slower rate than the 24-hour rate it usually takes.

For such moderately acidic fruits as blackberries, raspberries, plums, cherries, and eastern varieties of grapes and plums, about 3 gallons of water added to each 10 gallons of juice, or juice and skins, will yield good results. For the highly acidic fruits such as Loganberries, currants, and gooseberries, 7 gallons of water per 10 gallons of juice are suggested. (Add $1/3$ ounce of sodium bisulfite to each 10 gallons of fermentable material.)

The yeast should be added next. Home wine makers will probably find a dry granular or powdered form of baker's yeast the best to use for this. Fleischman Dry Yeast or Red Star Yeast (in dry powder or compressed yeast cake) are the two brands most commonly employed. Add one-half teaspoon of baker's yeast to each gallon.

Cover the top of the fermentation container with some cheesecloth or affix a specially made fermentation trap in place.

Add the remaining sugar (as previously directed) at the appropriate time intervals. Strain out the pulp when sugar is added for the final time. Transfer to clean storage containers and let the fermentation complete itself under a fermentation trap.

Bottle directly or after sweetening (if desired). But if you do sweeten the wine be sure to pasteurize or else refermentation will occur, which can cause tightly sealed bottles to explode almost like a Molotov cocktail. To prevent this from happening, put the sweetened wine into crown-sealed or screw-cap jars. Fill well into the neck of each bottle. Seal with plastic-lined closures and place the bottles on their sides in a large cooking pan. Fill with hot water out of the tap and heat *slowly* to 130°F. Remove the pot from the stove and leave the bottles in the water for another 10 minutes. Then pour off the water, remove the bottles, and allow them to cool back to room temperature. Some clouding is apt to occur from heat but is harmless and will settle to the bottom if left undisturbed. Store bottles in a dark, cool place standing up or slanted at a slight angle.

Nice Vinegars

Vinegars are another clever method of preserving delicious berries for a very long time. The fruits (raspberries and blueberries work particularly well) are steeped in *apple cider* vinegar (obtained from any health-food store or supermarket) for several weeks in fruit jars. About two cups of berries are soaked in four cups of apple cider vinegar and gently shaken once a day. Large two-quart glass fruit jars are ideal for this; the metal-ring lids should barely be turned or very loosely screwed on to allow for penetration of air inside.

The berry vinegars can be used in myriad ways: sprinkled over sliced fruit, basted on chicken, mixed with jam as an accompaniment to chicken or duck, or made into vinaigrettes. For instance, a huckleberry vinaigrette nicely complements roasted pigeon, quail, or pheasant. Here is an easy recipe for making 1 1/2 cups of it:

¹/₂ cup huckleberries (¹/₄ pint)
¹/₂ cup apple cider vinegar
1 tablespoon sugar or pure maple syrup
¹/₄ cup hazelnut oil
pinch of salt and white pepper, if desired

Steep the huckleberries in the vinegar and sugar or maple syrup for 24 hours. Mix thoroughly with the remaining ingredients for a fascinating vinaigrette that has been variously described as being "sweetly exhilarating, rambunctious and untamed, and tart and invigorating." Huckleberry, elderberry, or currant vinaigrettes nicely contrast with sharp-flavored, fresh leafy greens such as watercress, endive, escarole, or romaine lettuce.

Berry vinegars may also be used as efficient salt substitutes. I've added a teaspoon of cranberry vinegar to extra virgin olive oil in a friend's popcorn popper, heated them, then added the corn and popped it. Man, what a lip-smacking experience that was for our taste buds, but without adversely affecting our blood pressure levels. Or how about oven browned fries with elderberry vinegar? Just toss some frozen french fries with cold-pressed flaxseed oil, then bake according to the directions on the package. While still hot, sprinkle with elderberry-apple cider vinegar, some herbs, and a little granulated kelp. Now *there* is a treat well worth trying!

For those wishing to make their own vinegars from different homemade berry wines, I suggest they read E. LeFevre's *Making Vinegar in the Home and on the Farm* (Washington, DC: U.S. Government Printing Office, USDA Bulletin 1424, 1924; 28 pages).

Salted Berries

Jeannie Westover lives in the far north of the Alaskan wilderness, "miles and miles away from the nearest human habitat," she is fond of telling anyone. "A place teeming with big Kodiak bears, roaming wolf packs, wily foxes, ornery badgers, clumsy moose, aristocratic elk, and gentle does with big, moist, round eyes," she exclaimed when I met her for the first time at a health conference in Seattle, to which she had flown mostly out of curiosity.

When I mentioned I was intending to do a book on berries, nuts, and seeds, she volunteered this interesting method for preserving berries when you're completely removed from the services of available electricity. "I boil my bath water on an old wood stove and read by kerosene lamp," she joked. "But I salt much of my food to preserve it during the short summers up there when my long winter months of refrigeration have temporarily ceased.

"First, check your berries over, setting aside any broken, bruised, or over-ripe juicy ones for immediate use. Put the firm ones, dry (never wet), into quart fruit jars leaving about 1 1/2 inches of head room. If they can't be stored in a totally dark area, then I recommend a person use colored glass instead of the clear.

"Once the berries are in the bottle, add one teaspoon of salt and agitate gently, just enough to work the salt down through. Seal it—a screw-top, hand tightened, is adequate. Without further shaking, put into storage in some dark place. I guarantee they'll keep indefinitely!

"Now these berries will create a small amount of juice but for the most part, remain firm. They won't ferment or spoil."

But she added a caution to these directions. "If kept, as mine were, where the temperatures change from hot, when my wood stove was roaring in the dead of winter, to sub-freezing temperatures around 30°F below zero, pressure in those bottles will build up for sure. The first time I preserved my berries this way by salting them down and then went to open up a bottle of them later on in the year, they exploded everywhere. I had the wooden ceiling beams, inside log walls, and myself completely covered with saskatoon berries. But those remaining in the bottom of the jar tasted mighty good," she explained with a wink and nod. She said that if it is warm inside but it has been freezing, to relieve the pressure just let the bottles cool outdoors a few minutes before opening. Another method employed is to unscrew the lid (covered with a handheld cloth) carefully and slowly until the release of trapped air inside issues forth with an audible hiss.

"My preserved berries are quite delicious throughout the long—and I do mean l-o-n-g—white winter season with its many icy moments and snowcovered wonders. I use them just as I do the fresh ones in summertime. The salt doesn't flavor them one bit and extra sugar isn't needed.

"Salting (1 teaspoon per quart) is excellent for storing berries like currants, wild cherries, elderberries, or just about any berry that is fairly small with firm skin. But I don't recommend this for the soft skinned or large ones like raspberries, strawberries, or grapes," she concluded.

APPENDIX VI

THE FOOD VALUE OF BERRIES

The Importance of Trace Elements

All berries, especially those grown in the wild, are rich in many different trace elements. But in and of itself, this doesn't mean much unless a person knows just what is meant by the term "trace elements." At the present time it is known that the human body requires eighteen different mineral elements for good health and growth. Certain ones—calcium, phosphorus, sodium, chlorine, potassium, magnesium, and sulfur—are found in the body in appreciable amounts (0.05 percent or more) and are, therefore, called macrominerals, the others—iron, iodine, manganese, copper, zinc, cobalt, fluorine, selenium, molybdenum, chromium, and boron—appear in only very small amounts or traces and thus are called "trace elements" or microminerals.

Scientists have now concluded that deficiencies in many of these trace elements play a bigger role in human health than previously imagined by doctors. At the 1985 meeting of the American Association for the Advancement of Science, a series of papers focused on this. Many of these reported definite links between trace elements and health problems.

For instance, deficiencies of copper in the diet in older people is widespread and believed to be connected with bone fragility, anemia, connective tissue diseases such as arthritis and lupus, heart arrhythmias, elevated blood cholesterol levels, blood sugar imbalances, heart attacks, and coronary heart disease. Such deficiencies of copper have been attributed to the excessive intake of refined and processed foods that, for the most part, are lacking in this very necessary trace element.

Another research paper presented by Walter Mertz, then the director of the USDA's Human Nutrition Research Center in Beltsville, Maryland, focused on chromium. Chromium is recognized as being essential to bring the hormone insulin together with insulin receptors on a cell's surface. When this occurs, glucose (blood sugar) in the circulating blood plasma is immediately converted into energy for body muscles and organs to utilize in their various physical and biochemical activities. But without sufficient chromium, insulin is practically useless, resulting in elevated blood sugar, eventual diabetes, obesity, and fatigue. Hertz noted that "this is one of the few trace elements that consistently declines with age." So it stands to reason that as we get older our bodies require more of this vital trace element.

Elsewhere, scientists have discovered the importance of other trace elements, of which the public is just now beginning to hear reports. Jonathan V. Wright, a Washington State alternative physician, had been successfully treating many different allergy cases with intravenous and oral solutions of molybdenum right up until FBI agents, working in conjunction with state troopers and local county sheriff's deputies, raided his clinic sometime in 1993 and confiscated all of his nutritional supplements and patients' medical records on the false pretext that he was prescribing "dangerous" things that could purportedly "harm" people.

A study by a scientist from the department of Pharmacology and Toxicology at the University of Texas Medical Branch in Galveston was published in the February 1986 issue of *Federation Proceedings* (45:123–32). It dealt with another micromineral, vanadium, which was reported to indirectly affect liver, kidney, pancreas, and heart functions in positive ways. And *Chemical Marketing Reporter* for November 9, 1987, reported that scientists from the USA's Agricultural Research Service in Grand Forks, North Dakota, found that boron, an element long used as a water softener and mouthwash, is remarkable in conserving body calcium or preventing bone demineralization. Along these same lines my own research into paleolithic nutrition has shown that strontium was very high in the diets of cave dwellers, which accounted for their incredibly hardened bone structures. Other USDA scientists working out of the Agricultural Research Service's Plant, Soil, and Nutrition Laboratory in Ithaca, New York, investigated the role that nickel might play in liberating nitrogen wastes from different biological systems (In this case, plants).

Tin is used as the final example of the growing body of scientific evidence to support the very important role that trace elements such as these play in the body. A trio of scientists from the University of Akron in Ohio published an interesting article entitled, "Tin as a Vital Trace Element" in the *Journal of Nutrition, Growth, and Cancer* (1:147–153, 1983–84). They reported that "tin has an affinity for the thymus, as iodine does for the thyroid." But "as the individual ages beyond puberty, thymic atrophy is observed." However, the inclusion of more tin in the body from dietary sources is believed to slow down this thymic shrinkage to some extent: at least that was the speculation arrived at. They also noted, in passing, that "if...tin and zinc...are in proper balance" in the body, "mammary oncogenesis" (or breast cancer) will not occur."

As already noted, trace elements can be lost from the system by imprudent eating habits, highly processed foods, and old age. Another common factor that causes substantial losses of vital micronutrients is *any* kind of stress. And if a variety of mental, emotional, and physical stresses are combined all at once on an individuals then the losses can be more dramatic within a shorter period of time. An interesting study of this effect was reported some time ago in the *American Journal of Clinical Nutrition* (53:126–31, 1991). One hundred and nineteen U.S. Navy Sea, Air, and Land (SEAL) trainees recruited from two training classes of the Basic Underwater Demolition School/SEAL Training Center in Coronado, California, gave permission for military doctors to draw blood samples from them between September 1986 and February 1987. This was done during an intensive five-day ordeal known as Hell Week. Samples were taken before Hell Week (BHW) and immediately after Hell Week (AHW).

During the Hell Week period the trainees were subjected to unbelievably excruciating physical and psychological stress. Physical stressors included simulated combat exercises and obstacle courses, running, swimming, and boat races. In addition to undergoing physical activities, the trainees were permitted only about five hours of *total* sleep for the entire period. Psychological stressors included performance anxiety, verbal confrontations, activities with no-win situations, and anxiety due to the uncertainty of the nature of events during Hell Week and the length of Hell Week. A very high percentage of participants dropped out for one reason or another during the course of these brutal military tests.

The most fascinating part of this study concerned the status of three trace elements before, during, and after Hell Week. Levels of zinc, iron, and selenium were relatively normal BHW; during Hell Week they averaged 23.6 mg/d, 35.4 mg/d, and 92.5 micrograms per deciliter of blood, respectively. But values AHW for these three trace elements noticeably plunged by 33 percent, 44 percent, and 12 percent, respectively. What better proof could anyone ask for than this to show that stress—not to mention *extreme* stress—results in a serious loss of many different micronutrients, thus leaving the body in a helpless and exposed condition of poor health.

Berries as Rich Sources of Trace Elements

Until quite recently, not much attention had ever been paid to the food value of berries. But as paleonutritionists and others have thoroughly investigated the diets of ancient cave peoples the world over, they were drawn more to berries as potential sources of important nutrients for those they were studying. In fact, in the book *The Analyses of Prehistoric Diets* (Orlando, FL: Academic Press, Inc., 1985, p. 350) scientist Robert I. Gilbert, Jr., stated conclusively: "Nuts and berries, unlike the majority of foods, contain *extremely high concentrations* of trace elements!" [Italics and exclamation point added for emphasis.]

Such "hunting and gathering" societies (as designated by anthropologists) were not always able to secure adequate game for their needs. And leafy and tuber vegetables weren't always readily available either. Nor did such groups ever utilize eggs very much, let alone have access to any type of animal milk, which was almost as nonexistent in those times as the proverbial "hen's teeth" have always been. Some cereal grains (mostly corn, though) were utilized later on when such societies became more settled in their ways and adopted village forms of life instead of their customary wanderings. Those fortunate enough to live by lakes, rivers, or oceans were able to add fish to their meager diets.

When food inventories are taken of such groups as a whole, however, paleonutritionists and anthropologists such as myself are left wondering where on earth these Stone-Age primitives got all their incredible energy and stamina from. Well, believe it or not, after all the kitchen middens (refuse heaps) had been carefully explored and innumerable coprolites (human feces) from the front or back of many damp caves were thoroughly analyzed (in *well-*ventilated laboratories, I might add), an inescapable fact repeatedly surfaced: nuts, seeds, *and berries* were the premier choices of most snacks and meals by prehistoric hunters and gatherers! No wonder they had thicker bones, stronger muscles, tougher skin, greater nerve, clearer vision, healthier lungs, better hearts, and vastly improved digestive and eliminative systems!

Some years ago I bought a car from some friends (the Tiptons) in Plainview, Texas, and drove it all the way back to Salt Lake City. Along the way, to stave off some of the monotony in driving, I stopped for a day and night in Las Cruces, New Mexico. I went to the local university there and took advantage of their library. While looking through some of the scientific periodicals they had, I came across one in particular, which caught my interest. It was *Acta Agriculturae Scandinavica* (Supplement 22:89–113, 1980) and contained one of the most informative articles I believe I've read in years. It was entitled "Mineral Element Composition of Finnish Foods: Potato, Vegetables, Fruits, Berries, Nuts and Mushrooms," and was authored by four scientists from the department of Food Chemistry and Technology at the University of Helsinki.

I made a photocopy of their lengthy report and have frequently referred to it in many of my writings and public lectures since then. To put it mildly, it was a *literal* godsend from Providence, so far as this religious-minded scientist is concerned, for nowhere else in all of my extensive literature research have I found anything quite like this that definitely supports what paleonutritionists and allied researchers have been finding out for some time now: *Berries are chockfull of many trace elements!*

Samples of fresh vegetables, fruits, berries, and mushrooms were obtained during the growing season of 1976, either from gardens, produce markets, or the forest. Additional samples of frozen, canned, and dried commodities were collected later in the same year. The produce was sorted, washed, in some cases peeled, dried or freeze-dried, homogenized in a blender, and then finally analyzed for trace element contents.

The following berry fruits constituted a significant part of this research work: bilberry, lingonberry, cranberry, cloudberry, strawberry, currants (black and red), gooseberry, rosehip, rowanberry, raspberry, and grapes. Berries represented about 20 percent of the total foods thus evaluated. Space doesn't permit the reproducing of those tables of percentages for the variety of trace elements listed, but the micronutrients themselves can be mentioned in passing. The dozen berries cited were found to contain "statistically significant" (meaning "impressive") amounts of the following trace elements: iron, copper, manganese, zinc, molybednum, cobalt, nickel, chromium, fluorine, selenium, silicon, rubidium, aluminum, boron, bromine, and others. Wild berries sometimes showed trace element amounts "about ten times as high as cultivated berries and fruits"; still, those that were home grown yielded more micronutrients, as a rule, than most vegetables did.

In the years that I have been doing this type of research, I am continually amazed at just how efficient an energy food berries really are on account of their tremendous nutrition, measured out in minute proportions, however. Who says that great things can't come in very small sizes? It's been definitely proven with berries, for sure!

The Ellagic Acid Connection

In recent years scientists worldwide have been looking at something else in berries that holds great promise in the field of medicine. The substance is called *ellagic acid* and is found in fruits such as black currants, grapes, raspberries, strawberries, and some nuts such as Brazil nuts. Gary D. Stoner and his fellow coworkers from the Medical College of Ohio in Toledo began investigating its effects on cancer growth caused by different chemicals in the mid-to-late '80s.

By providing ellagic acid in the diet, these scientists hope to see the incidence of cancer greatly reduced throughout the country. But Stoner was quick to emphasize in his report to the American Cancer Society's thirtieth annual science writers' seminar in Daytona Beach, Florida, in late March to early April 1988 that "ellagic acid can only be used as a preventive" and *not* as a treatment, "because it has to be added to the system just before or during carcinogen exposure." It does very *little* good if taken *after* cancer has occurred.

Although Stoner and his team had not, at that time, yet defined the exact mechanism of cancer inhibition, later research seems to indicate that ellagic acid competes for DNA receptors that are also used by the carcinogens. More recent studies in 1993 point to raspberries as "containing more ellagic acid than any other common food." "Administered as a drug," read one newspaper account, "ellagic acid prevents esophagus, liver, skin and lung cancer in rats and mice...." ("Raspberry Farmers Eager to See Fruits of Crop in Cancer Research" in the *Salt Lake Tribune,* Friday, January 22, 1993, p. A-12).

A much earlier study on ellagic acid with black walnuts in the October 1968 *Journal of Pharmaceutical Sciences* (57:1730–31) demonstrated that when certain mice were injected with this solution *before* undergoing electroconvulsive shock, they remained alive for a longer period than did other rodents without the benefit of ellagic acid. This suggests in some way that it must have an undetermined protective effect on the myelin sheathing (fatty protein substance) encasing each strand of nerve.

Another unusual test for ellagic acid was done on semi-arid plants by scientists working out of the NPI-Plant Resources Institute at University Research Park in Salt Lake City. James A. Klocke and Brad Van Wagenen informed me that this substance has proven to be a rather good inhibitor of certain insect larvae growths when sprayed upon the same before maturation was reached.

Finally, a study by Dr. Elizabeth Barrett-Connor of the University of California at San Diego and Dr. Kay-Tee Khaw of Cambridge University in England reported almost a decade ago that an extra helping of fresh berries or other fruit and vegetables every day could cut the risk of stroke almost in half. Ellagic acid and different trace elements in the berries themselves was attributed to this. Their report was published in the January 29, 1987, issue of *The New England Journal of Medicine.*

Let it be said that berries are good for you in more ways than one. The evidence offered here is but a small sum of the total body available, which underscores this point very nicely.

Appendix VII

Some Delightful Berry Recipes

Blackberry Ice Cream with Sauce

1 pint fresh blackberries
$1/_2$ cup honey
$1/_8$ teaspoon sea salt
$1/_2$ cup milk
1 cup cream, whipped

Crush the berries and combine them with honey. Cook for 5 minutes, then strain through a sieve if a smooth mixture is desired. Stir in salt and let cool. Then add milk and fold in whipping cream. Freeze in refrigerator tray, stirring every half hour when mixture begins to turn to mush. After three stirrings, let freeze another couple of hours. This makes an excellent topping for berry pie or tarts, and is equally delicious by itself when served with blackberry sauce:

$1^1/_2$ pints blackberries
2 tablespoons blackberry brandy
2 tablespoons fresh orange juice
3 tablespoons clover honey

Pick over and reserve 1 cup of the smallest and most attractive berries. In a VitaMix whole food machine or equivalent food processor, puree the remaining 2 cups of berries with the brandy, orange juice, and honey. Transfer the mixture to a sieve set over a medium-sized bowl. Press the puree through the sieve and discard the seeds. (This sauce can be made 8 hours ahead and refrigerated, covered, until needed). Stir the remaining berries into the sauce just before pouring over the blackberry ice cream.

Fresh Blueberry Soup with Blueberry Corn Muffins

2 cups fresh blueberries

1 1/2 cups water

1/2 cup sugar

1/2 tablespoon finely grated orange peel

1/4 cup orange juice

2 cups buttermilk

1 cup sour cream

lemon juice to taste

pinch of nutmeg

Heat berries, water, sugar, orange peel, and juice; bring to a boil. Simmer for 15–20 minutes; let cool. Process until pureed in a VitaMix whole food machine or equivalent food machine. Whip in buttermilk and sour cream. Taste for salt and add lemon juice, if needed. Chill for two hours. Serve garnished with fresh blueberries.

1 1/3 cups all-purpose white flour

2/3 cup yellow cornmeal

1 tablespoon baking powder

1 teaspoon ground cinnamon

1/4 teaspoon salt

1 cup blueberries

1 egg

2/3 cup skim milk

1/2 cup honey

3 tablespoons extra light virgin olive oil

Preheat oven to 400° F. Lightly brush a muffin tin with canola or sunflower oil. In a large bowl, whisk together by hand the flour, cornmeal, baking powder, cinnamon, and salt. Add the blueberries and toss to coat with flour mixture. In a smaller bowl, lightly beat the egg. Add the milk, honey and oil, whisking until well combined. Add the liquid mixture to the dry ingredients and stir just until combined. Don't overmix. Divide the batter equally among 12 muffin cups, filling each about two thirds full. Bake for 22 minutes, until well-risen and golden. Turn out onto a rack to cool. Makes a dozen muffins, which is more than enough to go with the fresh blueberry soup.

Boysenberry "Souffle"

2 cups boysenberries
2 tablespoons honey
2 tablespoons lemon juice
1 cup whipping cream
whole berries for garnish

Blend berries into a fine puree with a VitaMix whole food machine, or equivalent food machine. Add the honey and lemon juice to just $1\,1/2$ cups of the berry puree. Whip the cream and fold it into the mixture gently. Chill, then dish out individual servings. Top each with the remaining $1/2$ cup pureed berries and garnish with a whole berry. This makes a very nice, light, and wholesome "souffle."

Buffalo Berry Indian Stew

I am indebted to Joy Yellowtail Toineeta of the Crow Tribe in eastern Montana for sharing this recipe with me years ago. She had no specific amounts in mind and used whatever portions she judged to be "right" for whatever she happened to be making at the time.

Because the buffalo berry is quite tart, one half as much as chokecherry or other berries is needed for this type of pudding or Indian "berry stew." Marrow-bone stock is the recommended liquid for all berry stews; the bones from butchered elk or deer make the best broth. However, plain water is just as acceptable.

Soak the loose berries in enough water to cover until the buffalo berries are tender. Add more water to replace the amount soaked up by the berries, then add at least 2 more cups. Cook the berries to a brisk boil. Make a paste of flour and water and add to the berries. Stir vigorously to prevent lumping. Add sugar to taste and a lump of butter or marrow fat. Serve with Indian fry bread.

Tangy Blackberry Chutney

Chutney is an elegant way to enjoy blackberries as an accompaniment to a main-course dish. A sparkling glass of stout English ale or mead or dark Bavarian beer and a crusty piece of fresh rye, pumpernickel, or wheat berry bread complete this hearty meal, which serves eight.

1 medium onion, chopped
1 tablespoon minced garlic
3 tablespoons extra light virgin olive oil
1 1/2 teaspoons salt
1/4 cup apple cider vinegar
1/2 to 3/4 cup light brown sugar
1 teaspoon ground cumin
1/4 teaspoon cayenne pepper
1/2 teaspoon ground cinnamon
1/2 teaspoon nutmeg
4 cups sliced peaches (about 1 1/2 pounds worth)
1 1/4 cups fresh blackberries
1/2 cup walnut halves (about 2 1/2 ounces)

In a large frying pan, sauté the onion and garlic in olive oil over low heat. Add the salt, vinegar, sugar, cumin, cayenne pepper, cinnamon, and nutmeg, blending everything well. Next add the peaches, blackberries, and nuts. Continue cooking over low heat for 15 minutes until the fruit is lightly cooked. Then let cool. For the best taste possible, cover the mixture and refrigerate the chutney overnight before using it. It keeps for months when stored in a covered jar, as do commercially available chutneys.

This particular condiment makes an excellent accompaniment to any type of wild game, pork, lamb or mutton, duck or goose, and, believe it or not, even fresh or saltwater fish.

Choke Cherry Jelly

I am indebted to Joy Yellowtail Toineeta of the Crow Indian Reservation in eastern Montana for this recipe.

Wash and destem the chokecherries. Add just enough water to cover the fruit in an iron kettle. Let boil until the skin breaks. Then mash the fruit and press through a jelly bag and strain. Measure the juice and bring that to a boil. For each cup of juice add one cup of white sugar. Boil rapidly to the jelly stage. Skim and pour into sterilized jars. Pour melted paraffin over the jelly when cold. Slightly rotate the glass as soon as the paraffin is poured on so it will stick to the glass at the edges above the surface of the jelly.

In the event the reader doesn't know how to test the liquid to see when it has reached the jelly point, here is what I saw Joy do. She dipped a spoon in her boiling jelly. As the jelly neared the jelling point, it would drop from the side of the spoon in two drops. When the drops ran together and slid off in a flake or sheet from the side of the spoon, she proclaimed the jelly finished and promptly removed it from the heat.

She skimmed off the foam from the top of the jelly and poured it at once into sterilized jars and glasses she had previously made ready for this procedure. The dry glasses were all filled to within half-an-inch from the top. (I've seen empty baby bottles with screw-top lids used to hold this jelly.)

Cranberry Nachos

Surprising as this appetizer sounds, it is actually a delicious way to serve cranberries. The crisp nachos and creamy coulis and salsa makes a hearty finger food, which serves four.

Red and Yellow Pepper Coulis ($^1/_2$ cup each)

1 whole yellow bell pepper
1 whole red bell pepper
4 tablespoons extra light pure virgin olive oil
granulated kelp to taste

Salsa (1 cup)

$^1/_2$ cup cranberries ($^1/_4$ pint)
$^1/_4$ cup fresh orange juice
$^1/_4$ medium red onion, diced
1 fresh jalapeño pepper, diced
2 tablespoons chopped cilantro
$^1/_4$ cup fresh lime juice
pinch salt
freshly ground pepper to taste
sugar to taste

Nachos

12 blue and gold tortilla chips
$^1/_4$ pound chèvre cheese
    (preferably a mild Californian or French variety)
radicchio
4 sprigs cilantro

Red and Yellow Pepper Coulis: Char the whole peppers over an open flame or under a preheated broiler. Place in a metal bowl and cover tightly with plastic wrap. Let sit for 15 minutes. Then wash off all the charred skin and purée in 2 batches (1 for each pepper) in a VitaMix whole food machine or equivalent food machine until smooth. Drizzle olive oil over each coulis batch and season with salt and pepper.

Salsa: Cook the cranberries in the orange juice for a couple of minutes, until tender. Place cranberry mixture in a bowl and add onion, jalapeño, and cilantro. Toss with lime juice and add salt, pepper, and sugar.

Nachos: Preheat the broiler. Arrange the blue and gold chips on a cookie sheet. To each chip, add 1 teaspoon each of yellow and red pepper coulis and top with salsa and chèvre, broken into pieces by hand. Put the pan under the broiler until the chèvre softens (about 5 minutes; it can get slightly browned). Remove from the broiler. Arrange the chips on a serving plate. Form a bowl out of the radicchio leaves and fill with the extra salsa. Garnish with cilantro sprigs and serve immediately.

Currant Summer Pudding

Although red currants are classic in summer pudding, other combinations of berries, such as raspberries, blackberries, or blueberries, can be used. Just be sure that at least half of the berries are red for the pudding to have the nicest color.

1 pint red currants

1 pint loganberries

2/3–3/4 cup sugar, depending on the sweetness of the berries

1/4 bottled pure seedless raspberry or strawberry jam

1 tablespoon eau-de-vie de framboise or crème de cassis

1 teaspoon fresh lime juice

8 slices firm white sandwich bread, crusts trimmed

1 cup vanilla nonfat yogurt

In a large, heavy saucepan, combine the currants, loganberries, sugar, and 1 tablespoon water. Bring to a simmer, stirring. Simmer over medium-low heat for 2 minutes. Remove from the heat, stir in the berry jam, liqueur, and lime juice. Let cool a while.

Line a 1-quart soufflé dish with plastic wrap, leaving a 4-inch overhang all around. Cut the bread slices in half diagonally, then fit them in the bottom and sides of the bowl, trimming further to fit snugly if needed. (You will have extra slices left over to be used for the top.)

Spoon the berry mixture into the bread-lined bowl; trim bread slices level with the top. Use remaining bread slices to cover the top. Fold the plastic wrap over the top of the pudding, then top with a plate slightly smaller than the diameter of the bowl. Weight the plate with a heavy can. Refrigerate at least 8 hours or up to 24 hours.

To serve, remove weight and plate, then fold back the overlap of plastic wrap. Set a rimmed serving plate over the bowl, then invert the pudding onto the plate. Remove the bowl and plastic wrap. Carefully cut the wedges with a serrated knife and serve each portion with a dollop of yogurt. Serves 6.

Elderberry-Barberry Jam

For many decades Maurice Mességué was one of Europe's most famous folk healers, treating the likes of kings, queens, popes, prime ministers, artists, novelists, and other famous people with his many wonderful herbs. The following recipe was freely translated from his book *C'es la nature qui à raison* (Paris: Opera Mundi, 1972).

In August the elderberry bushes are loaded with fruit. Make use of them, for they furnish an excellent marmalade with laxative properties. The task of stripping the berries from their clusters is somewhat tedious, but not if someone else is helping you. Be sure to wash the berries carefully, because they tend to be dusty.

Weigh the elderberries and combine them with sugar, using 1 1/2 pounds of sugar to every pound of berries. Cook in a large pot or kettle over low heat until the jam has the consistency of marmalade.

Other wild berries make delicious preserves. The blueberry is highly prized; but did you know that the red fruit of barberry can also be cooked into a jam? As with elderberry, you will need 1 1/2 pounds of sugar per each pound of fruit.

Gooseberry Jam

I am indebted to Joy Yellowtail Toineeta, A Crow Indian, for this recipe. Cook one quart of berries in just enough water (about a cup) until the skin breaks. Then mash the fruit. Next measure three cups of sugar and cook to the desired thickness and pour into clean hot jars or glasses. Seal at once with paraffin.

Huckleberry Fruit Batter Pudding

This is another of Joy's recipes that I obtained from her some years ago. Place a thick layer of cleaned and drained huckleberries in the bottom of a greased baking dish and pour cottage pudding batter over it. Then bake in a moderate oven at 390° F. for half an hour.

Here are the other ingredients you'll need for the cottage pudding batter that goes over the huckleberries:

$1\frac{1}{2}$ cups white flour

3 teaspoons baking powder

$\frac{1}{4}$ cup shortening

$\frac{1}{2}$ cup sugar

$\frac{1}{2}$ teaspoon salt

Sift the flour and baking powder together. Cream the shortening with a spoon in a bowl, then add the sugar, salt, and egg. Stir by hand. Last of all add the milk and flour alternately and continue to stir each time. Pour this batter over the fruit and bake as previously instructed.

Lingonberry Sauce

Here is a delightful sauce concocted by the two chefs of Henry's End Restaurant in Brooklyn, New York. It goes well with duck, goose, pheasant, or quail. In the Scandinavian countries, reindeer meat is the classic choice for serving with lingonberry sauce. This recipe serves four.

> $1/_2$ cup fresh lingonberries ($1/_4$ pint) or lingonberry preserves
>   (If you use lingonberry preserves, add about $1/_4$ cup ($1/_8$ pint)
>   of fresh berries for garnish if serving to company.)
> $1/_4$ cup lingonberry liqueur (optional)
> $1^1/_2$ cups poultry stock (duck or stewing hen)
> salt and freshly ground white pepper to taste
> 4 tablespoons unsalted butter, cut into pieces

Mix all ingredients, except the butter, in a small metal pot. Cook over medium heat for about three minutes or until the sauce reaches a medium thickness and coats the back of a spoon. before serving the warm sauce, swirl in the butter.

Mulberry-Agar Jello

> 2 tablespoons agar-agar
> 2 cups water
> 1 cup mulberry juice
> $1/_2$ cup honey
> 1 tablespoon fresh lemon juice
> 2 cups fresh mulberries

Mix agar (a gelatinous extract from red alga) with water and let sit for a minute. (Agar may be purchased at any Oriental food market or health-food store.) Boil two minutes, cool, and then add the other ingredients. Cover the bottom of a dish with the fresh berries. Pour the liquid over them and set aside for a couple of hours to jell.

Raspberry Breakfast Boboli

1 boboli crust (12-inch prebaked Italian pizza bread)
1/2 cup cream cheese, softened (4 ounces)
1 cup red raspberries (preferably fresh, but defrosted berries will do just fine—about 1/2 pint)
1 tablespoon Grand Marnier
fresh sprigs of peppermint leaf for garnish

Preheat the over to 450° F. Place the boboli crust on a baking sheet. Spread the cream cheese over the boboli crust. Bake for about 10 minutes. Next, sprinkle the raspberries with Grand Marnier. Remove the boboli from the oven and arrange the raspberries on top. Garnish with the fresh mint sprigs. Slice into wedges and serve warm. Serves eight.

You should be aware that boboli is somewhat difficult to find in parts of the United States. If your local specialty-food store doesn't carry it, make your own dough from a packaged hot-roll mix, following the directions on the packaging. Partially bake it until very lightly brown. If you are preparing the dough in advance, freeze or refrigerate it, depending or just how long it will be before you make the dish. You can also use it immediately after lightly browning it. Simply remove it from the oven and place the ingredients on top of it, following the directions above for the boboli. This option also permits you to mold the dough into different shapes, such as a heart for Valentine's Day to share with someone special in your life.

Rowanberry Jelly

An expert grower from Somerset, England, who raises all types of delicious berries in her back garden provided this recipe. She suggested it be used as an accompaniment to lamb or venison. You can also add cooking or crab apples to the berries to give the jelly more of a tart taste, if you wish to "keep a stiff upper lip" as the British say. This recipe makes 4 half-pints of jelly.

4 cups rowanberries (2 pints)
2–3 peeled apples
1 cup sugar for each cup of juice
lime juice

Place the washed berries and peeled apples in a saucepan, cover with water, and simmer for awhile, until the goodness has been extracted from the fruit and it is pulpy. This takes about 30 minutes; the fruit must become quite soft. Put the mash into a jelly bag and let it drip into a bowl overnight. Don't prod or help the liquid in any way or it will get cloudy.

Measure the juice and add the sugar accordingly. Add a dash of lime juice to the contents in the saucepan. Dissolve the sugar slowly. Then boil it until the jelly sets when tested. (Dip a cold spoon into the mixture. If the mixture runs off the spoon in a single sheet, as opposed to two drops, the jelly has set.) Pour into sterilized baby food jars. Cover with melted paraffin, let cool, and seal.

Strawberries in the Snow

6–8 large ripe strawberries
1 cup yogurt (or whipped cream)
2 tablespoons honey
1 tablespoon finely chopped spearmint left
3 tablespoons chopped Brazil and cashew nuts
1 cup shredded coconut

Hull all but the six largest strawberries and chill. Combine the yogurt. honey, and spearmint and also chill. When cold enough, arrange the strawberries and yogurt in alternate layers in sherbert glasses, beginning with a spoonful of yogurt. End with yogurt as the top layer and sprinkle with nuts and coconut. Place a whole berry on top of each glass.

Wild Grape-Fruit Smoothie

1 cup wild fox grapes (or cultivated purple grapes)
1 banana
1/2 orange, including the white part of the peel
1/4 cup peaches, frozen
1/2 cup plain yogurt
1/4 cup ice cubes

Place all the ingredients in a VitaMix whole food machine or an equivalent food machine in the order given. Secure the complete two-part lid by locking under the tabs provided. Move the black speed control to HIGH. Lift the black lever to ON position and allow the machine to run for 1 1/2 minutes, until smooth. Serve immediately. makes 2 1/2 cups.

To purchase the Vita-Mix whole food machine mentioned in this section, call or write to:

Vita-Mix Corporation
8615 Usher Road
Cleveland, OH 44138
1-800-VITAMIX (800-848-2649)
Fax: (216) 235-3726

Appendix VIII

Numerous phone calls and inquiries by mail from this author were made to almost 75 nurseries throughout the United States and Canada to determine which ones would have the greatest variety of berries available. Those mentioned here have a rather extensive range of edible berries. Just about all of the berries cited in this book (with only a few exceptions) can be purchased for planting purposes from one or several of them.

A. I. Eppler Ltd.
P.O. Box 16513
Seattle, WA 98116-0513

Makielski Berry Farm and Nursery
7130 Platt Road
Ypsilanti, MI 48197

Rayner Bros.
Box 1617
Salisbury, MD 21801

Van Bourgondien & Sons
P.O. Box A
245 Farmingdale Road
Babylon, NY 11702

White Flower Farm
Route 63
Litchfield, CT 06759-0050

Bigelow Nurseries
P.O. Box 718
Northboro, MA 01532

Burgess Seed & Plant Co.
904 Four Seasons Rd.
Bloomington, IN 61701

Johnson Orchard and Nursery
R.R. No. 5, Box 325
Ellijay, GA 30504

Jung Seeds and Nursery
335 S. High St.
Randolph, WI 53957

New York State Fruit Testing Association
P.O. Box 462
Geneva, NY 14456

Beaverlodge Nursery Ltd.
P.O. Box 127
Beaverlodge, Alberta, Canada TOH OCO

McConnell Nurseries, Inc.
Port Burwell
Ontario, Canada NOJ ITO

Farmer Seed and Nursery Co.
Reservation Center
2207 East Oakland Ave.
Bloomington, IL 61701

APPENDIX IX

TIPS ON SEED SPROUTING

Why Sprout?

The sprouted seed has been recognized for a long time as one of the most nutritious foods available from nature. Something wonderful transpires as each little seed swells and sprouts; it is the unlocking of an energy force and its expansion into vital nutrients, such as vitamins, minerals, amino acids, and enzymes, which the body needs for its daily sustenance.

In the King James Version of the Bible we find mention of the curious words "pulse" in Daniel 1:12;16. A number of bible commentaries I consulted have defined this word to mean several different but related things. For one, "pulse" can be "any herbs or vegetables derived from seeds." For another, it can be "sprouted seeds." And a final definition implies "any edible seeds that are cooked, as lentils, peas, beans, and the like."

We know from the wonderful story of Daniel and his three friends how well they fared on "pulse" while the rest of their Hebrew friends ate and drank the same rich food and wine that their captor, King Nebuchadnezzar of Babylon and his princes, routinely subsisted on. Daniel and his comrades had better complexions, felt stronger, and were more energetic than the others. This certainly is a fine testament to why sprouts out to be used frequently in the diet.

Sprouts Taste Good

Health foods may be good for you, but they don't always taste good. You may enjoy a delicious thick and creamy papaya milkshake. But I guarantee you won't smack your lips for very long if some powdered brewer's yeast is added; in fact, there will likely be an inducement to put a clothespin over your nostrils after that!

Luckily for us, though, sprouts have nearly universal appeal. There are so many varieties, each with its own texture and taste, that there will be at least one or two sprouts to please everyone. The classic mung bean, used so often in Oriental cooking, is mild and crunchy. If you enjoy nibbling on raw greens—lettuce, celery, or green bell pepper—then you will surely enjoy the mung-bean sprout.

Some raw sprouts, such as soy, have the distinct fresh taste of just-picked garden peas, which delights some but repels others. When you steam the same raw sprout for a few minutes, though, the taste is transformed to a nutty and crisp flavor that would not offend anyone. Other seed sprouts, such as alfalfa and wheat, are unbelievably sweet and can satisfy even the worst craving *for* sugar but without it. Rye sprouts are often mistaken for the flavor of wild rice when served in soups and rice combinations. Gourmets looking for exotic flavors will soon discover that fenugreek seed sprouts suggest Indian foods and go well with curries, while raw lentil sprouts add a zippy tang to otherwise boring salads.

Make no mistake about it, there are sprouts somewhere that will caress your palate, delight your brain and tickle your tummy!

Sprouts Are Economical

In an era of high food costs, simple meals prepared from ordinary sprouts will definitely save you money. This becomes even more apparent when feeding a family of four or more. Here is something so inexpensive that a little bit goes a long way. Sprouts are one of just a few foods I know of that cost *pennies* to grow and serve.

To show you just how economical this can be, consider the following true episode. Almost 21 years ago there was a Mormon family of 7 residing in the little northern Utah community of Providence. The father was unemployed, and very little money was coming in to support such a large household. Being too proud to ask for their local ward bishop (pastor) for some church assistance, they decided to seek alternative ways of putting food on the table every day.

The parents started sprouting a wide assortment of seeds, some in different combinations with each other. Soon their children got into the act, too, and began sprouting their own favorite seeds. The family spent a total of $59.71 for the cost of all their seeds and lived mostly on sprouts for almost half a year. Total food cost per family member figured out to be about $.018 per meal. No one suffered any ill effects from this rather spartan diet. And, interestingly enough, during that six-month period none of children came down with so much as a sniffle!

While this is an extreme example, it attests to the great food potential to be found in sprouted seeds. Sprouts can help reduce the weekly food bill without causing hunger, boredom, or outright malnutrition. They are the best "meal value" around!

Sprouting Equipment

Although some individuals have always engaged in sprouting, the activity never gained much public support until a quarter of a century ago. Then in the early to mid-1970s, a number of sprouting books started appearing, explaining the whys and wherefores of this unique kind of indoor "healthy gardening."

I recall the late Ann Wigmore, who founded the Hippocrates' Health Institute in Boston. She had "used every conceivable pot, bowl, crock, opaque apothecary jar and storage container" for sprouting purposes and found "every one of them to be a success." Her basic sprouting system required any receptacle large enough to hold the finished sprouts, but she strongly insisted that the container must *not* be transparent, wooden, or metallic. Containers of plastic, china, enamel, and unglazed pottery were very good choices, she said. And since the sprouting container has to be kept covered, anything that comes with its own lid is a good choice, including bean pots, crocks, canisters, coffeepots, fondue pots, cookie jars, chafing dishes, and plastic ice-cream boxes. The most preferred by her were large plastic storage containers bearing the Rubbermaid or Tupperware logos.

A container with a wide diameter is best when sprouting larger quantities of sprouts. Don't use tall, narrow, or small-mouth containers. Try to have your sprouts in as few layers as possible for even circulation of moisture and air. If some sprouts on the bottom are weighed down by the others on top, the pressure will increase the chances for problems of rot and spoilage to develop.

Although I've already covered some of this basic information in the entry under ALFALFA SEED, I will repeat it here. Once you have selected your container, you will need only a few other pieces of equipment: (1) measuring cups (2– and 4–cup); (2) paper towels (preferably with double-layered strength); and (3) a large wire mesh strainer.

A measuring cup is used to measure the initial amount of dried seeds to be used and is also convenient for soaking the seeds. Ann Wigmore usually chose to sprout $1/4$ cup of dried seeds at a time for herself and soaked them in a 2–cup measure. Moist paper towels are placed on top of the sprouts to help provide the correct percentage of moisture in the sprouting atmosphere. Ann preferred white towels for this purpose. If the towels turn sour, replace them with fresh ones. Sometimes a dry towel at the bottom of the sprouter will help absorb moisture if you are having a chronic water-accumulating problem. A strainer will facilitate rinsing and draining your sprouts at regular intervals.

Theories on Sprouting

There are three basic factors that control the sprouting of a seed: (1) The amount of moisture; (2) the proper temperature; and (3) the circulation of air. When dried seeds become moist, they wake from their dormant state and begin their irreversible growth process. During this process of germination, chemical changes begin to take place; carbon dioxide, other gases, and heat are released. These gases and residues create wastes that will accumulate if not permitted to dissipate. One of the most important steps in the sprouting process is to keep removing these wastes by rinsing the sprouts with fresh water to prevent the crop from turning bad. Cool water ventilates the sprouts and prevents their overheating and destruction.

While sprouts demand a constant supply of moisture to grow, they cannot be permitted to sit in water or they will definitely *rot!* It's not difficult to sprout if you make certain that the sprouts are always moist, but are never left standing in even the smallest portion of water.

Sprouts grow fastest in warm temperatures, free from drafts, and away from direct heat. In cold weather, soaking times may be increased a few hours and sprouts can be rinsed in slightly warmer water. Between 75° and 85°F is the ideal sprouting temperature.

Air must be permitted to circulate in the sprouting container. There should always be about one third of the sprouter left empty for air circulation. Keep in mind that sprouts expand rapidly, so be sure to provide plenty of growing room for them.

Simply stated, these are the basic rules of sprouting:

1. Keep your sprouts moist, but never wet.

2. Keep your sprouts warm.

3. Rinse your sprouts as often as possible.

4. Give your sprouts adequate breathing room.

5. DO NOT cram your sprouts in too small a container.

For more details, consult "The Art of Sprouting" under the entry for ALFALFA SEED in the main text.

APPENDIX X

SOME CRUNCHY SPROUT RECIPES

Alfalfa Sprout Pick-Me-Up

1 cup orange juice

1 cup pink grapefruit juice

2 tablespoons Tahini (a paste made from finely ground sesame seeds and
   available in specialty food stores catering to Greek, Lebanonese,
   Syrian, and other Middle Eastern ethnic groups)

$1/_2$ teaspoon dark honey

1 cup alfalfa sprouts

Place all of the above ingredients in the Vita-Mix Total Nutrition
Center container or an equivalent food machine in the order
listed. Secure the complete 2-part lid by locking under the tabs.
Move the black speed control level to HIGH. Lift black lever to
ON position and allow the machine to run 45 seconds until
everything is nice and smooth. Makes slightly over 2 cups.

Sesame Seed Milk

$1/_4$ cup sesame seed

2 cups milk

1 tablespoon carob powder

8 pitted dates

Place the first two ingredients in the Vita-Mix machine or equivalent food machine. Secure lid and turn on as previously
described. Blend for 30 seconds. Then remove center part of lid

and add last two ingredients. Replace center lid and blend for another 30 seconds. For flavor variation substitute banana, raisins, or concentrates of apple or grape juice for the dates. Makes slightly over 2 cups.

Millionaire's Sprout Drink

The late Anne Wigmore, founder of the Hippocrates health Institute in Boston and juicer extraordinaire claimed this to be one of her favorite "all-time" drinks. I asked her why she called it by this peculiar name. "Because it makes you feel like *a million dollars!*" she answered with one of her gleeful laughs. Then, with a wink of an eye, she added playfully: "Even poor people can afford to make this one!"

3 cups pineapple juice
1 cup distilled water
1 cup alfalfa sprouts
1/2 cup comfrey leaves (or 1/2 cup parsley sprigs)
1/2 cup watercress

Place the ingredients in the Vita-Mix Total Nutrition Center or equivalent food machine in the order given. Secure lid and turn machine on as previously mentioned. Blend for 1 1/2 minutes. Pour into a plastic pitcher with lid and refrigerate for an hour. Makes 4 cups.

Doug Corcoran's Sprouted Wheat Pancakes

What's so unusual about this particular recipe is that the guy it's named after, Douglas Corcoran, *never* has tried it. He is my manuscript editor at Prentice Hall (the house that publishes my series of health encyclopedias) and a good friend besides. So why am I naming a recipe after someone who hasn't even tasted it, let alone made it? Simply because it may inspire him to try this recipe for himself. Then he can pass it on to other friends and will truly be able to call it *his* special pancake recipe.

1 cup flour
1 teaspoon salt
1 tablespoon brown sugar
2 tablespoons baking powder
2 tablespoons oil
1 cup milk
2 whole eggs
1 cup of any kind of sprouts

Combine the dry ingredients. Then combine the liquids, adding them to the dry ingredients and mixing well. After pouring each pancake into a hot greased skillet to cook, sprinkle on it 1 tablespoon sprouts. Don't combine the sprouts with the batter, as they will sink to the bottom, and all the sprouts will be in the last few pancakes. makes 3–4 pancakes.

Dr. Bernard Jensen's Green Delight Salad

I've known Dr. Bernard Jensen and his wife for many years. They were regular participants in many National Health Federation conventions, where he was a popular speaker for many years. I had the pleasure of introducing him to audiences of several thousand people on a few occasions, as well as "ghost-writing" an herb book for him a few years ago. I have always admired his cordiality, courage, and stamina. This is one of his favorite recipes, which his wife, Marie, was willing to share with me. (As of 1995, Dr. Jensen was still "hale and hearty, and going strong" in his late eighties!)

1 tablespoon unflavored gelatin
1 tablespoon cold water
$1/_2$ cup alfalfa sprouts
1 cup unsweetened pineapple juice
1 spring mint
1 leaf lettuce
some salad dressing (fat-free)
olives

Soften the gelatin in the water, and then melt the mixture over boiling water. Blend in the sprouts, pineapple juice, and mint. Then pour the gelatin mixture into the pineapple juice mixture, and combine them thoroughly. Pour into a wet mold and chill until set. Turn out on a bed of leaf lettuce and garnish with some salad dressing (fat-free) and olives.

Meat Loaf Surprise

The name comes from a dish made by the head cook who works in the kitchen of the Timpanogos Unit at the Utah State Prison near the Point-of-the-Mountain (just south of Salt Lake City). My journalistic duties as editor of Utah's largest senior citizens' newspaper requires that I make periodic visits to the penitentiary to interview inmates who are 50 years and older. I wandered back behind the serving line and asked the head cook what was for supper the afternoon I was there, and he growled, "Meat Loaf Surprise!" "Why is it called that?" I queried. Because the inmates *don't know* what I'll be putting in it each time—that's the *S-U-R-P-R-I-S-E* part!" he laughed menacingly.

1 1/2 pounds beef, pork, and veal mixture, ground twice
1 1/2 cups garbanzo or soy sprouts (packed down to measure)
2 beaten eggs
2 tablespoons parsley
1 medium onion
1 teaspoon salt
1/4 teaspoon pepper
1 teaspoon lemon juice
1/2 cup bread crumbs
1/4 cup wheat germ

Put sprouts and onion through a grinder. Mix them with the ground meat using your hands and adding all other ingredients. Shape into a loaf and place in a lightly greased loaf pan. Bake at 350°F. for about an hour. Serve with tomato sauce. Serves 4–6.

Sam Chow's Fried Rice

Sam Chow is a good friend of mine. He owns and operates a nice little restaurant in San Francisco. Whenever business or pleasure takes me to the Golden Gate city, I always drop in for a visit and to eat. One time while we were in the back kitchen talking as he deftly deboned a chicken in the shortest time I've ever seen it done, he offered me the following easy recipe for fried rice.

5 tablespoons vegetable oil

2 eggs, beaten lightly

1 cup diced roast pork

1 cup diced cooked shrimp

1 cup diced cooked chicken

2 cups sprouts (mung, soy, lentil)

2 scallions, chopped, with green ends intact

$1/_2$ teaspoon pepper

1 cup soy sauce

4 cups hot cooked rice

1 cup chopped lettuce

Scramble the eggs in 2 tablespoons oil over medium heat until the eggs begin to set. remove them from the pan and put aside.

Add 3 tablespoons oil to pan and heat. Add the pork, shrimp, chicken, sprouts, scallion, pepper, and soy sauce. Stir-fry 2 minutes. Add rice and stir well. Add lettuce and eggs. Stir to heat. Yields 4 large servings.

Sharlene's Apple-Sprout Salad

Sharlene Jensen is a female body builder residing in Barstow, California. Her idea of pleasure is taking in an occasional evening dinner and movie with what she terms, "a gorgeous hunk." But her idea of *fun,* she secretly admits, "is arm-wrestling with all the guys at the local truck stops here." She gets her incredible strength from meals such as this.

1 small head of cabbage, grated fine
1 large apple, chopped
1 cup alfalfa, clover, or mustard sprouts
4 tablespoons tarragon vinegar
2 tablespoons sugar
1/4 teaspoon salt
3 tablespoons sour cream

Combine the cabbage, apple, and sprouts. Next combine the vinegar, sugar, salt, and sour cream. Stir this dressing into the salad. Add more sour cream if desired. Serves 4–6.

A Mortician's Lentil Sprout Soup

In all of the health books written by me, I use real-life people I've met or know, and their names wherever possible. Sometimes, though, a name may be purposely withheld or even changed so as not to violate the privacy of that individual, when permission has not been granted to identify the person involved. In this particular case, not only can't I mention the man's name, but I must also refrain from revealing the city he lives in, since his is the only business serving this community.

The person I'm referring to is a retired mortician. Quite a few years ago there was a period of time that I worked for him. His residential quarters, oddly enough, happened to be on the second floor *above* his mortuary. One night, after showing me how to do some incredible cosmetic work on the faces of several very cold corpses, he invited me upstairs for dinner. We washed our hands thoroughly of the sickening formaldehyde smell on them. I accompanied him to the kitchen and watched with interest as he put together a very unusual and hearty soup.

3 cups lentil sprouts
1/4 pound Canadian bacon
2 onions, coarsely chopped
2 large carrots, chopped

16 prunes, pitted
2 tablespoons brown sugar
2 tablespoons apple cider vinegar
1/4 teaspoon thyme
salt to taste
4—6 cups water

Combine all ingredients in the 3 cups water. Simmer in a heavy pot for 2 1/2 hours until thick. Add more water if necessary. Serves 6.

Creole Sprouts

Louisiana is famous for its Cajun and Creole cultures and cuisines. The term Cajun applies to those who are at least partially descended from the Acadian exiles of Acadie in the wilderness of southeast Canada or who have French ancestry somewhere in their lineage. Creole, on the other hand, implies those who are descended from early Portuguese and Spanish conquerors, but can also include those with a French background.

Chef Martin Lafourche is a culinary genius when it comes to creating magnificent tasting jambalayas, grillades, stews, fricasees, soups, gumbos, sauce piquantes, and a host of stuffed fish and vegetable dishes. But he's also health-minded enough to periodically attend conventions emphasizing natural foods and alternative medicine, which is where I met him. He made this dish for me in his restaurant and then gave me the recipe afterwards.

1 tablespoon vegetable oil
1/2 cup chopped onion
1/2 cup diced celery
1 can (1 pound) stewed tomatoes
1 bay leaf
1/2 teaspoon salt
2 cups sprouts (mung, soy, lentil, or pea)

Heat the oil in a skillet, add the onion and celery, and sauté until golden brown.

Next add the tomatoes, bay leaf, and salt, and bring to a boil. Simmer uncovered for 12 minutes.

Remove bay leaf. Add the sprouts and simmer covered between 5 and 7 minutes if using tough sprouts. Serves 4.

Sprout Burgers

You won't find these at your local McDonald's, Burger King, or Wendy's. Not only are they tastier, but they're better for you too.

1 cup barely sprouted wheat sprouts

1 cup adzuki bean sprouts

1/2 cup soybean sprouts

1/2 cup pea or lentil sprouts

1 medium onion

1 egg, well beaten

1/2 cup milk

2 tablespoons wheat germ

granulated kelp to taste

Grind the sprouts and onion together. Put them in a bowl. Add the egg, milk, wheat germ, and granulated kelp. Mix thoroughly, using more milk if necessary. Shape into patties with both hands and put on a lightly greased baking sheet. Broil until brown but not dried out. Serve as you would any burger. If you don't have the exact quantities or kinds of sprouts called for, substitute what you do have in roughly the same quantities. Makes 2–4 servings.

John's Sprouted Alfalfa Bread

For the last 35 years of my life, my father, brother and I have been eating a very special kind of sprouted wheat bread sold under the trademark of "Jack Spratt's" and made by Gregory Clint's Wheat Shop in Bountiful, Utah (84010).

On the front wrapper is this little ditty:

Jack Sprat could eat NO FAT
His wife thought this was keen
She started eating
Jack Spratt's Bread
And now she too is lean.

The ingredient list on the side includes: 100 percent whole wheat that is sprouted and ground fresh daily in our bakery, water, what flour, whey, honey, salt, yeast, molasses, lecithin, and gluten. NO shortening, fat, or oil has been added. And guaranteed NOT to contain any preservatives, bleaches, or crystalline-synthetic vitamins. Two slices of this bread, either as toast for breakfast or to make a sandwich for lunch, will satisfy hunger for at least 4 hours.

Another sprouted bread I became acquainted with while spending some time in southern California on a research project in the summer of 1994 was sold under the trademark of "Flourless California Fruit Loaf." It is made by Oasis Breads, 400 Venture Street, Escondido, California 92029. It differs from Cinton's "Jack Spratt Bread" in one major respect—it contains absolutely *no* flour! The ingredients are as follows: ground wheat sprouts, water, raisins, honey, sunflower seeds, dates, yeast, and salt. Like the other bread, just two slices will create a feeling of fullness for several hours.

I've come up with my own sprouted bread that is an amalgamation of several other bread recipes given to me in the past, with some modifications along the way to improve both texture and flavor. Not only is it different, but you can't seem to get enough of it once you've become acquainted with its flavor.

3 cups alfalfa sprouts
1 medium yam with skin
3 1/2 cups warm water
2 cakes yeast (or 2 envelopes dry)
1/2 blackstrap molasses
3 tablespoons cooking oil
2 teaspoons salt
1 teaspoon powdered cardamom
9 cups flour (1/2 white and 1/2 whole wheat)

Dice the yam and cook in 3 cups water until tender. Blend the
yam and water in a Vita-Mix machine or equivalent food
machine until smooth. Dissolve the yeast in $^1/_2$ cup warm water.
Add blackstrap molasses, salt, cardamom, cooking oil, and yam
liquid. Mix thoroughly. Add towel-dried sprouts and about 5
cups of flour. Knead well with fists and knuckles. Place in an
oiled bowl, cover, and let rise in a warm place until double in
bulk. Punch the dough down and form into 2 loaves. Place in
2 oiled 9" × 5" pans and let rise again until double in bulk. Bake
in 350°F. over for 1 $^1/_4$ hours. Remove from pans and cook in
wire rack. Makes 2 wonderful loaves of bread!

Appendix XI

A Florida business concern, owned and operated by my good friends Ron and Louise Hamilton, carry many of the seeds mentioned in this book. They supply customers all over North America and in some foreign countries with a wide variety of nuts, berries, and seeds.

Great American Natural Products, Inc.
4121–16th Street North
St. Petersburg, FL 33703
(813)-521-4372
Fax: 1-800-522-6457

Alfalfa Seed

Amaranth Seed

Anise Seed

Annatto Seed

Cabbage Seed

Caraway Seed

Cardamom Pods and Seeds

Chia Seed

Coriander Seed

Cress Seed

Dill Seed

Fennel Seed

Fenugreek Seed

Flax Seed

Mustard Seeds
  (Yellow and Brown)

Poppy Seed

Pumpkin Seed

Psyllium Seed

Red Clover Seed

Sesame Seed

Sunflower Seeds
  (Raw, Salted, Unsalted, Shelled, Roasted)

To order the Sprout Master—the ultimate device in simple and easy sprouting, write or call:

Life Sprouts
P.O.B. 150
Paradise, UT 84328
1-800-241-1516

APPENDIX XII

HOW TO CONTACT THE AUTHOR OF THIS BOOK

Most authors I know like their privacy. They don't want to be bothered with a lot of letters and phone calls from their fans and critics. They essentially want to be left alone. I guess they're entitled to this if that's what they want.

But my philosophy is much different. I believe that when a person writes books for the general public, he or she ought to be accessible to their readers. That is why within the last decade I've been putting my name, address, and phone number in the back of several of my health best-sellers. This way, people who want to get in touch with me can do so at their leisure.

I have one full-time staff person who does nothing but open and answer most of my mail, putting the really difficult or unusual ones on my desk for me to personally respond to. The phone number I give out happens to be my home phone. You can't find it in the local telephone book, nor can you get it from information directory. You see, it's *unlisted*. Ironically enough, though, it's probably *the* most widely known unlisted number in America.

The reason I put my home phone in my books it because I've *never* had a telephone in my research center. Not in 26 years; not ever! At home I take my calls in the morning before I leave; but in my office I have total peace and quiet. In that sublime environment, I can think and create, letting the spirit of wisdom inspire me with good things to write about that will help people a lot.

Furthermore, for your information, I have never had, nor do I ever intend to have a *computer* on the premises. I don't like computers; I don't trust them. And at home I have *no* answering machine, *no* VCR, *no* microwave, *no* cellular phone, and *no* pager to beep me. My life is very *low* tech and I've managed to keep it that way for almost 50 years.

When I mention these things every so often to different people I get smiles, strange and sympathetic looks, mild astonishment, and even outright admiration. I find that my life is relatively stress free, because I'm not bound to the sophisticated gadgets produced by our fancy technology. Electronic gimmickry enslaves the mind and soul of man; if you don't believe that just doing without a computer, radio, television, or movies for several months. Then you'll better appreciate the meaning of my last statement.

So, if you want to sit down and pen or type me a few lines, you can do so by sending your correspondence to this address; if you want a reply, then have the courtesy please to send along an SASE (self-addressed, stamped envelope). Sorry, computer fanatics, but I get *no* E-mail!

John Heinerman, Ph.D.
Director, Anthropological Research Center
P.O.B. 11471
Salt Lake City, UT 84147

Of if you want to call and "chaw a spell" on your nickel, then call me at this number *only before 8 A.M. MST (Mountain Standard Time)*: 1-801-521-8824. Otherwise, I'm unavailable.

I'd love to hear from you at your convenience regarding this volume. Thanks for buying it and some of my other books. As Red Skeleton used to say years ago: "Good-bye and God bless!"

To Order Rex's Wheat Germ Oil

I am not in the habit of selling health food products to customers. My business is usually confined to research, writing, and lecturing. But for the past several years I have been recommending something called "Rex's Wheat Germ Oil" in my various books. I have discovered that it is the *only* pure and unrefined vitamin E oil on the market. However, it is only sold to veterinarians, animal supply houses, and research centers like mine; otherwise it is unavailable to the general public. This is because it is intended for "Animal Use Only" because of its potency—meaning a little bit goes a long way!

Since some readers of my different books in which this product is occasionally mentioned haven't been able to procure it for themselves, I decided to carry it as a convenience to readers. It comes in a one quart heavy metal can and retails for $65. If taken in the recommended amount of one teaspoon every 2 days, it should last a person about 2 $1/2$ months. When ordering, make your check out to John Heinerman and for the correct amount, then send it to the above address. Allow up to two weeks' shipping time by U.S. Mail.

INDEX

Rosehips, 243-44
    description of, 243-44
    and infection, 244
Rosenbach's disease, and gooseberries, 144
Roundworm:
    and betel nuts, 36-37
    and pumpkin seed, 237-38
Rowanberries, 245-46
    description of, 245-46
    Rowanberry Jelly (recipe), 363-64
    and sore throat/tonsillitis, 246
Rowanberry Jelly (recipe), 363-64
Rubus chamaemorus, See Cloudberries
Rubus idaeus, See Raspberries
Rubus loganobaccus, See Boysenberries
Rubus phoenicolasius, See Japanese
        wineberries
Rubus ursinus loganobaccus, See Loganberries
Rubus villosus, See Blackberries

S

St. Johnswort berries, 247-49
    and anxiety, 248-49
    and bedwetting, 248
    and burns, 249
    and depression, 248-49
    and wounds, 249
Salted berries, 341-43
Salvia columbariae, See Chia seeds
Sambucus species, See Elderberries
Sam Chow's Fried Rice (recipe), 379
Saskatoons, 329
Saw palmetto berries, 250-52
    and allergies, 251-52
    and benign prostatic hypertrophy, 251
    description of, 250
Scalds, and sumac berries, 273
Scaliness, and jojoba nuts, 171-72
Scarification, and cashew nuts, 76
Sciatica:
    and coriander seeds, 101-2
    and flax seed, 131-32
Scratches, and sumac berries, 272-73
Scrates, and jojoba nuts, 172
Scurvy, and cashew nuts, 75-76
Seeds:
    sources for, 385-86
    sprouting, 6-8, 369-73
    See also Nuts and seeds
Seizures, and alfalfa seeds/sprouts, 8-9
Selenium, 302

Senile dementia, and ginkgo nuts, 139
Serenoa repens, See Saw palmetto berries
Serviceberries, 253-56
    description of, 253-54
    and diarrhea, 255
    and eye problems, 254-55
    and female problems, 255-56
    and loss of appetite, 255
Sesame Seed Milk (recipe), 375-76
Sesame seeds, 257-64
    and burns, 258-60
    and colitis, 260-61
    description of, 257-58
    and fracture wounds, 261-64
    and gastritis, 260-61
    and heartburn, 260-61
    and indigestion, 260-61
    Sesame Seed Milk (recipe), 375-76
    and underweight problems, 258
Sesamum indicum, See Sesame seeds
Sexually transmitted diseases, and coconut,
        99
Sharlene's Apple-Sprout Salad (recipe),
        379-80
Shaving agent, bayberry as, 25-26
Shengji, 261
Shepherdia argentea, See Buffalo berries
Shingles, and sumac berries, 273
Shortness of breath, and poppy seeds,
        231-32
Sichuan Chicken with Gingko Nuts
        (recipe), 320-21
Silybum marianum, See Milk thistle seeds
Simmondsia chinensis, See Jojoba nut
Skin disease/problems:
    and boysenberries, 55
    and cashew nuts, 75-76
    and pokeberries, 227-30
Smoking, and elderberries, 122
Snakebite:
    and cashew nuts, 73-74
    and flax seed, 130-31
Sodium, 303
Sore gums, and cashew nuts, 74-75
Sores:
    and American hollyberries, 19
    and bayberries, 24-25
    canker, and bayberries, 26
    and elderberries, 122
    and flax seed, 129-30
    and hackberries, 149-50
    and jojoba nuts, 172